The Call to Discernment in Troubled Times

The Call to Discernment in Troubled Times

New Perspectives on the Transformative Wisdom of Ignatius of Loyola

DEAN BRACKLEY

A Crossroad Book
The Crossroad Publishing Company
New York

The Crossroad Publishing Company
www.CrossroadPublishing.com

Printed in the United States of America

The text is typeset in 11/15 Optima, the display font is News Gothic, and text in the shaded boxes is Palatino.

Library of Congress Cataloging-in-Publication Data

Brackley, Dean.
The call to discernment in troubled times : new perspectives on the transformative wisdom of Ignatius Loyola / Dean Brackley.
p. cm.
Includes bibliographical references.
ISBN 0-8245-2268-0 (alk. paper)
1. Spiritual life – Catholic Church. 2. Ignatius, of Loyola, Saint, 1491-1556. Exercitia spiritualia. I. Title.
BX2350.3.B73 2004
248.4′82 – dc22

2004016204

6 7 8 9 10 10 09

To my parents, Nan and Dean, Sr.,
to whom I owe the most after God —
with deep admiration, gratitude, and affection.

Contents

The Copyeditor's Conversion: A Foreword for Skeptics

Ellen Calmus

In the course of copyediting the manuscript of this book, something extraordinary happened to me—despite the fact that I started the job without the least bit of interest in the subject matter, assuming that all books of theology were by definition dense, abstruse, and dusty. I had only the dimmest notion of who Ignatius of Loyola was, and I had never heard of his Spiritual Exercises, but I imagined they would be dense and dusty, too.

Still, having done plenty of copyediting in the course of many years as a starving writer, I figured I could do my usual job of tightening up the manuscript in terms of the issues that arise in just about anything written in my beloved and so frequently misused English language, regardless of subject matter. I warned the author that my reading would necessarily reflect the fact that I was not a "believer" (whatever that meant) in any traditional sense of the word: my education had been heavily weighted first in the sciences, particularly physics, and later in the arts, while my religious upbringing had been a hodgepodge sampling of churches in the areas where I'd grown up the child of atheist parents (they'd washed their hands of religious education but allowed me to go along with friends to an assortment of Protestant Bible schools in Florida, Jewish temple in New York, and an occasional Catholic Mass with an Italian-American neighbor in San Antonio). In my family, religion was appreciated mainly as a source of material for jokes and evidence of human gullibility. Although anything depending on a traditional Christian education would be sure to go right over my head, I thought I might be of some use as a test case for the author's idea of making Ignatian thinking accessible to the postmodern, post-religious reader: in addition to the usual copyeditor's role I would be a sort of skeptic acid test for the manuscript.

Why did I even take on the job if I had so little interest in the subject? To explain, I'll have to tell you a little about the author, Dean Brackley, and how I came to meet him—and I'm afraid I'll have to tell a bit of my own story, too. I was first introduced to Dean in San Salvador at the UCA, the University of Central America, during an all-night vigil held in memory of the six Jesuit professors assassinated there during the war. It was the sixth anniversary of their death, the first of these vigils I had been able to attend. I was terrified of going, not so much for fear that there would be some act of repression (I'd lived through many moments of that kind of fear during the war years, but those days seemed to be over). No, what scared me was a fear of the memories the event might revive.

I had hardly set foot on the UCA campus since I'd attended the six Jesuits' funeral in 1989—a strange time that was, with war in the streets of San Salvador, sounds of explosions echoing off the volcano, helicopters flying overhead with machine guns protruding from their doors, the air in certain neighborhoods smelling of cadavers left in the heat during days of inconclusive combat. I'd been too stunned to be afraid. Memories of those weeks remained a kaleidoscope confusion of too-brightly-lit impressions, remembered details sharp as broken glass, strangely juxtaposed, hard to reconcile. One of the six, Ignacio Martín-Baró—"Nacho" to his friends—a dedicated, innovative social psychologist and vice rector of the UCA, had been my advisor and friend during the year I spent in El Salvador interviewing people for a book about the war, and I was devastated by his death, falling into a depression so deep it left me unable to write.

I felt like a ghost the night I attended the vigil, a ghost among ghosts. I wandered silently among groups of people along that road winding up the hill past the UCA buildings to the library steps, shivering in the tropical night. A procession of people with candles walked past, the light warm on faces I didn't recognize, standing in my own circle of darkness. I scanned the crowd, wondering if I would see people I'd known during those war years—so many who might possibly be there, or who might not have survived. Then I heard my name called. I looked around and saw a group of people from Nacho's parish out in Jayaque. I was amazed that they remembered me from the time Nacho took me there so many years before. Morena (one of the most motherly women on the face of the earth, who had been Nacho's assistant in the parish) and I threw our arms around each other and cried, and I realized I'd been needing to do that for years. As I dried my eyes, Morena told me: "You have to meet el Padre Dean!" — pointing to a tall, skinny foreigner in glasses standing nearby. She explained that this was the American priest who had taken the parish of Jayaque after Nacho died. While I had been thrilled to see Morena and the group from Jayaque, I frankly didn't much care to meet some American priest who had come to take Nacho's place in the parish — if he wasn't even Salvadoran and had come only after Nacho was gone, then I figured he couldn't have known my friend, so what possible use could there be in talking to him? — but Morena was not to be resisted. So we were introduced. Considering all the points against him, el Padre Dean Brackley seemed like a nice enough person. Not that I had much use for nice people in those dark times.

It wasn't until I returned to El Salvador on the tenth anniversary of the assassination that I began to gain an appreciation of Dean's depth of understanding. I stopped by his office in the theology department at the UCA to say hello and somehow felt the *confianza* to tell him that during this visit I — at last — intended to visit some of the difficult places for me in El Salvador, in hopes that this would help me resume work on my book. Dean amazed me by offering the kind of moral support one might expect from family or very old friends (if one happens to be particularly fortunate in the family and old friend department). His office became a regular stop for me during that visit: after a challenging interview or a visit to a memory-laden place I hadn't seen since the war, Dean and I would go have lunch at a little Mexican restaurant uphill from the UCA, where I'd tell him where I'd been and what I'd heard, and cry into my enchiladas. It was with Dean's support and encouragement that I was finally able to face that initial reencounter with the places there that had so deeply affected me and to talk about Ignacio Martín-Baró with someone who actually seemed to have a real sense of the great man I had known, which I believe Dean gathered from working with Nacho's former colleagues, students, and parishioners.

Receiving his support as I faced what I needed to face there, benefiting from that accompaniment exactly when I most needed it as I took the first hesitant steps toward getting my book back on track, left me so deeply grateful to Dean Brackley that I couldn't imagine how I could possibly repay such kindness. It was this gratitude that prompted me, when Dean told me he was writing a book himself, to offer to read the manuscript of the book you hold in your hands. A book about theology. As I said, I figured it would be dense and dusty going, but I was so thankful to begin to emerge from that cloud of paralyzing, blocking grief that I told Dean I would be more than glad to be a reader for his manuscript, secretly vowing that no matter how dense the theology might turn out to be, I'd do my best, in the course of my usual copyeditor's labors, to dust it off.

My — what to call the impediment a nonbeliever works under while reading a book about religion? — my *theological handicap* made this daunting at the outset. Upon encountering the first reference to God I immediately wanted to red pencil in the margin: Define your terms! I knew this wasn't supposed to be algebra, but all my education had been based on the idea that in order to talk about something we need to agree on what that something is. Yet here we seemed to be plunging from page one right into the ineffable. I decided to think of the word "God" in the text as a sort of unknown variable, the *X* whose value might emerge as I solved the rest of the equation. Does that sound ridiculous? It was how I went about suspending disbelief in order to try to follow a logic that seemed quite foreign to me. The mental leap involved reminded me of poetry, which helped me toward a sort of working definition: *the force that through the green fuse drives the flower, brooding over the bent world with – ah! – bright wings.* Not exactly Euclid, but it would do for the moment. It was a little unsettling to find myself setting off across such unplumbed waters, but Dean's clear and sensible writing carried me forward, and I read on.

Within the first few paragraphs the current carried me directly into the ideas of Ignatius himself — which I was surprised to find immediately began to fascinate me. I was struck (thanks in part to Dean's paraphrasing) by the modernity of the thinking of this sixteenth-century Spanish soldier-turned-religious. No dust! In fact, it seemed to me that Ignatius had been centuries ahead of our modern psychologists in his awareness of the difficulties we encounter in life due to the essential ways in which we fail to understand ourselves, making decisions that run counter to who we are and setting forth in the most self-sabotaging directions. I was impressed by the sheer intelligence behind the meditation exercises Ignatius designed to help us make the important decisions in life for which we are—by definition—unprepared. How can we possibly know, before we have committed ourselves to years of following a path which may or may not be right for us, what it will mean to marry a certain person, or choose a particular career? Well, it turns out that Ignatius of Loyola has some very specific methods to help us figure such things out. I found myself wishing someone had given me this book to read years ago.

As I sailed on into the text, I couldn't help feeling the occasional moment of alarm brought on by the sustained suspension of my native skepticism, but I did my best to steady the keel by careful exercise of my craft, tucking in commas where they were needed, removing them where they were not, closing quotations, keeping the clauses in trim. Still, there were further shoals of vocabulary to run aground on. "Faith," for example. The concept of faith, used in the religious sense, had always been one of the most problematic of terms for me. The idea of believing something just because you decide to believe it, or—worse—because you are told you ought to believe it, had seemed to me the very seed of authoritarianism, the first step toward giving up what I consider to be human beings' greatest treasure: our ability to question, to think things through and make up our own minds based on the evidence presented to us. But in a sudden shift of perspective brought on, I believe, by Dean's fresh discussion of religious ideas in a modern context, I began to wonder if this quaint-sounding concept of faith might not have a more interesting meaning altogether than the one I'd learned as a child, something akin to the notion, so dear to us postmoderns, of self-esteem, the belief in our ability to act effectively in the world, the sense of our worthiness to be loved which so many of us seem to be lacking. I found myself wanting to rethink a number of ideas I'd rejected years before as childish things to be cast off upon entering rational adulthood. These weren't shoals at all, but the shores of entire new continents of concepts to be explored.

As the combination of Ignatius's acuity and Dean's wide-ranging discussion of Ignatius's meaning and how his ideas might be used to address the particular needs and problems of today's more interconnected society drew me further into the text, I continued to read in the close-up, magnifying-glass-in-hand way of copyeditors. What happened next – the extraordinary thing I've mentioned – is difficult to describe. In fact, I think it may be impossible to describe exactly what happened, but I can try to describe *how* it happened.

Back home in Mexico, I'd been working on and off on Dean's manuscript for several months while recovering from a painful divorce. I saw Christmas approaching that year with a degree of dread: under the circumstances, I just wanted to be alone. Festivities were out of the question, so I decided I'd make use of the down time to get as much of that stack of chapters copyedited as I could. I made some soup and set up my computer on a dining room table empty of everything but a potted fern. Dean had questioned my decision to do this, saying I should only devote my holidays to the copyediting if I really wanted to. "I really want to," I said. To the few friends who asked about my plans, I answered with a laugh that I intended to spend Christmas with St. Ignatius, which they seemed to find amusingly original.

The streets emptied as masses of Mexico City's residents left town to be with family in the countryside or on the beaches. My apartment building was nearly deserted, and the whole city grew very quiet. On December 23 I sat down in front of my computer and started work on the chapter entitled "Humility and Solidarity." I worked away, barely stopping to heat the occasional bowl of soup, which I ate sitting in front of my computer as I continued to study the text. The next day, Christmas Eve, I found myself, almost without knowing how I'd gotten there, deep in the next chapter, "Expanding the Soul." At that point, I didn't feel like stopping even for soup. I was so absorbed in the text that the dining room table was starting to seem like the most appealing place in the city. Pausing for a moment, I noticed how beautifully a shaft of late-afternoon sunlight was illuminating the fern and my little laptop. Bach's Mass in B Minor was playing on the stereo, the closest thing to Christmas music I had on hand. Did I work straight through the night? I think I must have rested at some point, though by this time I was so wrapped up in the work—one chapter melting into the next—that sleeping began to seem of as little interest to me as eating. Without my quite knowing how it happened, Christmas Eve turned into Christmas morning.

Now, there is a sort of trick I play on myself when I am copyediting. I imagine I am the author myself, or, perhaps more accurately, that I am inhabiting the author's mind. I find this useful, since it helps me sense where the text is heading, and it is easier in this way for me to figure out when the author has something in mind which hasn't quite made it onto the page. It may sound like an odd way to copyedit, but it works for me. However, I had never copyedited a text by an author with a mind like Dean Brackley's—let alone like Ignatius of Loyola's. The experience of imagining myself inside these two exceptional minds began to have a curious effect: I would discover myself sitting still in front of my computer, staring off into space, thoughts soaring. What I think was happening was that, without any intention of doing so, I was just naturally falling into the kind of meditation that Ignatius—and Dean—were recommending in these chapters. It felt as if, even while my rational mind continued to function, some deeper intelligence in there was beginning to awaken and engage.

This was when it happened—though I hardly know what to call it. If I were writing in an ordinary, nontheological context, I wouldn't hesitate to call it a miracle (we use the word so loosely these days as an all-purpose superlative for anything at all), but here the word seems in danger of being so literally appropriate that it seems almost presumptuous to write it. Maybe I'll put aside trying to name it and just try to describe what it felt like. Though that isn't easy, either, and I'm not sure how possible it is to communicate with any clarity about this kind of thing.

I'll try. It was as if the two meanings of the word "light" were suddenly the same, the world both brilliantly illuminated and, as if by entirely logical correlation in a non-Euclidian geometry of some highly advanced physics, all heaviness had been converted into buoyancy. The sun beamed in like a celestial knowing wink, and the light became a happiness I hadn't experienced since before Nacho died. Twelve years of depression evaporated, just lifted from my shoulders. The happiness wasn't at all a champagne-high sort of giddiness, no bubbly golden-hued confusion. It was more like a wonderful clarity, a transparence. Thinking back to that moment, what it most reminds me of is the time when, as a very lucky teenager who got to hear a truly brilliant physicist explain the proof of Einstein's theory of special relativity, after following the physicist through realms of calculus that stretched the limits of my abilities, I suddenly, struck breathless with awe and delight, *got* special relativity.

What to do with this sudden grace? I looked out the window: it was still Christmas; I was still alone. What I did — with even greater pleasure than before — was simply to carry on with the copyediting, wondering as I did how long that marvelous feeling could possibly last. A short time later, having been silent for days, the phone rang. Somehow, though it was a long-distance extravagance and he had never called me before, I wasn't surprised to hear Dean's voice on the line (the way I was feeling, it wouldn't have entirely surprised me if it had been Ignatius himself calling). Now I suppose that Dean must have been feeling some compassion for me, especially knowing how depressed I'd been and considering that I was spending Christmas alone doing nothing but copyediting his manuscript, and I think the call was simply an act of kindness on his part. But at that splendid moment, it seemed entirely of a piece with the sudden shift in the universe I had experienced an hour or so before. Dean sounded surprised to find me in such good spirits, but it was beyond me to explain what had happened. I told him I was very well, enjoying the work a lot, and we wished each other Merry Christmas.

Would I have been surprised to know that exactly one year later Dean would be baptizing me? Though I think nothing could have astonished me after what happened that morning, certainly the thought never crossed my mind. But that is in fact what happened, after a year of asking questions and talking theology with Dean and a number of other patient religious friends, at a Mexico City church called La Resurrección, in a simple Mass containing a baptismal ceremony so moving it left me feeling legally adopted into that parish of good souls, who continue to treat me with the kindest affection. Whenever I go to Mass at La Resurrección it seems to me that what the liberation theologians say about Christ being present in the poor is visibly, palpably true. The true miracle is that the happiness of that glowing Christmas morning is still with me, showing no signs of abating, even though with the September attacks and the war that followed—not to mention illness, family griefs, deaths of friends, money troubles—it's taken a few blows along the way.

There was, I admit, one faith-shaking moment when I wondered what on earth a feminist like me was doing contemplating joining an institution as male-dominated and plagued with error and contradiction as the Catholic Church. When I told my theologian friends, they acted quickly, arranging interviews with Catholic feminists and nuns of impressive intellect and spiritual strength. I reflected (as I continued my copyediting) that even our sixteenth-century Catholic Ignatius comes across as having had something close to a feminist sensibility himself. A political analogy occurred to me: I certainly wouldn't expect immigrant friends deciding to become U.S. citizens to endorse the foreign policy of whatever administration was in power at the moment, but would rejoice in their bringing a questioning mind into our evolving democracy. Wasn't it equally reasonable for me to join the Church while maintaining my conviction that male domination is archaic and un-Christian, wrong for a thousand reasons, and must go? Who knew: maybe I'd put my own two cents' worth toward helping that evolution along.

On the other hand, I knew I could never join the Catholic or any other church if this would require distancing myself from other churches and religions important to me: the Judaism of my New York cousins and friends with whom I have shared Seders, the Christian Science of my beloved Aunt Anne and cousins in Maine, the Presbyterian Churches that have made me feel at home in Princeton and other American cities. Dean told me that many Catholics have close ties to other religions, mentioning one of his Jesuit brothers whose religious practice includes celebrating Sabbath in the Jewish tradition, and assured me that the Catholic Church would not exclude me for my associations with other religions: another obstacle melted away. And though I'd previously understood the word "conversion" to mean the renouncing of a supposedly inferior religion in favor of a supposedly superior one — a concept I'd found too patronizing to take seriously — I came to understand the concept of conversion in the sense of a spiritual transformation. Not patronizing at all, but deeply interesting.

All the while, that sustaining moment of Christmas joy carried me through these and other grave doubts and kept me in what may possibly have been an almost annoying state of good cheer during exhausting months of working with Catholic Relief Services' 2001 earthquake relief effort in El Salvador. Best of all, though, the sturdy happiness that evolved during the year of successive epiphanies which followed that moment of Christmas light has given me the courage to face the pain of the past, overcome my writer's block — and I am writing again.

I can't promise that if you read this book you will have the kind of transforming experience I did. But I think there is a good chance that, if you read it with some attentiveness and reflect on the ideas presented here, doors may well be opened. Consider the fact that I started reading the book with no interest at all in its contents: having picked up this book on your own, you are already five steps ahead of where I was when I began reading. You may be way ahead of me in being able to talk about spiritual things, as well, since I confess that the word "God" still makes me uneasy; my variable *X* continues undefined for me, at least in words. However, it is clear to me that the formulas presented here *can work* — albeit, as they say, in mysterious ways. If you happen to be, as I was, a skeptic without any adult experience in Christian spirituality, I encourage you to suspend disbelief for the time it takes to read this book and give these exercises a try: I think you will find this to be a particularly accessible approach to understanding what that experience is about. What Ignatius of Loyola set out to do four centuries ago, and what Dean Brackley has set out to make accessible to people of our time, is a sort of spiritual methodology which helps us to prepare the ground in order to become as well-equipped as possible to make the decisions which will lead us toward living better and more fulfilled lives. Whether or not reading this book brings you to your own transforming spiritual experience, these exercises are designed to help you gain deeper insights into yourself, your talents, your yearnings, and your relationship to the rest of the world — no small accomplishment in this fragmented day and age of ours.

Malinalco, Mexico
April 2004

Acknowledgments

In writing this book, I have drawn a great deal on others' experience and testimony. This humbling process has helped me appreciate better how all that we have are gifts received.

Many others have helped make the book possible. I want to thank my colleagues at the Universidad Centroamericana (UCA) in San Salvador who freed me from other tasks, as well as the many friends who shared their knowledge, hospitality and resources at the Woodstock Theological Center in Washington, D.C.; the Jesuit Center for Spirituality in Wernersville, Pennsylvania; Ciszek Hall at Fordham University in the Bronx; Schell House and John Carroll University in Cleveland; and St. Alphonsus House and Loyola Center at St. Joseph's University in Philadelphia.

I am especially grateful to Gwendolin Herder and Roy Carlisle of Crossroad for their patient collaboration and assistance. I also wish to thank Tom Clarke, S.J., Elinor Shea, O.S.U., Miriam Cleary, O.S.U., Sagrario Núñez, A.C.J., Mary Campbell, Jack Barron, S.J., Gene Palumbo, Dan Hartnett, S.J., Arthur Lyons, Vincent O'Keefe, S.J., Jon Sobrino, S.J., Peter Gyves, N.S.J., José Antonio Pacheco, S.J., David López, Martha Zechmeister, Xavier Alegre, S.J., Robin Waterman, Jean Stokan and Trena Yonkers Talz for their helpful suggestions, and Zulma Alvarado for her secretarial assistance.

I owe an unpayable debt to Ellen Calmus, whose talent and generosity have immensely improved the book in style and content.

DB

San Salvador
April 2004

GETTING FREE

These turbulent times disclose our need for a discipline of the spirit. To respond to our world we must get free to love. That involves personal transformation, which includes coming to terms with evil in the world and in ourselves, accepting forgiveness and changing.

1 Spirituality for Solidarity

We live in troubling times. While people can connect as never before, the world seems more fragmented. We are awash in information, yet it is hard to get a sense of the whole. As communities and families crumble, we feel more alone. The voracious monsters of greed, unchecked market forces, and violence prowl the planet, leaving a trail of misery and exclusion in their wake. AIDS spreads and environmental crisis deepens. All this leaves many people dispirited and apprehensive.

But there are signs of hope. One is a growing interest in spirituality. As the desert of materialism expands, people are seeking fresh water. By "spirituality" I mean a discipline of the spirit (which we are), a way of life. For believers, spirituality is a way of life "in the Spirit," capital S, a way of living-in-the-world in relation to God. For Christians, it is a way of following Christ.

The disorientation that so many experience today hit home for me, personally, in college. The trouble began as I reflected on how all the geniuses that we were reading disagreed among themselves. To me, each one's vision of life seemed as valid, or invalid, as the others'. This provoked a deep crisis. I had been brought up a Catholic, was instructed in the faith, and had wonderful role models. Now it seemed that Christian doctrine hovered over an abyss. Looking back, I can see that I was short on experience, especially the kind that helps us make sense of life and its conundrums. I had little acquaintance with the suffering of the poor.

Fortunately, my upbringing provided resources for this crisis, which lasted four years. I clung to basic morality and a sense of vocation (I was a Jesuit in training at the time). I sought guidance and made use of tools I'd recently acquired, like St. Ignatius of Loyola's "Rules for Discernment." Though I had doubts about God, Ignatius seemed to me to make good practical sense. His Rules got me through workdays of depression and anxiety and offered promise that I could ride out the storm. They helped me notice that when I drew near to suffering

I experienced a sense of solidity and some relief. Letting the drama of life and death break through my defenses – the drama of down-and-out adults and youth at risk in Lower Manhattan where I lived and worked – helped me gather together my scattered self. It did me good to get close to these people.

Since then, that kind of experience has continued to nourish me. The crucified people of today lead us to the center of things. Eventually they helped me rediscover Christianity. Through those difficult years and ever since, the Ignatian path, Ignatian spirituality, has been crucial for finding my way.

I discovered I had company. Plenty of others were walking a path like mine, especially members of my own middle-class "tribe." For many, engaging the victims of history became a turning point in their journey, leaving them "ruined for life," as the Jesuit volunteers say (ruined, that is, for the conventional life they once aspired to). The victims help us find a deeper purpose in life. They help us discover our vocation to solidarity.

In these times of transition, the world cries out for that. One "order" is coming apart, and its successor is not yet in sight. I'm not sure what the best political strategy is for making the world a more liveable place. I do know that the world needs a critical mass of people who will respond to suffering, who are ready for long-term commitment, and who will make wise choices along the way. Without such "new human beings," I doubt that any amount of money, sophisticated strategies, or even structural change will make our world much more human.

IGNATIUS: TENDING THE FLAME

Sustaining a life of generous service requires a spirituality. Which is where Ignatius comes in. A genius of the spiritual life, he lived in Europe at the dawn of the modern age, and he addressed a growing need for personalized spirituality. During the Middle Ages, that was deemed proper mostly for church professionals – monks, nuns, and the clergy. Religious commoners had to be content with the minimum of sacraments and popular devotions, including public practices like processions. With hindsight, we can appreciate how the crumbling of the Middle Ages brought to light the need for a personalized spirituality for lay people. By Ignatius's time, the official and collective devotions were proving less helpful for sustaining serious Christian commitment. The Renaissance, the rediscovery of the Bible, the invention of the printing press, the birth of modern science, the discovery of "new worlds" — all this undermined exclusive reliance on ancient authority and venerable custom. Commerce facilitated travel; people could see that their traditions were local, not universal. The situation raised questions similar to those we ask in our own wildly pluralistic times: How do we ground our convictions and sustain commitment, and how do we do this together?

In the cities of a Renaissance Europe in the throes of the Reformation, reasonable people increasingly disagreed on life's basic questions. In an environment of critical questioning and viable alternatives, there could be no substitute for personal conviction founded not on faith alone, but also on experience and reason.

Ignatius responded to his changing times with uncommon originality. As a Basque soldier, Iñigo (as he had been christened) pursued the pleasures and prestige of courtly life until he was thirty. But in 1521, while convalescing at Loyola from a battle injury at Pamplona, he underwent a profound experience that he later interpreted as God's direct action on him. He experienced within himself the birth of a great love and a powerful desire to spend his life in God's service. He later spoke of being "on fire with God."

Departing Loyola in 1522, he took up residence in a cave at Manresa, near Barcelona, where he spent several months in intense prayer and reflection. Having resolved to imitate the exploits of the saints, he practiced harsh penances and took other rash actions with little regard for circumstance or consequences. He later concluded that in this period his passion to serve was contaminated with egoism and lacking in "discretion." At Manresa he fell into such deep desolation that he thought of suicide. He begged God to show him the way forward. Soon after, he says, he was learning to let God lead him and to order his tangled loves.

With this progress came powerful illuminations about life, the world, and God. He understood people better, perceived his surroundings more clearly, and developed a better grasp of how the world worked. In time, he would speak of finding God easily and communicating "familiarly" with God.

Endowed with exceptional insight and a habit of reflection, Iñigo soon discovered that his gifts benefited others. He could help them understand their experience, above all how God was working in their lives. His passion became, and always remained, to help people steward the flame of love that God had lit within them, the better to serve the world around them. That flame spread through the many deep friendships he formed. The spirituality we associate with him is all about tending that flame in us, as it is purified, flourishes, or even flags, and stirring the fire in others.

Iñigo was a layman with no thought of becoming a priest, still less of starting a religious order. His desire to help people led him to shape his new insights into a series of meditations, or "spiritual exercises," which he administered to others. For those who were properly disposed, his retreat lasted about thirty days, grouped into four uneven "weeks," each devoted to a different theme. For about ten years after Manresa, he refined his retreat notes, fashioning them into a manual, *Spiritual Exercises,* for others to use in guiding "exercitants." (I will refer to the retreat itself as the Spiritual Exercises and to the manual as *Spiritual Exercises,* in italics. These days those who make a retreat are commonly called "retreatants.")

The *Spiritual Exercises* crystallizes most of Ignatius's key insights — but not all. He went on to study for several years and to gather the group of close friends who became the first Jesuits. Meanwhile, his vision evolved. This is evident from his voluminous correspondence (over seven thousand letters and instructions have come down to us!), the so-called *Autobiography,* fragments of his *Spiritual Diary,* the *Constitutions* he wrote for the new Society of Jesus during his last years, and from testimonies of others about him. For Ignatius in his mature later years, to live meant to seek and find God everywhere, in order to collaborate with God in service to others.

Ignatius's outlook was revolutionary. While he was a child of his times, he also transcended them. He even transcends our own. According to the great theologian Karl Rahner, Ignatius's originality will be understood only in the future. His spirituality "is not typical of our time; it is not characteristic of the modern era which is nearing its end. It is, rather, a sign of the approaching future."[1] Today's booming interest in Ignatius seems to confirm Rahner's prophecy. Ignatian spirituality is now promoted and practiced beyond the Catholic Church where it was born, among members of other Christian churches and among non-Christians, as well. Its contemporary vigor is evident in the welcome it has received from many feminists.[2]

READING THESE PAGES

Although Ignatius's vision evolved, it remained grounded in his experience at Manresa and the insights set forth in his retreat manual. The Spiritual Exercises always remained his preferred instrument for introducing people to a life of deeper faith, hope, and love. When he discovered someone who was open to generous commitment, he would invite that person to make the Exercises.

Here I follow his lead. Like the Exercises, this book offers readers an opportunity to reflect on their experience in an ordered way and to grow in commitment. Like Ignatius's retreat, it (re)introduces them to Christianity, as an experience more than a set of doctrines. For that purpose, I can hardly improve on his basic pedagogy. As I said above, the full Exercises lasted about a month, divided into four uneven "weeks." I use the same schema for the scaffolding of this book. At the same time, I incorporate Ignatius's more mature insights, which "flow back" over the themes of the Exercises, so that all the essential elements of his spirituality are included.

This book is more than an introduction, however. It seeks to adapt the Ignatian vision to our times, as many have already done, but with special attention to our global social crisis. Obviously, there is a need to re-present Ignatius's wisdom in contemporary language, including more adequate theological language. But we must also explore its *social implications* — a point of particular emphasis in this book. In the Spiritual Exercises, attention centers on the individual and God's action in the life of the individual, which is only fitting in a retreat where people take stock of their lives. But the Exercises are not all of Ignatian spirituality. Moreover, we can be certain that, were he alive today, Ignatius would develop the social significance of his insights. We are more aware today of the social and institutional dimensions of our lives. Christians are more aware of the social implications of their vocation and of the mission of the church. We are *all* more conscious of the scope of misery in the world, of the institutional mechanisms of injustice, and of the global dimension of our moral drama. Responding to massive injustice according to each one's calling is the price of being human, and Christian, today. Those looking for a privatized spirituality to shelter them from a violent world have come to the wrong place.

I explain my interpretation of the social significance of some key Ignatian themes in two appendices at the end of this book – one on the exercise of "The Call" (or "The Kingdom"), the other on the "Two Standards" meditation. Readers with less interest in these more scholarly arguments can skip the appendices without losing the main lines of thought.

The First Week of the Exercises (corresponding to Part 1 of this book) deals with sin and forgiveness; the Second, with following Christ and making major life choices (Parts 2 and 3); the Third Week considers the passion and death of Christ (Part 4); and the Fourth Week, the risen Christ (Part 5). Although prayer is discussed throughout the book, its final three chapters treat prayer systematically (Part 6). They do not depend on earlier chapters and can be read at any time.

As the progression of "weeks" suggests, Ignatius recognized a typical pattern in God's dealings with us, that is, a typical pattern in our growth in freedom and love. Not that people pass lockstep through stages, never to return to them. Rather, as in a symphony of four movements, the themes of the four weeks recur in different ways throughout the life of the maturing person.

At the same time, Ignatius stressed that each individual is unique and that God deals freely with each one. He always tailored his counsel to each one's needs, sternly warning others against steering everybody along the same road. In these matters, one size does not fit all.

Nor is every truth always timely. We need different types of nourishment at different points of our journey. Some people may not be ready for certain vital truths, and dwelling on them could do them harm (cf. John 16:12–13). Others may have no need to rehearse the basics, but should instead "leave the elementary doctrine of Christ and go on to maturity" (Heb. 6:1).

Readers should therefore read this book with the prime Ignatian virtue of discretion. They should take from it what illuminates their experience, what heals, and what challenges them to step forward onto new terrain. Ignatius advises us to dwell on and savor just such things. And better still than reading this book would be to make the Exercises, for which no book can really substitute.

These pages speak the language of faith. However, others besides convinced Christians have derived great profit from Ignatius (as I did myself during years of agnostic doubt). I have tried to make this book "searcher-friendly" and to speak of Transcendence without mystification, decoding theological language as much as possible. That is one reason I introduce prayer only gradually. Most often, I take human experience, rather than revelation, as the starting point for each theme. At the same time, our lives are too rich for precise scientific explanation, ordinary common-sense discourse, or both, to encompass. If the holy Mystery called God pervades our lives, as I believe it does, then we need religious symbols to point to reality as it actually is. Without that language, we sell our experience short. I invite readers, as Ignatius invited those he counseled, to give a fair hearing to language that might at first put them off [22].*

CONCLUSION

With major institutions in crisis, we find it hard to say where the world is headed. Some believe this affords groups of deeply committed people a better chance to shape the future than they would have under more

*Numbers in brackets in the text, without further indication, refer to the standard paragraph numbering of the *Spiritual Exercises.* To streamline references, I will avoid the double-bracketing of a (cf. [36]) in favor of [cf. 36]. It will be helpful, though not necessary, to have a copy of the *Exercises* at hand while reading this book. See the bibliography at the end of this book for versions.

stable, less fluid conditions: an encouraging way to think about this state of uncertainty. In any event, we urgently need a critical mass of such people to make this century the century of solidarity and turn the swelling tide of misery, violence, and environmental crisis.

The good news (gospel) assures us that it makes sense to struggle against the odds and to celebrate along the way. I do believe, as the song says, that we shall overcome some day. I hope these reflections will stoke the inner flame of generous readers and provide them with resources to help bring that day closer.

We now turn to the "Foundation," a kind of overture of first principles, which Ignatius invited people to ponder at the beginning of his retreat.

2 Free to Love

For you were called to freedom, brothers and sisters; only do not use your freedom as an opportunity for self-indulgence, but through love become slaves to one another. For the whole law is summed up in a single commandment, "You shall love your neighbor as yourself." (Gal. 5:13–14)

The Beatles were right: all you need is love. But real love does not come cheap. Dorothy Day used to quote Dostoyevsky, saying, "Love in practice is a harsh and dreadful thing compared to love in dreams."[1] What love requires is not always obvious. Above all, love demands sacrifice, and we are slow to sign up for that. And even when we do, the path of love is full of traps and blind alleys that steer us off track or turn us around. Our frailty and our fears block our way to serious commitment. To respond with love to a world which seems to have gone wrong in fundamental ways, a broken world, we must get free to love—we need to find a way to love better and over the long haul.

THE FOUNDATION

Popular wisdom and songs are full of advice about how to live and to love, but how far does that advice lead us? This book offers a way based on the spiritual wisdom of Ignatius of Loyola, the sixteenth-century founder of the Jesuits.

A set of basic propositions called "The Foundation" stands at the beginning of Ignatius's *Spiritual Exercises*. The Foundation speaks to the heart of life's drama. It is about getting free to love. With the addition of a clarifying amendment at the beginning, it reads as follows:

> Human beings are created to love God with their whole heart and soul, essentially by loving and serving their neighbors. In this way

> they participate in God's plan to bring all creation to completion and so arrive at their own ultimate fulfillment (eternal life).
>
> The other things on the face of the earth are created for human beings, and to help them to pursue the end for which they are created.
>
> From this it follows that we ought to use these things to the extent that they help us toward that end, and free ourselves from them to the extent that they hinder us from it.
>
> For this reason it is necessary to make ourselves indifferent to all created things, in regard to everything which is left to our free will and is not forbidden, in such a way that, for our part, we not seek health rather than sickness, riches rather than poverty, honor rather than dishonor, a long life rather than a short one, and so on in all other matters, wanting and choosing only that which leads more to the end for which we are created [23].[2]

The original text begins: "Human beings are created to praise, reverence and serve God our Lord, and by this means to save their souls," but I have translated "save their souls" as "attain their ultimate fulfillment." I have specified what Ignatius left implicit: that we praise and serve God essentially by loving our neighbor.

The Foundation outlines a vision of life and the most basic criteria for making choices. It says that we live well and attain our ultimate purpose by loving just one thing, or rather some One, and that this requires interior freedom — freedom to choose, habitually, the most loving thing. According to the Foundation, serving God is what makes us happy. If that is true, then the sensible way to deal with "all other things on the face of the earth" is to embrace them to the extent that they contribute to that goal and shun them when they do not. We should be ready for riches or poverty, honor or dishonor, health or sickness, a long life or a short life, depending on whether they serve this goal. It makes no sense to have nonnegotiables in life: for example, to pursue economic security or social prestige no matter what, or to determine to do nothing, ever, that might endanger our health. Rather, says Ignatius, we should be "indifferent" to such alternatives.

"Indifferent" is probably not the best choice of words. As the Ignatian scholar George Ganss says, "indifference" here means:

> undetermined to one thing or option rather than another; impartial; unbiased; with decision suspended until the reasons for a wise choice are learned; still undecided. In no way does it mean unconcerned or unimportant. It implies interior freedom from disordered inclinations.[3]

"Indifference" means inner freedom. It is the capacity to sense and then embrace what is best, even when that goes against our inclinations. Indifference is neither stoic impassiveness nor the extinction of desire that some currents of Eastern religions advocate. It means being so passionately and single-mindedly committed, so completely in love, that we are willing to sacrifice anything, including our lives, for the ultimate goal. It means magnanimous generosity, abandonment into God's hands, *availability*. It is not so much detachment from things as "detachability."[4] It means being like a good shortstop, ready to move in any direction at the crack of the bat.

Of course, we are not indifferent to murder or adultery. Nor are we indifferent to our spouse, family, church, or anything else that serves the ultimate goal here and now. Once we determine that X is more conducive to that goal than the alternatives, we pursue X passionately. Our one great love works itself out as passionate loves of people, projects, and all creation.[5] But we need a radical interior freedom in order to "want and choose" what is more conducive to this goal. And, in the course of following our particular commitments, we must be free to move on when the supreme goal requires it.

"Indifference" means living "without being determined by any disordered inclination" [21]. Inclinations are likes and dislikes, "habits of the heart," that direct the will toward food, possessions, sexual gratification, or sleep; or toward beauty, order, or knowledge. They can be ordered or disordered. Disorder can take crude forms of compulsion or more refined, socially constructed forms, like legalism, racism, elitism, or conformity to convention.[6] Paul speaks of slavery to "the flesh" (by which he means human nature on all its levels) and even to "the law," which comes from God.

Inner freedom is not the total absence of disordered desire. Otherwise, no one would qualify. Rather, it means being able to overcome contrary desire, especially disordered desire, when we have to. That requires *ordering our desires,* or rather allowing God to order them [16; cf. 1], like a magnet pulling iron filings into line, and to enlist them in single-minded service. That is what happens when we fall in love: the one we love engages our feelings and aligns them toward a single reference. This liberates us for spontaneous and creative action. Tracing the biblical roots of the Foundation can help us understand all of this better.

COVENANT, FEAR, AND FAITH

Assyria will not save us;
We will not ride upon horses;
We will say no more, "Our god,"
to the work of our hands.
In you the orphan finds mercy.
(Hos. 14:3)

The central story of the Hebrew Bible is the Exodus. Yahweh, the god of Israel, freed the Hebrews from slavery in Egypt and led them to the land of promise. Once out in the desert, Yahweh made a covenant with Israel and promised them security and well-being (*shalom*). That is what gods were supposed to do for communities at risk from war, disease, wild animals, and crop failure. In turn, Israel promised to look to Yahweh alone. This covenant of exclusive adherence was revolutionary. Ancient Near Eastern peoples usually worshiped several gods simultaneously, looking to one for copious rainfall, another for the fertility of the flock, still another for national security. Yahweh rejected this divine division of labor, assuming exclusive responsibility for Israel's well-being and making an unheard-of demand: "You shall have no other gods besides me" (Exod. 20:3). The Great Commandment of the Book of Deuteronomy, the *Shema,* restates this: "Hear, O Israel: Yahweh is our God, Yahweh alone. You shall love Yahweh your God with all your heart and with all your soul, and with all your might"

(Deut. 6:4–5). You shall not give Yahweh 80 percent of your heart and the remaining 20 percent to some other god, for "Yahweh is a jealous god" (Deut. 6:15). Israel must live entirely by "hearing" Yahweh's word and following his instruction (*torah*). This exclusive "love" is love and trust all in one—the fundamental religious attitude we call faith.[7]

With this, humanity takes a decisive step forward. Serving many gods pulls a people, or an individual, in more than one direction, like someone trying to manage two spouses. To serve Yahweh alone means having an undivided heart. A single super-loyalty puts all others in perspective. That means not being tyrannized by anything in heaven or on earth. It means freedom. This is the taproot of the Ignatian Foundation.

The Bible, Ignatius, and traditional spiritual theology all target "disordered inclinations" as key obstacles to freedom. The Bible stresses the *objects* of these inclinations, which it calls idols. Israel was to embrace the God of life and reject the idols of death (cf. Deut. 30:15–20). Idol-language discloses the public dimension of our internal disorders.

Here the Bible takes aim at one disordered inclination: fear. Insecurity stirs our fear—of hardship, rejection, and death. Fear "disorders" our desires; we grasp for idols which promise security, but fail to deliver it. Idols enslave their devotees and demand human sacrifice.

Today we have different insecurities, and different idols. Although we can control our surroundings better than our ancestors, we are still afraid. We cling to the means of control—money, power, status, and weaponry. "Indifference" is the freedom to let those things go. As the song says, "Freedom's just another word for nothin' left to lose."

I live in El Salvador, where I have been amazed at people who seem to have lost all fear, including mothers and spouses of those "disappeared" and massacred during the civil war of the 1980s. In a tense situation during the war, one woman told me, "*Mire,* when you've hunted for your children among piles of corpses, you are no longer afraid. They can't do anything to you anymore."

Although fear is natural and beneficial in the presence of danger, it can dominate us. It need not, however. When terror invaded Jesus in the garden, he overcame it, by placing his destiny in his Father's hands:

"Let your will, not mine, be done." He repeatedly called his disciples to radical trust: "Why are you fearful, you of little faith?" "Do not be afraid!" Pointing to the birds and the lilies, he told them not to worry about food or clothing. His message was that God knows and cares for you. Seek first God's Reign and its justice, and all your personal needs will be met (cf. Matt. 6:25–33). The Letter to the Hebrews says Jesus cut the root of fear. He set "free those who all their lives were held in slavery by the fear of death" (2:15).

"Indifference" to food, shelter, clothing—and death—might sound foolish, or even dangerous. Yet even those things we most need, and to which we have a right, can dominate us. And none of these things, nor all good things together, can make us happy by themselves.[8] They can relieve suffering and give pleasure. Going without them brings pain, even death. But all the satisfaction that things can give us does not add up to happiness; and all the pain of loss does not add up to unhappiness.

Happiness goes deeper than pleasure; misery goes deeper than pain. When peace and happiness are present, they flow deep within us like a river, even when we lack things that are good, even when we lack things that are essential (cf. John 7:37–39). That living water does not depend decisively on what we have or where we are. Paul wrote to the Romans:

> Who shall separate us from the love of Christ? Shall tribulation, or distress, or persecution, or famine, or nakedness, or peril, or sword? ... No, ... For I am sure that neither death, nor life, nor angels, ... nor anything else in all creation, will be able to separate us from the love of God in Christ Jesus our Lord. (Rom. 8:35–39)

Thus Paul could write, "In any and all circumstances I have learned the secret of being well-fed and of going hungry, of having plenty and of being in need" (Phil. 4:11–13).

The river of living water is not our private property but a river shared and "channeled" by friends who nourish a common vision and praxis. (This is what church is supposed to be and do.) In this sense, friends (and spouses) do "make us happy." But if one or another dies, despite our loss and grief, our happiness should remain. Its ultimate source lies

WITH ALL YOUR HEART AND SOUL AND STRENGTH

Radical trust and total commitment can seem like a lot to ask for. In the final analysis we will only find out whether the Great Commandment and the Foundation make sense if we take up their challenge. But perhaps it will help if we briefly address some of the obstacles that often block this path. These issues all deserve more extensive treatment and we will return to some of them later. The first difficulty is often faith itself.

- Faith includes both trust and belief: for example, the belief that God exists and acts on our behalf. Faith is not an irrational leap in the dark. While it leaps beyond the evidence at hand, faith leaps from the solid platform of experience and in the direction in which the evidence points. We exercise faith like this in the bus driver, the dentist, our friend or spouse. We trust them, based on our experience or on others' testimony, and we risk the leap because it is more reasonable to trust than not to. When Jesus chided his disciples for their lack of faith, it was not because he wanted them to act irrationally, but because "having eyes they did not *see* and having ears they did not *listen.*" Their senses were dulled, their capacity to experience deadened. They failed to penetrate reality (cf. Mark 8:18) and to perceive the Reign of God in their midst. Authentic testimonies of faith are based on experience. They shine like a beacon not on some imaginary world but deep into the heart of reality, which we experience all too superficially. The difference between religious faith and everyday faith (in the dentist, for example) lies in the type of evidence and the type of subsequent verification which, in the case of religious faith, almost always leave room for doubt. But doubt also stalks our faith that someone loves us. In neither case does doubt invalidate faith, or necessarily weaken it.

• But how is total commitment to God compatible with freedom and human fulfillment? The God of the Bible is not another "entity" in the universe. This God acts like no other agent, desiring only our freedom and full humanity and to bring all creation to fulfillment, and working only for that. God is Love, says John's famous letter, a God with whom we can fall in love. Otherwise, total commitment would make no sense.

• The "praise, reverence and service of God" [23] consists, essentially, in loving our neighbor as ourselves, especially our neighbor who is a victim of injustice (cf. Luke 10:25–37). That is our sole obligation (Matt. 7:12; etc.).[9]

• Instead of an impossible burden imposed from outside us, the New Testament understands love to be an internal dynamic of freedom (James 1:25), which the divine Spirit helps us live out with joy and satisfaction.

• Finally, there is the problem of how exclusive loyalty to one god has served to legitimate patriarchal-authoritarian societies, families, and churches, as well as fanatical intolerance and imperial conquest. In fact, like anything else, religion, too, can be abused. However, that does not invalidate monotheism any more than Hitler's *Mein Kampf* invalidates books. But it should serve as a warning. Religion only liberates when it is prophetic, that is, when it denounces abuse, defends the weak and announces a credible utopia. Such a vision inspired people like Martin Luther King, Dorothy Day, Oscar Romero — and Jesus of Nazareth.

elsewhere. Landscapes, a party, or a community victory can swell our joy, but they do not create it.

That peace and joy is what we were born for. Its necessary condition is the freedom to love. Our happiness seems to depend on how we respond to the insecurities that besiege us. In the end, there are only two ways to deal with them: either we grasp for idols or we live by faith. When we grasp for idols, they turn on us and dominate our lives. To live by faith is to abandon ourselves to the Ultimate Reality which surrounds and penetrates us and which alone satisfies us.

The people of Israel expressed this faith in song:

> God is our refuge and strength,
> a very present help in trouble.
> Therefore we will not fear though the earth should change,
> though the mountains shake in the heart of the sea;
> though its waters roar and foam,
> though the mountains tremble with its tumult....
> Yahweh of hosts is with us;
> the God of Jacob is our refuge. (Ps. 46)

St. Teresa of Avila prayed with similar faith in the midst of conflicts and trials:

> Let nothing disturb you, let nothing dismay you;
> All else changes; God alone remains.
> Patient endurance attains to all things.
> The one who has God finds she lacks nothing,
> and God alone suffices.

The psalm and Teresa bear witness to the radical trust and total commitment of the Great Commandment and the Ignatian Foundation.

CONCLUSION

According to the Foundation, our fulfillment depends on getting free to love. The insecurities of life stir our fears — of hardship, rejection, and death. As fear grows, it "disorders" our loves and drives us to serve idols that enslave and dehumanize.

By faith we can abandon ourselves to the Mystery that surrounds us, confident that the universe is in good hands. Faith in this radical goodness overcomes fear and orders our loves. But to come to terms with radical goodness, we must also come to terms with evil. The truth — the double truth about radical evil and radical goodness — will set us free.

3 The Reality of Evil

People loved darkness rather than light
because their deeds were evil.
(John 3:19)

One freezing night, I nearly ran into a homeless man on a sidewalk in Manhattan. Wrapped in plastic sheeting against the cold and laced with frost, he looked like a creature from the deep. I was startled. It took me a while to recognize what, or who, stood before me. How to react? What to do? When I approached the frostman, he looked at me with hostility. I shrank back and withdrew, making my way home in a troubled state of mind. Each confused thought led to others. Could he survive much longer? How many more were there like him? Should I have taken him home? Would he have come? How would my housemates react? Should I have taken him to a hospital?

I had come face to face with homelessness in the richest place on earth, and I didn't know what to do. After that, I would think about people in the street as I took hot showers on cold mornings. I will never forget the frostman. He brought me up against evil—the horrible injustice of homelessness—and up against myself.

Evil is difficult to deal with. The nightly news assails us with murder and mayhem, lying and corruption. Still, it is necessary to face evil and the part we play in it if we are to live in accord with our dignity. The gospels open with John the Baptist's call to repentance, reflecting that urgent need.

The Spiritual Exercises also begin with an invitation to reform our lives and accept forgiveness. It is here in the First Week of the Exercises that Ignatius addressed the issues of sin and forgiveness most extensively.[1] Part of what he says jars our contemporary sensibilities. Following centuries of tradition, he begins by presenting one-time acts, including the sin of the angels and the sin of Adam and Eve, as leading many into eternal damnation [cf. 50–52]. (This preoccupation recedes in Ignatius's later writings.) Here we must sort out what is essential and instructive from what is not. When Ignatius discusses the reform of life, which is the heart of what he has to say about sin and forgiveness, we can follow him more closely.

Today, if we want a hearing when discussing moral evil and reform, we must avoid scare tactics and the guilt-peddling and cheap moralizing that stress the bad news of sin at the expense of the good news of deliverance. There are churches and other institutions, as well as many parents, that promote a morality of obedience, more in service to control than to human development, straining out the gnat of everyday peccadilloes and swallowing the camel of massive injustice. Ignatius stresses coming to terms with evil, including our own, in view of God's healing and liberating forgiveness—which was Jesus' approach, as well.

THE TRUTH WILL SET YOU FREE

When Jesus said that the truth will set you free, what he meant by truth was the bad news of sin and the good news of divine love. Knowledge of this reality is not something we can easily grasp by ourselves. The depth and breadth of evil eludes us. Evil hides under a pile of virtues, wreaking havoc in the name of freedom, property rights, national security, and religion. Liberal society trivializes evil and practically denies sin.[2] Its standard discourse goes something like this: "We have found the solution to happiness (getting and spending, elections and markets). We are now in a mop-up operation on the way to paradise. We just have to eliminate terrorists and drug traffickers, clean up toxic waste sites and check global warming. But if we stay the course, better technology will solve our problems." This is a cover-up.

The cover-up continues as the villainy of public enemies erupts in our living rooms in images of gratuitous violence, disconnected from the way society is organized. Street crime and terrorism—real evils, to be sure—dominate the news. Meanwhile, poverty kills many times their victims. But if a nightly news program were to begin each evening with the announcement that 120,000 people had died deaths related to malnutrition that day, and then devote the time necessary to help us understand why, the news program probably would not last a week.[3]

INTERIOR KNOWLEDGE AND CONTEMPLATION

Empirical science requires dispassionate observation and something like pure reason. That is not enough for understanding life. Since life is a moral drama, understanding it requires moral empathy. We need to enter into that drama and allow it to enter us. That is the way we come to know another person, a foreign country, a new neighborhood or place of work.

Interior knowledge is like absorbing important news, like the good news that I passed my final exams or that Chloe agrees to marry me or the bad news that I've been fired or that my father has died. I might grasp the facts quickly, but it will take time for the truth to sink in. Not just my head, but all of me has to adjust to the new reality, perhaps as parts of me resist. This is how we appropriate the reality of injustice. We first absorb its impact. Then we "sit with" it, working through the feelings and thoughts it evokes. In that way, the experience reshapes our likes and dislikes, our will and our thoughts. Engaging that reality draws us out of ourselves and even moves our hands and feet to act.

Sitting with reality, allowing it to work on us, working through the feelings and the thoughts it stirs is what we mean by *contemplation*. Contemplation arises naturally out of our need to be in touch with reality in its rich complexity. Contemplation in this sense is the opposite of flight from reality.

Neither demonizing the enemy, nor threats of punishment, nor obsessive guilt discloses the truth about evil. Understanding this truth comes from contemplating the real world, its sin, and our part in it. This gives us what Ignatius called "interior knowledge" [cf. 63, 104, 233, etc.]. Interior knowledge changes us and frees us. "It is not much

Rightly understood, spirituality is the opposite of escaping from reality. We encounter Ultimate Reality not by leaving the world, but by plunging into it, as Jesus did. (A "retreat" is really a tactical withdrawal from distractions, in order to advance more deeply into reality.)

Contemplation is also communion and communication with Ultimate Reality, that is, with God. It is prayer. We do not have to scale distant mountains or practice strange rituals to contact God, as if God were far away or hard to find. In that case, closing the gap would be beyond our powers. The good news, the gospel of the New Testament, is that God has closed the gap, especially in the person of Christ. God has drawn near as the holy Mystery that surrounds us and presses upon us from all sides, embracing and filling us. God is always at our very center, even though we are frequently somewhere else. God actively offers and communicates God's own self (the Spirit).

Ignatius insists that God works on us directly, enlightening and guiding us [cf. 15]. With this in mind, he prescribes a prayer for "what I want and desire" [48] at the beginning of each prayer exercise of his retreat, depending to the subject matter of the prayer. That gives focus and direction to the exercise. We ask for the interior knowledge that comes from immediate experience of God: knowledge of the meaning of life, of Christ, and so on. In the present case, we ask for interior knowledge of evil.

knowing that fills and satisfies the soul," says Ignatius, "but feeling [*sentir*] and savoring things internally" [2]. The Spanish verb *sentir* means both feeling and understanding. Interior knowledge is experiential knowledge, involving intellect, imagination, will, the "affections," even action. It does not depend decisively on IQ or schooling. It is not esoteric knowledge. It is rarely dramatic. Most often it comes in the form of a new insight and the development of a new feel for important truths about life. Interior knowledge means walking and dwelling in the truth (2 John 4).

To really understand evil, Ignatius has us ask for interior knowledge, a "feel" for how the world works and deep repugnance for its disorder [63]. We want clear-sighted realism about people and institutions — governments, militaries, churches, companies — and ourselves. We want to be able to sniff out the evil lurking behind warm smiles, political platforms, pious rhetoric, and advertising.

THE BEAN CRISIS AND THE GREAT PLUNDERING

Taking in the truth about evil can require patient effort, as I learned one day while visiting my friend Gabriela Reyes in Talnique, El Salvador. Gabi is a grandmother and catechist who bubbles with ironic humor. Since times were tough and she had been ill, I asked if she had been eating well. She leaned close and lowered her voice so others could not hear. "It's more important that the little ones eat, don't you think?" she said, smiling.

I only asked because of what I've come to learn about rural communities like hers. On another occasion, as Gabi served me breakfast, I complimented her on the beans. "Are you eating beans these days?" I asked. The price of beans had lately shot through the roof. "Well, no," she answered. She kept such delicacies for special occasions like this. It turned out that Gabi's household hadn't eaten beans for some time. I shuffled my feet in the dirt.

Just then Toña arrived from next door. "Are you eating beans?" I asked her. "Well, no," she said. "They're pretty expensive." "How are you getting by?" I asked. "We eat tortillas and sometimes rice." "Anything else?" I asked. *"Mora,"* she answered, referring to the edible greens for which the people forage in the woods in order to make a thin soup.

I squirmed on my wooden stool. This was hard to take in. My automatic gringo reaction was to walk up to Delia's store to buy beans for

Toña and Gabi. Along the way I wondered: How do these households manage?

I was in for another surprise: Delia had no beans to sell. "Why not?" I asked. "The people can't afford beans," she explained, "and I can't afford to buy them if they can't pay for them." Hmm. "Maybe Don Chico has beans. Try him," Delia suggested.

I did, but Don Chico wasn't selling beans either. The situation in Talnique was beginning to sink in, and Don Chico opened my eyes a little more. "Look," he said. "The situation is really messed up. Last year the *campesinos* around here had to sell their products at a very low price. They couldn't even cover their costs. Now, they can't buy beans to eat!" (Most *campesinos* rent land to cultivate, since the land was robbed from their ancestors long ago.)

"How is that possible?" I asked Don Chico. "What happened between last year's harvest and this year?" "It's the middlemen," said Chico. "The merchants made a killing." The merchants had exported part of the national crop, with the government turning a blind eye to antispeculation laws.

In the days that followed, rich lessons unfolded for me from this experience. One was that reality is often much worse than it appears at first. It takes effort to observe and listen carefully to uncover how bad things are. The truth has to work its way through our internal resistance.

Second, the more we appreciate victims like Gabi and Toña, the worse the evil looks to us. The good people harmed, the projects and values undermined show up evil for what it is.

Finally, conditions in Talnique threw light on the situation of the whole countryside. As Don Chico explained, the local tragedy was tied to wider structures that enmesh the local community in a lethal web of injustice. That web extends farther still. As I write these words, the U.S. and Central American governments are negotiating a "free trade" agreement. Uncle Sam wants U.S. agricultural companies to be free to dump their heavily subsidized produce in Central America, a practice that will devastate local producers.

People in Talnique are part of the more than 800 million who are chronically undernourished on the planet despite an overabundance of food supplies. More than 30,000 children under five die in the world each day from preventable causes.[4] By some accounts, more than two-thirds of the world's poor are women.[5] More than 100 million inhabitants of the rich countries are poor, more than 5 million homeless, almost 40 million jobless — and most of the homeless and jobless are young people. Thirty million in the U.S. suffer hunger.[6]

Since 1960, the gap between rich and poor countries has multiplied many times.[7] The rich-poor divide may be the single greatest cause of environmental degradation due to both overconsumption by the rich and the desperate methods of survival the poor are forced to employ.[8] Power is concentrated in the centers of world finance, with no accountability to the billions who lack basic necessities. We have organized a world that excludes billions from the banquet table and the decision table. Inequality is not a defect of the system; it is the system.

Things need not be this way. Rich countries do not have to subsidize local agribusiness to the tune of $300 billion a year. They could easily remove barriers to imports from poor countries. It would probably require no more than $150 billion in well-targeted aid to pull poor countries out of poverty. Compare that to the $160 billion spent each year on beauty products.[9]

THE ANTI-REIGN AND IDOLATRY

Poverty is not primarily a technical problem. Above all, it is a moral problem, the great sin of our time. We rarely think of sin in these terms. We usually apply that label first to personal actions — theft, adultery, lying, homicide — and then, analogously, to original sin, habitual sin (vice), and, perhaps, structural sin. From one standpoint, this is correct. Personal sin is at the root of all sin. However, that is only part of the picture. Taking personal sins with utter seriousness, the New Testament locates them in a wider context, as part of the "sin of the world" (John 1:29). Sin is a large-scale enterprise, a kind of "anti-reign" opposed to the Reign (or Kingdom) of God (see 1 John 5:19; Luke 4:5–6). Sin "reigns" (see Rom. 5–7) in individuals and also in relationships and institutions. Personal sin is a participation in the anti-reign.

When we look through the wide lens, the systemic despoilment of the poor is the most obvious, the most massive and death-dealing sin. (I mean "the poor" in the biblical sense: the economically deprived, first of all, and all other vulnerable and oppressed groups, as well.) It is the great sin of all times, the nucleus of the sin of the world. It is a structural sin that is more than the sum of individual sins. Today, our growing global interdependence discloses this more clearly. Unless we place this sin at center stage, we risk trivializing sin, including personal sin (which is one reason for starting here rather than with Adam and Eve).[10]

The language of idolatry helps us penetrate the logic of sin. Idols thrive on the insecurity we feel in our bones. Freudians speak of our traumatic expulsion from the womb and our total dependency as infants. The existentialists call us the anxious animal, because, unlike other animals, which react only to present dangers, we humans imagine future threats as well. Insecurity generates fear. We cope mostly by trying to control our surroundings, and nowadays we have unprecedented means of control: locks, razor wire, security cameras, attack dogs, and nuclear deterrents. When fear dominates, we turn these means of control into absolutes. We make idols of money, law, the party, efficiency, the church, my job, my rights, status, approval. Idols foster compulsive rituals and addiction. They demand sacrifice. We sacrifice such real security as housing, health, and education to bloated military budgets and prison construction.

Some idols are more bloodthirsty than others. Jesus assigned priority to Mammon, riches (see also Eph. 5:5; Col. 3:5). Mammon demands the most victims. As Jon Sobrino says, the present organization of the economy is the most sacred of our sacred cows. It is untouchable and self-justifying ("Business is business"). So are its essential components — the "free" market, private property, profit (the "bottom line"). The economic system generates additional idols, including untouchable military establishments and the incontestable logic of war.[11]

CONCLUSION

To sum up, evil is a vast enterprise that follows the logic of idols. Above all, it is the pillaging of the poor and the weak. We must come to terms with evil to become more fully human. The knowledge of evil that helps set us free is that interior knowledge which involves the whole person. It makes a slow, sometimes difficult entry.

The evil that each of us most needs to face, however, is our own. That unsettling challenge is easier—in fact, liberating and life-giving—when we know that we are accepted and forgiven. We now turn to consider that message.

Forgiveness 4

The father said to his servants, "Bring quickly the best robe, and put it on him; and put a ring on his hand, and shoes on his feet; and bring the fatted calf and kill it, and let us eat and make merry; for this son of mine was dead and is alive again; he was lost and is found!" (Luke 15:22–24)

THE THIRTY-NINTH WITNESS[1]

In the predawn hours of March 12, 1964, Kitty Genovese was assaulted and murdered in New York City. Her screams awakened at least thirty-eight neighbors who heard or watched how, for another half hour, her assailant stalked, stabbed, raped, and finally killed her. No one wanted to get involved or even call the police. The story attracted international attention. It was not just that many identified with the victim and understood that something like that could easily happen to them. Killings happen all the time. What could account for the public's intense fascination with this crime? Many who have studied the case attribute it to people's deep-seated fear that, had they been there, they would have been the thirty-ninth silent witness. In this crime people caught a glimpse of the "bad Samaritan" in themselves.

The story of Kitty Genovese resonates with our sense of being guilty bystanders in a cruel world. We are more aware than our forbears of the scope of injustice. We are all its beneficiaries, if not its agents. We know we should not mug or exploit people, but this is not enough. There is no neutral ground in the war between good and evil. All that is needed for evil to triumph is that good people do nothing. The silence of decent folks standing on the sidelines troubled Martin Luther King more than the racists who threw rocks.[2] As we know, if you're not part of the solution, well then.... Even when we try to be part of the solution, can we claim to have done enough? And don't less-than-noble motives contaminate our noble actions? The point is not to get down on ourselves but to awaken from a lonely hypocrisy. We are all in this together. Better to feel our solidarity in sin and our need for forgiveness than to cling to a phony righteousness. Getting free to love requires facing up to our part in the sin of the world.

ACCEPTANCE FIRST

Where does that leave us? Can we face up to our sin? Can we conquer those old habits? What about responding to the world's suffering?

But, wait. Doesn't "responding to the world's suffering" sound overwhelming? Are we up to that? Could we make a life of it? The most legitimate demands can dishearten rather than move us to act.

Are we starting out on the wrong foot here? The gospels suggest as much. They turn the whole thing around. There we find God taking the initiative in conversion, like a good shepherd seeking after stray sheep. Jesus welcomes sinners *before* they repent. "This man welcomes sinners and eats with them" (Luke 15:2). He "hangs out" with them in festive meals that celebrate God's acceptance. He offers public sinners the respect that society denies them.[3] Jesus' acceptance is a recognition of their dignity. It includes the offer of forgiveness before they ask for it (Luke 5:20; John 8:11). He empowers people like Zacchaeus and the sinful woman to acknowledge their sin. Their lives change because they have first been surprised by his acceptance (Luke 19:1–10; 7:41–43).

There are two sides to forgiveness. It must be offered, and it must be accepted. Accepting it entails admitting we need it and assuming responsibility for our actions. Still, Jesus' offer of forgiveness in no way depends on our past "merits." It is gratuitous: grace. He is saying that God offers forgiveness to everyone, no matter what they have done. That offer is first; it is always there for us — 24/7. Repentance is a response to that offer.

Facing our faults and reforming our lives is not primarily a matter of willpower and effort. Although we have a part to play, it is not the most important part. From a gospel point of view, appreciating God's healing mercy is more important than fixating on our defects. For what frees us is knowing that we are acceptable and accepted, not as a prize for being good, but in spite of being not so good. Otherwise, it is well-nigh impossible to face our sinfulness – let alone to take on world hunger.

To fully appreciate this we have to get clear about the thorny issue of guilt.

GUILT AND FORGIVENESS

You are not under law but under grace.
(Rom. 6:14)

One day when Marta Dimas stopped by, I invited her in to lunch. Marta was about twenty. She and her family had been driven from their hamlet by the Salvadoran army years before. The family is extremely poor. As I set a plate of chicken before Marta, she stood up without a thought, bowed her head, and offered thanks. As she finished her serving, I urged seconds on her. "No thanks," she said politely. "Come on," I said, "who knows when you'll be able to have this again." "Really, that's it," she said, smiling. "I can't get accustomed to what I can't have."

Marta had learned to steward her hunger. She knew that eating a lot today only makes things worse tomorrow. I was confused, then a little embarrassed, as the truth of Marta's life sank in. Not that I should feel bad about eating. Rather, it is appropriate to feel sorrow that Marta does not eat well – and moved to do something about that.

You may have felt something like this when coming across homeless people or someone denied medical care. Dorothy Day felt it while passing a bread line in lower Manhattan on cold mornings in 1937. "Every morning about four hundred men come to Mott Street to be fed," she writes. "It is hard to say, matter-of-factly and cheerfully, 'Good morning,' as we pass on our way to Mass.... One felt more like taking their hands and saying, 'Forgive us – let us forgive each other! All of us who are more comfortable, who have a place to sleep, three meals a day, work to do — we are responsible for your condition. We are guilty of each other's sins. Forgive us and may God forgive us all!' "[4]

Dorothy expresses the "shame and confusion" that Ignatius urges us to beg for [cf. 48, 50, 74]. These are not the bitter guilt-feelings that lash us for offending authority or failing to live up to our ideal self-image. This is a humanizing shame and confusion, that arises out of sorrow for trampled dignity and a sense of oneness with the victims. Unlike bitter remorse, these sentiments move forward, toward reconciliation.

Modern society produces fragile egos. Consumerism makes us feel inadequate for how we look, how much we weigh, or how old we are, because we don't measure up to the ideals promoted by advertising and multiplied by peer pressure. In this context, the prospect of facing our moral failures can look like one more putdown, this time by a divine prosecutor. How can we get beyond that? We have to replace these bad-news lies with the good news that we are acceptable and accepted, and this doesn't depend on measuring up to anything. If we're not okay, well, that's okay. That frees us to face our failings and leave them behind. It gives us a handle on guilt.

Guilt feelings arise spontaneously when we transgress a law or disobey authority. The superego Freud describes is a subconscious reflex mechanism that develops in early childhood. It embodies the criteria of authorities that we internalized long ago and that now constitute a kind of ideal self we subconsciously crave to be. Failing to measure up triggers the sting of remorse. To avoid this, some people strike out in rebellion, while others strive to placate authority. Both are dead-end strategies. The first, throwing morality overboard, can lower the volume of a hyperactive superego but at the cost of dehumanizing myself and harming others.

Writing to the Romans, Paul describes the opposite strategy, that of trying to make ourselves acceptable in others' eyes, in God's eyes, and ultimately in our own eyes, by strictly observing the moral rules. The more we strain to keep the law, says Paul, the more we perceive its demands to escalate. Meanwhile, prohibition stimulates desire for the "forbidden fruit." This vicious circle produces intense anguish (cf. Rom.

IN OTHER WORDS...

The Letter to the Hebrews says that since Christ died once and for all we are forgiven once and for all.[5] Before him, sacrifices were offered repeatedly to expiate sins. But Christ's love-unto-death was a kind of all-sufficient "sacrifice" that achieved definitive forgiveness. Now, we need only accept that forgiveness and reaccept it when we fail. There is no further need for sin-sacrifices, either cultic or moral. The church's practice of confession and Eucharist has not always reflected this revolutionary truth.

Another way to express this reality, perhaps the most radical way of all, is to say that God has decided to cancel our moral debt (cf. Matt. 18:27).

7:17–25).[6] The project breaks down. Besides, says Paul, when we seek justification (that is, forgiveness) through our own good works, we are rejecting the justification that God offers regardless of our merits. This is trying to buy love from someone who offers it freely. If Christ died out of love for us, no other work is needed to "buy" forgiveness.

What the gospel says about our situation is that the holy Mystery (God) presses upon us from without and within with a permanent offer of forgiveness, no matter what we have done. Believing that and accepting the offer leaves us at peace with God and with ourselves (cf. Rom. 5:1–2). It removes the bitter sting of guilt.

After that, we can still expect to fail; and when we do, we should feel remorse and "godly grief" (2 Cor. 7:11). After all, that is a sign of self-respect indicating we have done something unworthy of ourselves. However, if we offend someone we love who we know is disposed to forgive us, that makes reconciliation easier. Remorse is swallowed up in the welcome-back party that the Father throws for his prodigal child. We will have to admit our offense, clear up misunderstandings, and repair harm done. But trust and love will propel us to the fresh light of reconciliation.[7]

"BY THEIR STRIPES WE ARE HEALED"

While this is revolutionary good news, for most of us it doesn't sink in as we would like. We continue to struggle with guilt. Some experience guilt feelings that are disproportionate to any real harm they have done. Their superego insists not just "You have done something wrong" (which may be true), but "You are no good!" (which is nonsense) or "You're still guilty no matter what." These people, and all of us, need to resist such inner voices, confident that they do not come from God who "is greater than our conscience" (1 John 3:20). As Paul says, "there is no condemnation for those who are in Christ Jesus" (Rom. 8:1).

But, as I say, for most of us the good news of radical forgiveness rarely takes over our lives. And though people rightly say that we need to accept and forgive ourselves, few seem able to self-administer this medicine in the dosage required. Healing, liberating forgiveness is a gift we cannot force. If it comes ultimately from God, however, it normally comes through others. It is channeled by people who accept and forgive us in their own human way.

Jesus mediated radical pardon to his disciples and public sinners. Later, confessing their sins to one another and forgiving one another, his followers mediated divine forgiveness (cf. James 5:15; John 20:21). The church community continues to do that for me and many others, though not for everyone. I have found the sacrament of reconciliation very beneficial, but it has not been enough to drive home to me the radical acceptance that heals and sets us free. Who or what can do that? I propose people like my friend Marta Dimas. My country sent the bombs that were dropped on her village. The grace-full acceptance by Marta and others like her of people like me places us before an acceptance more radical than their own. It seems that God has chosen people like them as ambassadors of grace for people like me.

Each year waves of foreign delegations visit El Salvador. Most of the travelers deplane a little anxious. Having been briefed about poverty, massacres, and earthquakes, they vaguely fear what awaits them. "Will these people lunge for my wallet?" they wonder. "Will I suffer a massive guilt-attack when we reach the first poor community?"

The visitors spend much of their time puzzling over why these poor people are smiling and why they insist on sharing their tortillas with strangers. If the visitors listen to the stories of unspeakable hardship, their hosts will break their hearts — and that will turn out to be the most important event of their trip. If the pilgrims let it happen, it can be a life-changing experience.

The victims stop them in their tracks. "My God! Their children die from malnutrition. The powerful steal from them at will. It's so unfair. And what has my government been doing here?" The visitors are shocked, not because the poor are saints, but because they obviously don't deserve this.

As the humanity of the poor crashes through the visitors' defenses, they glimpse their reflection in the eyes of their hosts. ("These people are just like us!") They feel gently invited to lay down the burden of superiority of which they were scarcely aware. They are brushed with a light shame and confusion, and feel they are losing their grip. Actually, it is the world that is losing its grip on them. I mean the world consisting of important people like themselves and unimportant poor people. That world starts to unhinge. The experience threatens to sweep them out of control like a stream in spring. It is like the disorientation of falling in love. In fact, that is what is happening, a kind of falling in love. The earth trembles. The horizon opens. They are entering a richer world.

We don't have to travel to Central America for this. Plenty of people suffer terrible injustice closer to home, in all our countries: abused women and children, oppressed minorities, homeless people, immigrants. Engaging them puts us in touch with the world, with ourselves, and with divine mercy.

It puts us in touch with the world. The victims draw us into the central drama of life. They show us that the world is a much crueler place than we supposed, but also that there is something going on that is far more wonderful than we dared to imagine. When the poor insist on celebrating life no matter how bad things are, and on sharing what little they have, they communicate hope. What accounts for that smile with so little grounding in the facts? There is more here than meets the eye. Sin abounds, but grace abounds even more (Rom. 5:20).[8]

Engaging the outcast puts us in touch with ourselves. The outcast calls forth from within us parts of ourselves that we have banished into unconscious exile, and heals us. (That this encounter can heal us suggests to me that our psychic suffering has deep roots in the kind of society we live in. Isn't psychic torment in the affluent suburbs the polar reflection of inner-city decay? If so, then healing our inner divisions depends on working to heal our social divisions.)

Finally, the victims place us before divine mercy. Many pilgrims experience deep peace at being so warmly received by the poor — before having cleaned up their act with them and billions of others like them. In such encounters, the poor masses of the world emerge from anonymity and take on flesh and blood as three-dimensional human beings. Actually, there are more than three dimensions here. The eyes of victims beckon like bottomless wells. The outcast is like a door that opens out to the divine Mystery.

Isaiah told of a Servant of Yahweh whose appearance was repulsive, who had suffered horribly but who turned out to be a source of healing and life for others:

> ...despised and rejected by people,
> a man of sorrows, and acquainted with grief;
> and as one from whom people hide their faces
>   he was despised, and we esteemed him not.
>   Surely he has borne our griefs and carried our sorrows;
>   yet we esteemed him stricken, smitten by God, and afflicted.
> But he was wounded for our transgressions...
> and by his stripes we are healed. (Isa. 53)

Today as in Isaiah's time, engaging such stricken people has something open-ended about it, like the opening of a chess match with its infinite possibilities. They arouse in us the awe and fascination that points to the Holy. They stir up the humanizing shame that says, "Depart from me, O Lord, for I am a sinner" (Luke 5:8).[9]

The victims of a divided world are uniquely qualified to forgive. Not all are inclined to do so; but when they do, they mediate an acceptance greater than their own. They enable us to acknowledge our part in the sin of the world and to stand before the holy Mystery that draws near to identify with their suffering and to befriend us, too. God continues to show up today in cold stables and on death row.

MY MIDDLE-CLASS "TRIBE"

Middle-class societies are newcomers to history, having existed for only about two hundred years. My own middle-class "tribe" is a peculiar bunch. We're not all bad people, by any means, just a minority under an illusion shared by many minorities, that we are the center of gravity of the universe. The poor can free us from that fantasy.

Don't get me wrong. The middle-class cultures of the North have made extraordinary advances in civilization. While many came at great cost to despoiled nations and races, they are nonetheless historic achievements. I mean even the ambiguous technological progress, but especially the spiritual, cultural, and political breakthroughs: the unheard-of opportunities, political liberties, democracy, modern science, the critical consciousness of the Enlightenment. No need to disparage these. Yet we too pay a high price for our freedoms and economic security. While they allow us to pursue our personal life-projects, they generate a spirit of go-it-alone individualism. They separate us from each other. More serious still, they distance us from the poor and their daily struggle for life. The vast majority of all the human beings who have ever lived have had to battle every day to keep the household alive against the threats of hunger, disease, accidents, and violence. By removing us from the daily threat of death, the benefits of modernity induce in us a chronic low-grade confusion about what is really important in life: namely, life itself and love. To make matters worse, our technology and media lead us to believe that our perspective on life is on target, indeed the norm. The victims stop us short; they show us that they, the marginalized, are at the center of things. We who nosh in Washington and Paris cafés are on the fringe. We clearly need these people more than they need us.

However, they also need us. Try this quiz. What do the following have in common: Dorothy Day, Mohandas Gandhi, Che Guevara, Mother Teresa, Martin Luther King, Simone Weil, Karl Marx? Answer: They were all well educated and from middle-class or well-to-do backgrounds. While we may not agree with everything that all of them stood for, they did put their talents and training at the service of people in need. It seems that there is hope for my tribe, and plenty for us to do.

CONCLUSION

The experience of acceptance and forgiveness empowers us to face our part in the evil of the world. The New Testament says that God offers this forgiveness no matter what we have done – not because we are good, but because God is good. People we have offended and other victims can mediate that healing and liberating news.

Of course, it takes two to reconcile. Our part in the bargain includes admitting our faults, and changing. We now turn to that challenge.

Reform of Life 5

While I kept silence, my body wasted away. . . .
I said, "I will confess my transgressions to Yahweh,"
and you forgave the guilt of my sin.

(Ps. 32:4–5)

In Arthur Miller's *Death of a Salesman,* Willy Loman is living a hell on earth. He cannot face the truth about his life. Willy has constructed a false identity and a false world to shield himself from past failures. Maintaining these fictions wreaks havoc all around him. His phony present depends on imagining a fake past and dreaming an impossible future.

There is a bit of Willy in all of us. Past sins and present weaknesses sit there in our lives like unwelcome guests. What are we to do with them? Working through them is surely better than evasion or wallowing in guilt. We may have broken with harmful behavior long ago. Maybe no major skeletons lurk in our closet. Even so, shadows from the past can darken our present if we have not come to terms with them, if our wounds are still raw.

Members of Alcoholics Anonymous and other twelve-step programs stress the importance of facing present errors. They then undertake inventory of the past, trying to understand why things occurred and repairing what damage they can.[1] In that spirit, Ignatius invites us to examine our present faults and to review our past. That stirs up sorrow, shame, confusion and repugnance [cf. 45, 50, 55, 63]. ("Was that me? I can't believe I did that!") But this is a redemptive sorrow and holy confusion that leads to new freedom and inner peace. Working through the past loosens its grip on us. Recent experience of societies emerging from civil war and atrocity confirms this. By bringing past horrors to light in South Africa, Central and South America, and Eastern Europe, truth commissions have helped war-torn countries move toward healing and reconciliation.

As A.A. members know, taking inventory also brings to light the way our friends and the Higher Power looked after and helped us, even as we did harm. Ignatius, too, invites us to recall how God and many creatures gave us life and sustenance, as we were acting selfishly. This exercise produces gratitude and enthusiasm for the future [cf. 60, 61]. It also gives us a more mature appreciation of sin as ingratitude and betrayal (as Ignatius stressed in later writings).

We can make this kind of examination in different ways. For example, we can set aside time each day for several days. Writing in a journal helps some people. Start with the present, asking questions like, Where am I going? Does my life have an overall goal? Is that goal worthy? How coherent are my choices? Is this who I want to be? Is this who I am called to be?[2]

We need a quiet time for this kind of reflection. Ignatius recommends imagining ourselves in God's benevolent presence. He suggests imagining Christ on the cross and asking ourselves: What have I done for him? What am I doing for him? What should I do for him [53]? The martyred university rector Ignacio Ellacuría suggested placing ourselves before the crucified victims of today and asking: Have I helped to crucify them? What am I doing to remove them from their crosses? What must I do so they can rise up again?[3]

More specific questions can also help us review: What idolatries hold me back? Do I care for my spouse, children, and parents? Do I pull my weight at home? How am I fulfilling work responsibilities? Do I dominate or manipulate others? Have I harmed others? Do I show concern for the poor and others in need? Do I share what I have, or do I hoard? Do I speak up for the truth and in defense of the weak? Am I prejudiced? Do I lie to get out of a jam? Am I lazy or cowardly? Overindulgent in food or drink? Immoderate in my use of TV or other forms of entertainment? Is there disorder in my sexual life? Do I care for the natural environment? Do I neglect prayer? Do I take rest and show reasonable care for my health?

Having examined the present, we can then inventory the past, reviewing our lives year by year, place by place, job by job, assessing not only our errors but also blessings received [56, 60].

In these exercises, we ask for a deep sense (interior knowledge) of the disorder in our lives; for appropriate sorrow, shame, and confusion; for repugnance toward evil; for profound gratitude toward God who forgives us no matter what we have done, and for the many blessings we have received [48, 55, 63]. These "graces" are appropriate for times of reform and conversion. Asking for them is part of our collaboration with the God who heals and frees us.

We can also collaborate by practicing penance, that is, by taking action that targets our weaknesses [cf. 82–87]. The best penance is responding to our neighbor in need. We might also benefit from an evening without television or fasting "not only from food, but also from frantic activity, stimulants, deadening amusements, [and] superfluous possessions."[4]

PERSONAL TRANSFORMATION

> *We know that we have passed from death to life*
> *because we love one another.* (1 John 3:14)

In the perspective of Christian faith, reform is more than a change of behavior. It involves personal transformation – or "conversion."

The book of Acts recounts Paul's conversion on the road to Damascus. Augustine and Ignatius of Loyola provided classic accounts of theirs. More recently, C. S. Lewis, Dorothy Day, Thomas Merton, and Etty Hillesum have done the same.[5]

The crucial change in life is the turn from selfishness to love. For some this takes place early in life, for others later; still others avoid it to the end. Some make the turn and later reverse direction. The fundamental change can be dramatic or barely perceptible; for most, it seems to happen in stages. It always involves struggle. After all, a false self is dying and a "new human being" is coming to life. One is "born again" (cf. John 3:3). The basic turn initiates an ongoing adventure that will include miniconversions and backsliding. Reform will always be in order. Archbishop Oscar Romero was already a saintly man when violent repression and the murder of his friend Rutilio Grande occasioned a further conversion that transformed him into a prophet and a martyr.

Conversion is a process of self-transcendence. From being turned in upon ourselves, we open up to our neighbor. Having sought what was merely self-satisfying and comforting, we now seek what is true and good.[6]

Conversion is religious as well as moral. It opens us up to Ultimate Reality. Augustine, Ignatius, and Etty Hillesum assure us that it is more God's work than ours. The first impulse comes from beyond us, and what happens is disproportionate to our efforts.

The saints describe conversion as a falling in love. A powerful new love ignites and works its way through the whole person. It pulls lesser loves into line, like a magnet aligning iron filings. Being in love gives life a deep sense of purpose. It gets us out of bed on cold mornings to face tough challenges.

Falling in love involves letting go, abandonment. A friend of mine, a recovering alcoholic, once confided, "Everything started to change when I resigned as chairman of the universe."

Conversion produces interior knowledge. Though there may be no visions or flashes of insight, our horizon expands; we see the world with new eyes.

ULTIMATE TRAGEDY

Jesus said to them, "It would have been better for that one not to have been born." (Mark 14:21)

With conversion, we change our moral direction. For, in the final analysis, our lives move in one of two directions. We either live basically for self-satisfaction, or we have opened up to respond to real needs around us. I say "basically," because no one is completely egotistical or perfectly loving. If fundamentally generous, we still have minor vices. Though fundamentally selfish, we may still be capable of kindness.

In the language of scripture, we are either serving God's reign or the death-project of sin. The former follows the logic of light (truth) → freedom → love → life. The anti-reign follows the dynamic of darkness (lies) → slavery → indifference/hatred → death.

CONVERSION

Theologian Bernard Lonergan writes:

> [We achieve] authenticity in self-transcendence.... Our capacity for self-transcendence...becomes an actuality when one falls in love. Then one's being becomes being-in-love.... Once it has blossomed forth and as long as it lasts, it takes over. It is the first principle. From it flow one's desires and fears, one's joys and sorrows, one's discernment of values, one's decisions and deeds.
>
> ...Being in love with God is the basic fulfilment of our conscious intentionality. That fulfilment brings a deep-set joy that can remain despite humiliation, failure, privation, pain, betrayal, desertion. That fulfilment brings a radical peace, the peace that the world cannot give.[7]

It is possible to surrender to the latter logic, to become a serial murderer, a torturer, a big-time or petty dictator. People can turn life into hell on earth. Or they can collaborate through icy indifference. For the final exercise of the First Week, Ignatius invites us to take a hard look down the second path, as far as we can see [cf. 65–71]. What would it be like to give ourselves over to that logic? Where would it lead us? He recommends letting ourselves feel (*sentir*) the bitter tragedy of moral and spiritual death. Here we can visit in our imagination some of the tragic examples we have of hell on earth.

Today we are advised to take things "lite," to take nothing too seriously, neither birth nor death. We can "change the channel" on war, plague (AIDS), and famine, but we can also waste our lives on trivial pursuits. In this climate, I think that it is salutary to recall that some lives—Hitler's, Stalin's, Idi Amin's, and less dramatic lives—have been disasters and that none of us wholly escapes the danger of personal disintegration and an ultimately tragic life.

As I understand the New Testament, we could never attribute that ("condemnation") to God, who works exclusively and relentlessly for our abundant life.[8]

CONCLUSION

Reform of life includes coming to terms with sin. It includes forgiveness, healing, and breaking free from past disorder. This involves struggle. It stirs deep sentiments in us. As we commit to change, we experience two kinds of feelings at a deep level: on the one hand, discouragement and strong desires to backtrack; on the other, enthusiasm, hope, and joy at the prospect of a new way of life. What do these feelings mean? What about the thoughts and inclinations-to-action that spring from them? How are we to interpret them? That is the subject of the first series of Ignatius's "Rules for Discernment," to which we now turn.

Rules for Discernment  6

Be strong in the Lord and in the strength of his power. Put on the whole armor of God, so that you may be able to stand against the wiles of the devil. *(Eph. 6:10–11)*

INTERIOR MOVEMENTS

Reform of life stirs up sadness and fear, but also enthusiasm for the future. The prospect of serious commitment (like marriage) provokes similar interior movements. These deserve serious attention, especially the fear and discouragement that block reform. What kind of interior movements are we talking about?

It might happen that, having decided to break off a harmful relationship or overcome a bad habit, I find myself feeling discouraged and sapped of energy. Or maybe, having made the break, I crave what I left behind and tremble for the future. Have I bitten off more than I can chew? Can I keep this up? Do I want to?

Apart from conversion and major commitments, everyday challenges can also trigger the fear and discouragement that derail wise choices. Having to confront a difficult person can leave us dispirited. Gross evil – violence, greed, mendacity, intractable injustice – can make us feel overwhelmed. Failure can make us want to throw in the towel. Six months into married life a spouse can get a sinking feeling and start to wonder, What did I get myself into?

In cases like these, how much do our feelings accurately reflect our situation? Can we trust them as a reliable guide for making decisions, especially since ideas-for-action frequently arise from such emotional states?

On the other hand, life-reform also awakens joy, excitement, and a sense of freedom. For example, someone entangled in dishonest business dealings, or a damaging relationship, now sees a "hole in the hedge," a way out, and that exhilarates her. A film like *Gandhi* or a religious service can stir up a deep desire to spend our lives in service.

A conversation with a prayerful person can stimulate enthusiasm about learning to pray, or to pray better. If I've been down on myself, feeling guilty for some past action, somebody might affirm me and remind me of God's forgiveness, leaving me feeling like I've just awakened from a bad dream. Our heart can go out to a homeless person, focusing our attention and feelings in ardent fellow-feeling. A random act of kindness can inspire an intense desire to be more generous. Or, on a quiet summer night with no thought for the morrow, I might feel strangely at one with everything around me.

These positive states of soul cause fewer problems, but, again, do they accurately reflect our situation? Are they a reliable guide for action?

These are the issues addressed by Ignatius of Loyola's Rules for Discerning Interior Movements.[1] He presents them in two parts. Here we examine the first set of Rules, which are especially useful during times of reform. Later, we will discuss the second set.[2] The Rules are based on Ignatius's experience and what he learned from helping others. They are criteria for understanding and responding to emotional states like those just described, which he calls "consolation" and "desolation." These are not just any emotions on the periphery of experience, such as pain from an illness or pleasure from a great piece of music. They are stirrings and moods, states and affective currents which affect us globally and endow ordinary emotions with a distinctive tone. That is because they come from so deep within us that they seem, paradoxically, to have their origin beyond us [cf. 32].

Like the writers of the New Testament, Ignatius presupposes that we live in a kind of double force-field. Human beings, their relationships, and their institutions exhibit two kinds of tendencies: movement toward light (truth), freedom, love, and life, and movement in the opposite direction toward darkness (lies), slavery, egoism, and death. Behind the former are Satan and his demons; behind the latter, God's Spirit and the good angels.

Just how we label the power of evil is less important than recognizing it in operation. We may consider the ancients primitive dupes for personifying evil. That is not the most serious issue. It is far more dangerous to miss what the ancients understood: that our minds and moral resources are no match for the "mystery of iniquity" (2 Thess. 2:7). That would make us naive postmodern dupes. Evil not only disguises itself; it has the uncanny "jiu-jitsu" ability to turn our best-intentioned schemes against us. "The best and the brightest" have ever marched down history's blind allies, with disastrous consequences, in the name of law and order, the fatherland, freedom, the true religion, the revolution, and countless less noble causes. Moderns are no wiser or less culpable. After two centuries of unspeakable tragedy, we are still boasting of our brainpower and our high-tech toys.

For all that, we are not condemned to succumb to evil. We can partly understand its logic, and, what is more important, we have a far stronger power on our side. So we must learn to recognize these subtle tendencies, toward life and toward death, in daily life and in ourselves. And we must know how to respond to them.

THE RULES OF DISCERNMENT, FIRST SERIES

The first set of Rules is addressed principally to people who are struggling to reform their lives. Most of the rules therefore have to do with the desolation that accompanies that struggle. The first four, however, are general introductory principles. (The numbers below roughly follow *Spiritual Exercises* [313–27].)

1. People who are moving from bad to worse experience the influence of the "enemy" as congenial and confirming of their ways. Since they are dominated by fear of pain and love of comfort, the enemy prompts them to imagine the delights of self-seeking. The divine Spirit operates in the opposite direction, "sting[ing] their conscience with remorse" [314].[3]

2. People who are advancing in spiritual and moral maturity experience the two forces in the opposite way. When someone is striving to reform, "it is characteristic of the evil spirit to cause gnawing anxiety, to sadden, and to set up obstacles. In this way the enemy unsettles these persons by false reasons aimed at preventing their progress" [315]. The enemy *discourages,* stirring up fear and sadness over the cost of perseverance (desolation). The divine Spirit *encourages* them, removing obstacles and giving peace, strength, joy (consolation).

All the rest of the rules for discernment apply to people who are advancing in maturity. Though they might suffer from strong temptations, and they may fail, they are committed to advancing. The Rules will help them understand their interior movements and respond appropriately. They must first recognize that the enemy discourages, sowing desolation, while God's Spirit encourages, giving consolation. They must resist desolation and reject the ideas that spring from it, and they must embrace consolation and follow its lead [cf. 313].

3. "Spiritual consolation" refers to the peace and joy that arise from our center and affect our interior state as a whole. For Ignatius (and the biblical tradition he draws on), consolation is much more than the mere comfort for the sorrowful which is the everyday meaning of the term. Consolation releases new energies, widens our vision, and directs us beyond ourselves. Dorothy Day describes her experience of consolation, when, as a young girl, she heard of the life of a saint. Dorothy felt "lofty enthusiasm."

> . . . my heart seemed almost bursting with the desire to take part in such high endeavor. . . . And the thrill and joy that stirred my heart when I came across spiritual truth and beauty never left me as I grew older. The sad thing is that one comes across it so seldom. Natural goodness, natural beauty, brings joy and a lifting of the spirit, but it is not enough, it is not the same. The special emotions I am speaking of came only at hearing the word of God. It was as though each time I heard our Lord spoken of, a warm feeling of joy filled me.[4]

A wonderful description of consolation!

Though pleasant, consolation is different from pleasure. Whereas pleasure passes with its stimulus, consolation produces abiding peace and joy. It is compatible with pleasure but also with pain and anxiety. Pleasure, like pain, engages a part of us. But since consolation arises from that unifying center where we are opening up to the world and to God, it affects our overall mood and outlook, our emotional and intellectual horizon. In consolation, the subterranean river within us overflows into conscious life, endowing ordinary feelings with a heightened tone and fullness.

In consolation, we feel God attracting us (cf. John 6:44), touching us. We feel drawn to prayer and revealed truth. Generous sacrifice seems easy. "Whoever goes forward with this fervor, warmth, and interior consolation finds every burden light and sweetness in every penance or trial, however great."[5] But consolation can also be mild as well as intense.

Consolation can take the form of a redemptive sorrow that heals and unites us to others – for example, when we are mourning the death of a friend and wish to be nowhere else but there, sharing that family's loss. We also feel consolation when we grieve for the sufferings of Christ, or for the crucified of today, and when we feel sorrow for our sins.

4. The opposite of consolation is spiritual desolation. Desolation is sadness and inner turmoil. It is not just any "feeling down" but a disturbance arising from deep within, and therefore touching us globally. Like its opposite, desolation can be occasioned by events outside us as well as by our emotional and physical state: a personal tragedy, a depressing news report, failure, persecution, frustration, and fatigue.

Dorothy Day describes her desolation on returning to New York from a trip:

> In town the usual crosses: Carney calling us all racketeers,... E. with his vile accusations; the misery of M. and P.; Kate's illness; the threatened suit against us; the bills piling up – these things to be topped by such a lack of understanding of the personalist idea from those from whom you expect the most, lays me low. Since I got back from Pittsburgh, I have had this completely alone feeling. A temptation of the devil, doubtless, and to succumb to it is a lack of faith and hope. There is nothing to do but bear it, but my heart is as heavy as lead, and my mind dull and uninspired. A time when the memory and understanding fail one completely and only the will remains, so that I feel hard and rigid, and at the same time ready to sit like a soft fool and weep.[6]

Desolation drains us of energy. We are attracted to the gospel of self-satisfaction. We feel drawn backward into ourselves.[7] Life feels burdensome, the thought of generous service repugnant, devotional practices boring and distasteful. God seems absent, God's love unreal. Though the sun may be shining above the clouds, everything here below is gray.

Desolation generates negative thinking. It narrows our vision. It can visit with enough force to obliterate all memory of consolation, or even normal calm. It reduced Jesus to fear and trembling in Gethsemane. He cried out in desolation on the cross. In desolation we can only think, "This will never end." "Things can only get worse." The enemy gets us asking ourselves, "'How are you to live your whole life in such penance [and privation]?'...[The enemy] fails to tell us of the great comforts and so much consolation which our Lord is accustomed to give" those who enlist in his service.[8]

Consolation is a little "Transfiguration," a taste of what Peter, James, and John experienced as they witnessed Jesus glorified on the mountain. Desolation is a little Gethsemane, which these same disciples also witnessed. We live most of our lives on the flatlands between the peak of one and the depths of the other. When undergoing conversion, however, we can expect storms of desolation to alternate with the joy of consolation, separated by periods of calm. (This pattern can also occur when facing a serious challenge like marriage, when risking our security, etc.). In times of conversion, since the egoist in us is dying, we feel desolation. But since a new person is coming to life, we also experience consolation. Consolation encourages us to go forward; desolation is withdrawal pains pulling us backward.

In times of reform, whereas consolation poses few problems, desolation is a major obstacle. The remaining rules of the first series deal with desolation.

5. Like consolation, desolation gives rise to spontaneous thoughts about action and inclinations toward (or away from) actions. The first rule when in desolation is, Don't make important changes! Why? When we are "in the pits," thoughts arise about changing our way of life. But when in turmoil, under the influence of the "enemy," we lack the peace of mind needed to assess alternatives properly. We should stick firmly to the decisions we made when we felt consolation (or at least calm). For "Just as in consolation the good spirit guides and counsels us more, so in desolation does the evil spirit" [318].

6. A time of desolation is no time to "go with the flow," since the flow is dehumanizing. Nor can we afford to wait out the storm. We must resist actively, because desolation is corrosive. The "enemy" acts like a schoolyard bully [cf. 325].[9] If you kowtow or try to negotiate, bullies will eat you alive. Like other predators, they smell fear in their prey. But behind the bluster, they are insecure cowards who turn tail in the face of stiff resistance. Resisting desolation might mean helping someone in need, keeping busy or praying, even begging for the opposite of where desolation inclines [cf. 16, 157]. Cheer up and cheer others up. Do some penance.

Going against the flow is countercultural in a supertolerant society. But we cannot afford to tolerate poison. However we label the power of evil, we are not up against a pragmatic adversary who might accept a compromise settlement. Ignatius speaks of "the enemy of human nature" who seeks our destruction and wages war to the death. When Jesus says the devil is a murderer, he means it. In the gospels, he does not dialogue with the demons. Firmness and decisiveness are essential. "Resist the devil and he will flee from you" (James 4:7; cf. 1 Pet. 5:7–9).[10]

That does not mean being violent with ourselves but calmly resolute about the kind of person we want to be. In practice we have to work out the balance between what some Jungians call "embracing our shadow" and firm refusal to let that shadow dominate us.

7. We can profit greatly from desolation. Patient resistance strengthens us. Life is no bowl of cherries. Grin and bear it. Poor people and old people have a lot to teach us in this matter. Desolation also helps us appreciate how weak we are when left to our own resources. It shows us whether we do the right thing only when it gives us a warm glow. Finally, desolation can be a wake-up call warning us that we have been slacking off.

8. When in desolation, remember that consolation is around the corner, which takes effort when desolation paralyzes memory and imagination. In consolation, don't get overinflated. Desolation will follow! (see John 16:20–22).

9. Two final criteria in the first series of Rules point ahead to the second series. First, the enemy operates like a seducer trying to sweet-talk

us into an illicit affair. For the plan to succeed, the suitor's ambiguous advances must be kept secret. When the person targeted confides the matter to a friend or advisor, the game is up. The lesson is that temptations lose their power when we disclose them to a wise confidant. It is highly beneficial to develop that habit.

Second, the enemy's attacks are personalized. Like a smart commander sizing up a military objective, the enemy sizes us up and attacks our weak points. So we need to know our weak points and fortify ourselves against attack.

Just as temptations are tailor-made for us, our experience of interior movements is conditioned by who and where we are. "The body, psychology, and also society and the economy, etc. *always* act, throughout one's entire conscious life," Daniel Gil writes. People's "sexual history, the social class to which they belong, the ideas and symbols of their economic condition, their political affiliations, etc., etc., always color with characteristic tones their spiritual movements."[11] With this in mind, before concluding it will be useful to explore briefly some of the social implications of these Rules and their relationship to empirical psychology.

DESOLATION IN SOCIAL GROUPS

The examples of consolation and desolation at the beginning of this chapter suggest that events outside us — a hostile encounter, a word of encouragement, a work of art, the nightly news, a liturgy — can occasion these interior movements. A prime example of provocation from outside is the way consolation and desolation are contagious. Moreover, if they are contagious, then they are collective realities as well as personal. Since the first set of Rules is chiefly concerned with desolation, I will consider its social dimension here, leaving collective consolation for later.

Desolation is contagious. We can spread it by becoming stumbling blocks, undermining the faith and idealism of others.[12] "Come on; you can't seriously believe that stuff!" "Be realistic. It's a dog-eat-dog world. You've got to look out for Number One."

This shows that members of groups — families, unions, parishes — share desolation (as well as consolation). Sex abuse scandals recently produced collective desolation in the Catholic Church. The first set of Rules can therefore apply to groups. When experiencing collective desolation, a group pursuing a good cause should not change its basic commitments and strategies [318]. It should combat discouragement [319, 325]. Desolation is an opportunity for purifying and fortifying the group [320, 322]. Group members should recall that desolation will pass; better times lie ahead, when it will be easier to hope, to sing, and to struggle [321]. Finally, the group should air its difficulties to others who can help clarify dangerous temptations [326] and pinpoint and correct group weaknesses [327].

INTERIOR MOVEMENTS AND PSYCHOLOGY

In the faith-perspective of Ignatius's Rules, empirical psychology cannot fully account for consolation and desolation. Their distinctive quality points to transcendent origins. That is why they affect our overall mood and outlook, rather than part of us, like a toothache or a good workout. How, then, are consolation and desolation related to everyday emotions? One extreme view, a kind of "spiritual imperialism," would confuse ordinary depression with spiritual desolation and ordinary exhilaration with consolation, attributing transcendent origins to phenomena for which empirical psychology can adequately account. The opposite extreme would construe consolation and desolation as miraculous, radically unlike ordinary emotional states and completely independent of empirical psychology. Neither extreme does justice to experience or to a correct understanding of transcendence.[13]

We human beings are highly complex systems which integrate biological, psychological, and intellectual subsystems within ourselves. Like other subsystems, our emotional life operates according to its proper patterns, in this case psychological principles (whether Freudian or Jungian or others). However, our psyche also feels the impact of God's activity (grace) and the resistance of human nature and sin to that influence.

How can consolation and desolation affect the way we feel without violating the principles of empirical psychodynamics? The answer is that they endow ordinary emotions with a distinctive tone which is qualitative and, ultimately, ambiguous. Precisely because of their transcendent origins, it is difficult to indicate clear boundaries for the qualitative change they produce in us.[14] Even though, on close inspection, consolation and desolation appear to be disproportionate (in quality and sometimes intensity) to their apparent causes, this is not measurable; and few people seem to recognize it for what it is. Most often consolation and desolation seem completely natural and normal. Desolation has a lot in common with ordinary depression (it is a kind of depression) and frequently accompanies it.[15] Consolation has a lot in common with emotional well-being, and well-being frequently accompanies it.

The experience of consolation confirms the traditional principle that God's saving action builds on human nature and perfects it. Starting with the raw material that we are, the good Spirit humanizes us (in fact, divinizes us). The Spirit heals us psychologically and even physically and enlightens us intellectually. The "enemy" targets our moral weaknesses and our neuroses in order to dehumanize and destroy. Since these subtle forces work through who we are and, especially, through our emotions, our psychological makeup conditions their operation.

CONCLUSION

It is difficult to overestimate the importance of consolation and desolation. We will return to them later when we examine the second set of Rules.

So far, we have been reflecting on evil and on getting free from past and present failings. But free for what? Reform for what? What does conversion turn us toward? Conversion opens us up to reality. It does not bring us to a final destination but sets us on a *path*. How do we recognize the path? Once on it, how do we make our way? That is what we turn to next, beginning with a central Ignatian theme — the call of Christ.

SOMETHING WORTH LIVING FOR

Getting free places us on a new path. Part 2 discusses the idea of a vocation, God's project for the world, and the way of life, or path, opened by Jesus of Nazareth, with its implications for today.

7 The Call

Then I heard the voice of the Lord saying,
"Whom shall I send, and who will go for us?"
And I said, "Here am I! Send me." (Isa. 6:8)

When I was in college, during the crisis I described in chapter 1, I was struck by the way those geniuses—Aristotle, Descartes, and the rest—disagreed about what is real, what is right, and what life is about. If they were so smart and still disagreed, what chance did I have to understand these things? From their disagreements I concluded that their different worldviews were ultimately based on first principles that could not be strictly proven but had to be accepted on some kind of faith. That insight (which I still consider correct) shook me deeply and triggered a top-to-bottom crisis. What did I believe in? On what basis? I couldn't give solid reasons for what I had been taught and had accepted up until then.

Though I didn't know it at the time, I had entered the postmodern world. Now I realize I have plenty of company. Sooner or later a crisis of authorities and inherited worldviews strikes most members of my middle-class tribe.

It took me much longer to grasp that this kind of crisis is not just about understanding the world around us. It is about finding a path in life, an identity. It is about discovering our vocation.

THE IDEA OF A VOCATION

What do we mean by vocation? That is an idea we have to reach for in contemporary society. Late capitalism might offer us a job, even a profession, but the only vocation it knows is getting and spending.[1] That robs us of our dignity.

Grown-ups ask children what they want to be when they grow up, and children answer: an astronaut, a firefighter. Later, dreams grow more realistic. Then economic pressures crowd in. The flame of adventure flickers, and dreams can die, either because they are impractical, or because of lack of courage or lack of opportunity, or because there is nobody there to stroke the dreamer in us. In the process, many, maybe most, fail to discover their vocation.

My vocation might be to raise children, discover new planets, drive a truck, or lead a social movement. It will not be something I just up and decide on, like picking out a shirt in a store. My vocation is something I discover. More than something to do, it is who I am or might be. For most people, music is a pastime or a hobby, but for Pablo Casals it was destiny: something that unlocked his most creative energies. When we discover our vocation, something clicks. We have found what we were born for.

After graduating from college, my friend Mark got a job in a hotel and soon found himself helping organize a union. He was good at it, loved it, and stayed with it, even though other lines of work would have paid better. Eventually, Mark made his way to Central America, where he collaborated with beleaguered labor leaders in wartime conditions. Once he was nearly killed when a union headquarters was bombed. After recovering from his injuries, he returned to Central America. More recently, thugs tried to kidnap and kill him for his support of fired union leaders. None of this has dampened Mark's enthusiasm for workers and their rights. He is currently pursuing graduate studies in industrial relations. Mark has discovered his vocation.

We can have several vocations. I can be a mechanic, an athlete, and a spouse, all at once. Still, we don't identify completely with these activities. I would still have a mission in life if I could no longer repair cars or if my spouse died.

Is there a deepest vocation that integrates the others? If so, it would be that way of life that fulfills me as a human being. What does that? Consider Forrest Gump of the movie by that title. Forrest is mentally retarded, and people are forever telling him he's dumb and not much good for anything. At one point he spits back: "I know what love is." Forrest is right. He can love; he's good at helping people. That does not depend on special talents, which he scarcely has. Case closed,

I'd say. Human beings are made to love, to help others. That is our deepest vocation.

A life of service is not something people normally muscle into by sheer willpower, however. It is, literally, a calling that they "hear," a "still small voice" which, in privileged moments, comes through straight and clear.

In his memoir, *Markings,* former U.N. Secretary General Dag Hammarskjöld describes responding to an invitation that transformed his life: "I do not know Who – or what – put the question," he writes. "But at some point I did answer 'Yes' to Someone – or Something – and from that hour I was certain that existence is meaningful and that, therefore, my life, in self-surrender, had a goal." Responding to this call cost him dearly: "I came to a time and place where I realized... that the price for committing one's life would be reproach, and that the only elevation possible to man lies in the depths of humiliation. After that, the word 'courage' lost its meaning, since then nothing could be taken from me."[2] Hammarskjöld's vocation led to his death, working for peace in war-torn central Africa.

Maryknoll sister Ita Ford paid the same price in El Salvador in 1980. The armed forces labeled Ita and her fellow sisters subversives for their work among refugees. Shortly before she and three companions were raped and killed, Ita wrote to her young niece, Jennifer, in the United States: "I hope you come to find that which gives life a deep meaning for you. Something worth living for – maybe even worth dying for – something that energizes you, enthuses you, enables you to keep moving ahead. I can't tell you what it might be. That's for you to find, to choose, to love."[3]

Ita invited Jennifer to discover her deepest calling.

Life is short; we only get to do it once. We can sleep through it, squandering it on trivial pursuits. The wake-up call to service resonates with our own need for something worth living for, our need to find ourselves by losing ourselves.[4]

MIDWIVES AND MEDIATORS

> *During the night Paul had a vision: there stood a man of Macedonia pleading with him and saying, "Come over to Macedonia and help us."* (Acts 16:9)

As the word suggests, vocations are called forth from us. We often discover them thanks to role models – people like our Aunt Mildred or that special teacher, Mr. Prescott, whom we admired so much. Role models evoke an echo deep within us. As in a mirror, we recognize in them part of who we are or might be. We grow into and out of emotional identification with role models as we discover and shape our identity.

Mentors also call forth our vocations. They are people with experience who point out our gifts and help us develop them. There are few greater gifts in life than the opportunity to apprentice with a good mentor.

Role models and mentors are special cases of the general rule: we discover our callings in response to the world. Mothers and fathers discover theirs in response to their children. Couples call forth from each other their vocation of spouse and lover. Martin Luther King discovered his prophetic calling during the Montgomery bus boycott. Dietrich Bonhoeffer in Nazi Germany and Dorothy Day in Depression-era New York grew into their vocations in response to their turbulent surroundings. Our surroundings shake us, sift us, and draw our vocation from us.

A lot depends on where we place ourselves. If King had spent his youth hanging out by the pool, would we remember him today? The crucified people are a privileged place for hearing the call to service. They provoke the crucial question: What will we do to take them down from their crosses?

Faith recognizes the call to love and serve as the voice of Christ. (We say this call is a constitutive dimension of the human condition, an "existential.") Christ invites people of every time and place to participate in the Reign of God.

THE CALL OF CHRIST

> *Jesus said to them, "Follow me, and I will make you fish for people." And immediately they left their nets and followed him.*
> (Rev. 3:20)

Between the First and Second Weeks of the Spiritual Exercises, Ignatius inserts the exercise traditionally called the Kingdom Meditation. I prefer the title "The Call" (for reasons I will explain). In this exercise, retreatants consider the call Christ makes to everyone to collaborate with God's work in the world. This exercise prepares them to hear that call in the future and to consider now, beforehand, what a fitting response should be.[5]

The call

Ignatius presents a parable about a great-hearted charismatic leader (a king) with a difficult, noble cause. The leader invites; he does not order. He shares the hardships of his troops in the field and promises that if they labor with him they will share in his victory. Ignatius compares Christ's call to this attractive leader's.

Kings are out of fashion these days,[6] and we are slow to follow the leader, even a humble, generous one. Sometimes that reflects a healthy, critical attitude. At other times it reflects an individualism that balks at collaborating in something wider than our personal projects. Today we might imagine a credible, selfless leader mobilizing others to combat poverty, war, discrimination, or environmental destruction. We could consider a personal appeal for help from someone like Dorothy Day or Oscar Romero, the kind of invitation only a small-minded person would refuse [94]. Christ calls each one personally like that with words like these:

> It is my will to win over the whole world, to overcome evil with good, to turn hatred aside with love, to conquer all the forces of death – whatever obstacles there are that block the sharing of life between God and humankind. Whoever wishes to join me in this mission must be willing to labor with me, and so by following me in struggle and suffering may share with me in glory [95].[7]

Christ invites all to participate in God's project, or "Reign," offering to be mentor and role model for those who respond.

The call is something people experience in real life. It comes in the form of *consolation,* drawing them to a freer, more generous way of life. In the Exercises, people normally experience it as consolation attracting them to Christ (whom they are contemplating) and his cause, the Kingdom. It is a personal invitation—"My sheep hear my voice. I know them and they follow me" (John 10:27)—to join others, working in community and for community.

The response

The aim of the exercise is not to experience the invitation during the exercise itself but to prepare for it. The petition ("what I want") at the beginning indicates the purpose of the exercise. We pray "not to be deaf to Christ's call, but ready and diligent" when it comes in real life [91]. It is a gift that we cannot schedule or conjure up. But we can prepare for it and reflect on how best to respond.[8]

Ignatius says that any decent person will respond to Christ's invitation without reserve [cf. 96]. We will all say, "Sure, count on me!" However, following through is another matter. When the call actually comes, greed and sensuality can prevent us from attending to it; fear of hardship and rejection can prevent us from following through. To neutralize this danger, people with "more" desire "to show devotion and to distinguish themselves in total service" [97][9] will appeal to Christ in advance, in terms like these:

> Eternal Lord . . . , I am moved by your grace to offer myself to you and to your work. I deeply desire to be with you in accepting all wrongs and all rejections and all poverty, both actual and spiritual—and I deliberately choose this, if it is for your greater service and praise. If you . . . would so call and choose me, then take and receive me into such a way of life. [98][10]

Those who are serious about having something to live for, maybe even to die for, will pray to share rejection and poverty with Christ! ("Spiritual poverty" in the prayer means detachment from possessions.) The prayer helps neutralize fear of hardship and rejection; it helps keep us vigilant, lest Christ's call should catch us napping (cf. Matt. 25:5; 26:41). The prayer also reflects the logic of companionship: Christ calls us to be his companions and share his lot ([95]; cf. Mark 3:14). We will return to these suggestive themes later on.

GOD ON OUR SIDE— OR RATHER, VICE VERSA

Christ invites all to collaborate with God. If this means ascribing divine sanction to our activities, it might strike some people as quaint at best and pernicious at worst. On the other hand, consider Tessie, a six-year-old African-American girl who helped integrate the New Orleans public school system around 1960. Each day for a full year, federal marshals escorted Tessie and two schoolmates past a mob of jeering white segregationists on the way into school. Some protesters stayed on to taunt and threaten the girls as they left school in the afternoon.

The young psychiatrist Robert Coles accompanied Tessie and her friends during the ordeal. Coles and his tape recorder were on hand one morning at Tessie's house when the girl, recovering from the flu, was chafing at having to face the hostile crowd again. Her grandmother Martha reminded her of her mission: "I'm not the one to tell you that you should go, because here I am, and I'll be watching television and eating or cleaning things up while you're walking by those folks. But I'll tell you, you're doing them a great favor; you're doing them a service, a big service."

Martha chased down and swatted a bee. "You see, my child, you have to help the good Lord with His world! He puts us here—and He calls us to help Him out. That bee doesn't belong here; it belongs out there. You belong in that McDonogh School, and there will be a day when everyone knows that, even those poor folks—Lord, I pray for them!—those poor, poor folks who are out there shouting their heads off at you. You're one of the Lord's people; He's put His hand on you. He's given a call to you, a call to service—in His name!"

Some weeks later, Tessie told Coles what her grandmother (and mentor) meant that morning: "If you just keep your eyes on what you're supposed to be doing, then you'll get there—to where you want to go," Tessie explained. "The marshals say, 'Don't look at them; just walk with your head up high, and you're looking straight ahead.' My granny says that there's God, He's looking too, and I should remember that it's a help to Him to do this, what I'm doing; and if you serve Him, then that's important. So I keep trying."

When integration was finally achieved and the jeering mob dissolved, Tessie confided to Coles: "We were supposed to get them to stop being so angry; then they'd quiet down, and we'd have the desegregation – and now it's happening," she said. "So we did the service we were suppose to for New Orleans, and Granny says, 'Next it'll be some other thing to do,' because you always should be trying to help out God somehow."[11]

Tessie was more than a young victim caught up in a racial confrontation. She understood herself to be deputized by God to help integrate New Orleans and win over embittered segregationists in the process. This gave her the sense of purpose she needed to persevere.

COMMITMENT OVER TIME

A vocation to service is a lifelong commitment that is fleshed out in concrete commitments that project into the future. Liberal society can be poor soil for this kind of commitment to take root.[12] Liberal culture's critical temptation is the corruption of its supreme value, freedom. It promotes a kind of "open-door" freedom. In this interpretation, being free is like standing in a room full of doors and being able to walk through any one. After walking through one door, however, I am reluctant to close it behind me, because that would foreclose returning to the original room and walking through those other doors. Freedom means being free to undo tomorrow what I decide on today.

Many balk at committing themselves more than two years into the future because they can't foresee circumstances two years from now. And by what logic should a couple commit themselves "till death do us part," tying their hands like that? After all, things change, especially in liberal society.

People also avoid weighty commitments because they lack information or feel pressured: I can't be sure that marrying Stephanie –

or going to medical school, or entering the ministry — is a truly free and responsible decision, that I am not responding to the press of circumstances. Will I regret my decision five years from now? Will I find myself asking, Did I really choose my spouse (or my career) freely? Was I mature enough? If I had it to do it all over again, would I choose as I did?

We need to question "open-door" freedom. We may have a hundred dreams, but ninety-plus will have to die for one or two to become reality. Consider Gladys and James, who have been together for forty years (going strong, more or less). While they have endured doubts and crises, their relationship deepened by working through them. The reasons they stay together now are not exactly the ones that first brought them together. When they got married, they walked through a door and closed it behind them. But in the new space they entered, other doors opened, new and unforeseen possibilities that have enriched their lives qualitatively.

Their life project unfolded over the years, the present building on the past: children, sickness, job changes, tragedies, and triumphs. Together they made a history they could not have made alone. They could accomplish what they have because each could count on the other being there as each had promised.

James and Gladys show us how the "open-door" caricature misconstrues freedom as the private property of isolated individuals. I can only undo tomorrow what I decide on today because I am alone in my decision, because I'm not engaged in any common effort, because no one has to count on me to be there tomorrow, because I don't have to answer to anyone. In this concept of individualistic freedom, each instant of time is an isolated moment. I start each day as if I had no past and no future in common with others. But is that freedom — or permanent childhood?

Liberal individualism fails to appreciate the drama of *interior* freedom by which we mature. It mistakenly takes this freedom for granted. In reality, inner freedom is a difficult conquest. Our choices shape us. Some expand our freedom, while others diminish it. Through our choices we forge our identity. Freedom grows and develops as we assume our vocation, making commitments that close some doors and open others.

Our vocations draw us to collaborate with others, and that requires being able to count on one another to be there in the future. Otherwise, there will be no clinic, labor union, or serious scientific endeavor. When it comes to a shared life project involving primary support, as in marriage or religious life in community, permanent commitment is essential. When we promise to walk with others into an unknown future, we have to assure them that they will be able to count on us.

If such a commitment has been responsibly made, we need to put our hand to the plow and hold on. It is debilitating for people like Gladys and James to keep looking back and asking, "But what if . . . ?" If the chosen path turns out not to be our vocation, that will become clear in practice without having to afflict ourselves with a hundred doubts and a divided heart.

Real life involves risks. Since total freedom and clarity are fantasies, commitment only requires sufficient freedom and information. Life sometimes forces decisions — school, career, job, marriage partner, etc. — before all the data is in. When the train is pulling out, we have to climb aboard or get left behind.

When we have sufficient reason to make a vocational decision, it is unreasonable not to do so. In The Call, we beg to be prompt to respond to Christ's invitation [cf. 91]. To one candidate, Christ said, " 'Follow me.' But he said, 'Lord, first let me go and bury my father.' But Jesus said to him, 'Let the dead bury their own dead; but as for you, go and proclaim the kingdom of God' " (Luke 9:59 – 60). The call of Christ, the call to service, is a gift that most often comes with force when people are young and unencumbered. The window of opportunity can close. If we demur, the seed sown will fail to bear fruit.

CONCLUSION

Abraham and Sara, Moses, Deborah, the prophets, Mary and the apostles all heard God call them. They said "Yes" to an uncontrollable future, and God made history through them. So did Sojourner Truth, Dorothy Day, Simone Weil, John XXIII, and countless workaday heroes — housewives and bus drivers — closer to our time. The story continues today.

What is the cause to which Christ calls us? And who is Christ, who calls? Ignatius could count on a common understanding of the cause, that is, God's saving work and the mission of the church. We cannot presume that today. In addition, people are skeptical of saviors, especially when saviors ask for total commitment, as in this case.

We first turn to consider the cause of Christ, God's "Reign," and then the caller, Christ himself.

The Reign of God 8

The time is fulfilled,
and the Reign of God is at hand;
repent, and believe in the good news.
(Mark 1:15)

In recent years, tens of thousands of people from all over the world have gathered at the World Social Forum in Porto Alegre, Brazil, and in Mumbai (Bombay), India, to celebrate their conviction that "another world is possible," a world free of mass poverty and environmental degradation, and to explore ways to bring it about.[1] Are they deluded? Can we overcome poverty, violence, and environmental crisis before they overcome us?

Every day thousands of parents, health professionals, and other dedicated persons spend their waking hours helping severely handicapped people just get through the day. Is their time well spent? Is a life serving "unproductive" people worthwhile?

What do efforts like these have to do with the call and cause of Christ, and what does his message say about their value and prospects? According to the New Testament, Christ invites all to labor with him for God's Reign of justice, truth, and peace (cf. 1 Cor. 15:24–25; Rev. 11:15; 12:10; and [95]). This sounds at once consoling and utopian. Yet while many may be open to a life of service, before signing up for the Christian version they will surely want to hear more about the "Reign of God."

In the *Spiritual Exercises,* the Contemplation on the Incarnation [101–9] follows immediately after The Call and opens the Second Week. By describing how Christ received his own mission, this exercise throws light on the cause to which he calls. Ignatius invites us to view humanity with the eyes of the Trinity: to observe the whole expanse of the earth, with the multitude of peoples and races, in their diversity of dress and customs. Some are at peace and others at war, some weeping and others laughing, some sick and others well, some being born and others dying [106]. But the Trinity sees that everyone is being lost, and, in merciful response to this tragedy, sends the Son to become human and save us all. It is this mission that Christ invites others to share with him.

God's concern for human beings is striking. Still, what does it mean to "save" humanity? Is that a real project underway or a wishful fantasy? If it is real, is it worthwhile? Is it worth total commitment? We need to face these questions today. Many people understand the God of Christians as a judge disposed to forgive sins and grant salvation in the afterlife. In this reading, God is relatively unconcerned with the suffering caused by war and injustice. Some believers conspire with secular culture to keep God out of worldly affairs.

For a long time I found it difficult to believe in God. I could not see where the victims of this world fit into God's plans. I felt my own Christian formation had failed to address this issue. Does the Christian God just promise heaven to the virtuous after death? Or does God have something to offer here and now to those who suffer? Years of struggle with this question, including study of the scriptures, bore fruit for me. A better understanding of the message of Christ made it easier for me to believe.

BLESSED ARE YOU WHO ARE POOR

Blessed are you who are poor,
for yours is the reign of God.
Blessed are you who are hungry now,
for you will be filled.
Blessed are you who weep now,
for you will laugh. (Luke 6:20–21)

What was Jesus' message and ministry all about? In Luke's Gospel, Jesus' "inaugural address" at Nazareth is a programmatic statement. He announces good news to the poor: God is about to liberate the oppressed and the captive (cf. Luke 4:16–21). In the beatitudes, Jesus explains further. God is coming as a merciful king who takes the side of the poor who are hungry and afflicted (Luke 6:21–26).[2] "Happy are the poor," not because they are poor, but because they will be filled and laugh. God rejects the injustice they suffer at the hands of the rich who are satisfied and laughing ("But woe to you who are rich . . . filled . . . laughing" [Luke 6:24–25]). There is nothing wrong with being full and laughing. The point is that the rich man, "Dives," is satisfied and laughing *while* his poor neighbor Lazarus languishes in hunger at his gate (cf. Luke 16:19–31). God, who loves both, takes the side of the latter against the former. According to Jesus, God is like a mother who sees her older child abusing her younger child. She takes the side of the victim (even if the victim is a brat!). The mother loves all her children, but she runs to the defense of the one who needs help.

There is nothing meritorious about being poor that might win God's love. God's option for those who suffer is unmerited; it is grace. God takes their side, not because they are good, but because God is good. Luke's beatitudes are not about the virtuous dispositions of the poor.[3] They are about the dispositions, and actions, of God. God gets upset when little people are pushed around.

The society of Jesus' time was divided not only into rich and poor but also into "righteous" people and sinners. Sinners were despised by those who kept the law and added pious practices to it. In the gospels Jesus exercises a preferential option for sinners as well as for the poor, and for the same reason. In the Reign of God that is emerging, God comes to restore the dignity of the poor, the outcast sinners, Samaritans, and all despised people.

God breaks into history rejecting unjust social relations and offering a new way to live together. The offer of brother- and sisterhood is unmerited, and it can be refused. If the oppressed factory worker goes home and beats his wife, then God, who took his side in the factory, now takes his wife's side in the home. The worker has rejected God's offer in practice. The Reign of God must be accepted — by rich, poor, women, men. All are sinners; all must repent and accept forgiveness. In practice, this means accepting the offer of new social relations. In Jesus' ministry, God gathers the poor, the outcast sinners, women, the sick and lepers, the children, Samaritans and eventually the gentiles — all the rejected and "unimportant" people — into a new community where they will serve one another and no one will dominate (Mark 10:42–45). Jesus invites the rich to repent, share what they have, and be "saved," as Zacchaeus was (cf. Luke 19:1–10).

The Reign of God is a banquet, a party, that all are invited to join (Matt. 8:11; 22:2; Luke 15:23). But since faith is lacking, God's revolution, which gathers us for that banquet, is slow, painful, under siege. Jesus said that God's Reign was underway in his ministry (see Matt. 12:28; Luke 17:21). Already a present reality, it will fully triumph only in the future, even over the grave. "According to his promise we wait for a new sky and a new earth in which justice dwells" (2 Pet. 3:13). All creation longs to share in this liberation and communion (Rom. 8:19–21). The Reign of God means new human beings, new communities, a new, transfigured world (Rev. 21:5). That is the cause to which Jesus calls.[4]

People participate by accepting the good news in faith and responding to the world in love. Love fulfills all the requirements of this "kingdom," especially love of the victim who is outside our circle, our family, our religion or nation (cf. Luke 10:25–37). The criteria for the final judgment measure us in terms of feeding the hungry, housing the foreigner, clothing the naked, visiting the sick and imprisoned (Matt. 25:31–46).

GOD'S REVOLUTION

I came that they may have life, and have it abundantly.
(John 10:10)

This sounds wonderful, but can we take it seriously? Aside from the problem of faith itself, it seems to many a little late to be talking about a great project for history. Hasn't history shown itself to be a story without a grand plot? Constant warfare, world poverty, and environmental crisis have exploded the myth that humanity's journey is a slow march of progress toward well-being by means of reason and science, universal education, suffrage, capitalism or socialism. Today none of these trains seems headed for the promised land. So is history a collection of unconnected short stories? Are we reduced to pursuing ephemeral

Lilliputian projects? Is love even possible; and, if so, can it ever be more than intimate concern for a few people around me? Is love irrelevant to our social situation and the direction of history? Should we forget about the suffering masses and about changing the world and just look out for ourselves and those seven or eight people we can actually try to love?

But is history really just a string of unconnected anecdotes? There is no utopia on the horizon, it is true; humans are constitutionally weak and egocentric and always need conversion. In fact, evil grows and "develops." But wait. Moral goodness also grows and develops. We have raised our standards and sometimes our behavior in modern times. Think of the Enlightenment, the labor movement, the abolition of slavery, democracy, decolonization, the women's movement, the awakenings of the handicapped and minorities, the renovation of churches, the environmental movement, rejection of the death penalty, progress in international human rights law, and, in general, the affirmation of human dignity. Might God have had a hand in this?

Faith affirms that God's Reign irrupts into this world and advances in the heart of history, within and beyond these often-ambiguous movements. In the end, faith is not based on those movements, but on a deeper experience, a shared sense that, despite the egoism, suffering, and death, life is worth the trouble. It springs from the internal conviction that sacrifice, love of neighbor, and celebration make sense, less because of the apparent facts than despite them. The easy smile of the poor and the severely handicapped and their readiness to celebrate have a basis in reality. While they show us that life is more cruel and evil more tenacious than we ordinarily admit, they also help us recognize that there is something going on in the world that is much more wonderful than we had imagined. The *experience* of this quiet assurance — that it makes sense to struggle and to celebrate — is our solid grounds for hope. It is experience of such a kind (consolation) that we cannot give a full account of it. And yet it furnishes sufficient reason to believe in God's Reign, reason enough to trump the evidence to the contrary. Though I cannot always explain why, deep in my heart I do believe that we shall overcome some day. The prophets and martyrs were not deluded. The thousands who gather at the World

Social Forum are onto something. So are those who care for "unproductive," terminally ill children. Love and community are possible, and not simply in the exceptional corners of an unloving world. And if life and truth and love will have the last word, then history has direction, although it has less to do with conventional measures of progress than with crosses and resurrections. Parents and laborers, and not just public figures, make history and contribute to a project whose depth and breadth surpass our ability to grasp it.

To repeat Jesus' words that "the Reign of God is at hand" and "in your midst" today is to say that God's power irrupts in our lives. The coming of God's Reign is the coming of a God who offers us the possibility of a new way of living. It is actually *God's self-offer.* God presses upon us from all sides, in and through the events of daily life, enabling us to live differently. The Reign of God happens when we accept this offer—when we make love, justice, and peace real.

CONCLUSION

Although the symbolism of God's Reign comes from the distant past, its general meaning is clear even today. It means good news in a world of bad news. It is a project of liberation from sin, poverty, injustice, and violence. It means new community where the dignity of all is respected. It means harmony with the natural environment. It means a new world.

Where do we fit into this? Christian faith responds that we find our place in this project by knowing and following Christ. We now turn to consider Christ, the one who calls. He offers himself as role model and mentor for a life of love and service. By contemplating and reproducing his way of life, his followers discover their place in the drama of God's Reign.

Contemplation of Christ  9

> *I have called you friends, because I have made known to you everything that I have heard from my Father. You did not choose me, but I chose you. And I appointed you to go and bear fruit, fruit that will last.* (John 15:15–16)

An inspired work of art—a painting or a poem—reaches out to us and *into* us, to question, enlighten, and inspire. A great story draws us into itself and discloses the deeper drama of life.[1] Stories shape us when we recognize part of our own story in them. That happens, for better or worse, when children identify with characters like Harry Potter, television celebrities, or sports stars. Even as adults, stories mark our lives. A first encounter with such figures as Nelson Mandela, Dorothy Day, Simone Weil, Gandhi, or Joan of Arc can kindle a desire to know more, to grasp what made them "tick." When personalities like Teresa of Avila or Francis of Assisi resonate and stir consolation, people profess "special devotion" to them.

Jesus of Nazareth occupies a special place in this regard. Probably no story has had a greater impact than his. Whatever our preconceptions, if we give him a serious hearing we find that Jesus stirs our feelings and invites a response. People who have pondered the gospels for decades continue to find surprises there. In the gospels, Jesus calls friends to labor with him. He will be their role model and mentor (cf. Matt. 23:8–10).

Today, believers still respond to his call. Their friendship with him grows as they apprentice with him. This is not imaginary, but it does require engaging his story with imagination. Earlier I described contemplation as "sitting with" reality, allowing it to penetrate us, and working through its impact on us. Contemplating Christ's life like this helps us to know him better (through interior knowledge), love him, and live more as he did [cf. 104–5]. Ignatius can teach us how.

CONTEMPLATING THE LIFE OF JESUS

> *The two disciples followed Jesus. When Jesus turned and saw them following, he said to them, "What are you looking for?" They said to him, "Rabbi, where are you staying?" He said to them, "Come and see." They came and saw where he was staying, and they remained with him that day.* (John 1:37–39)

We can contemplate the life of Christ by recreating a gospel story in our imagination and even entering into it as a bit player. Try it. Take the account of Jesus' birth in chapter 2 of Luke's Gospel.[2] Imagine the road from Nazareth to Bethlehem, "its length, its width, whether flat or through valleys and hills" [112]. Imagine Joseph and Mary, tired from the journey, searching for a place to stay. Paint the scene of the stable or cave where Jesus was born, a little dusty, lit by a single lamp. Picture the wide-eyed shepherds.

As the story unfolds in your imagination, attend to three things: the people, what the people say, and what they do. Reflect as you feel moved, drawing from the scene whatever seems of special interest. Pause where you find fruit, devotion. If you feel so moved, express to God (to Christ, etc.) what you think or feel. A "colloquy," or conversation in prayer, is made "in the way one friend speaks to another, or a servant to one in authority" [54].

This imaginative re-creation, reflection, and conversation is the heart of the prayer. However, Ignatius recommends some brief preliminary steps before plunging in: First, pause in silence before beginning the prayer, recalling how God regards you with love. Next, ask that the whole prayer be directed to the ultimate purpose of life, the service of God's project. Anchor the imagination by imagining the scene, as I said. Finally, make your request (Ignatius says to think about "what I want"): *to know this man Jesus more intimately in order to love him more deeply and follow him more closely.*[3]

This exercise is a little like filming a movie in our imagination.[4] Such an exercise helps us understand any historical figure (or even a present acquaintance). A biography provides only fragmentary data. We have to connect the dots, clothe the skeletal narrative with warm flesh, imagine how the person looked, sounded, and interacted with others.

We invent a little, spontaneously, exercising artistic license the way a filmmaker or historical novelist does. In contemplating Christ's life, we take a step farther, allowing the characters and the story to come to life. We imagine Christ doing or saying things, for example addressing others (or us!), beyond what the gospel story relates. In this way, we compose in our imagination the "Gospel according to Stephanie," or Bill, or Marge, for today. Naturally, there are limits to this creativity, as with any artistic re-creation. Subjective contributions should not contradict the gospel message.[5]

Dietrich Bonhoeffer's reflection on the birth of Jesus reveals an appreciation of this kind of prayer:

> If we wish to take part in this Advent and Christmas event,
> then we cannot simply be bystanders or onlookers,
> as if we were at the theater,
> enjoying all the cheerful images.
> No, we ourselves are swept up into the action there,
> into this conversion of all things.
> We have to play our part too on this stage.
> For the spectator
> is already an actor.
> He cannot withdraw.
> . . . we cannot approach his manger
> as if it were the cradle of any other child.
> Those who wish to come to his manger
> find that something is
> happening within them.[6]

Most exercises of the month-long Ignatian retreat consist of this kind of contemplation. They are all propelled by this same request: to know, love, and follow Christ better. Naturally, this form of prayer is appropriate in daily life as well as in a retreat.

COMPANIONS OF CHRIST

Contemplating Jesus' life is an imaginative exercise but not a fantasy. For believers, Christ is present in a way that Mozart and Joan of Arc

IS JESUS FOR EVERYONE?

Not everyone finds it easy to accept Christ as model. He was a Jew who lived two thousand years ago. He was male. Today, however, Christ is no longer confined to such categories. As Paul says, "Even though we once knew Christ according to the flesh, we know him no longer in that way" (2 Cor. 5:16). Sandra Schneiders reminds us that the risen Christ is present in his followers. The church (actually each local church) constitutes his body, which, in biblical terms, means his person (cf. Rom. 12:4–5; 1 Cor. 12:13–31; Eph. 4:14–16). We cannot consider the risen Christ as exclusively male, as Jesus of Nazareth obviously was. All of his followers share in his identity in equal measure. We can portray him today as black, old, female, or Chinese. "In Christ," says Paul, "there is neither Jew nor Greek, slave nor free, male nor female. You are all one in Christ Jesus" (Gal. 3:28).[7]

While Jesus' maleness complicates matters for some women, his being male does not make him the measure of humanity. Nor does his being the *son* of God mean that masculinity best represents divinity. God is neither male nor female; and "the second person of the Trinity came to be called 'son' because Jesus is male, not the other way around."[8] One could even say that Jesus' manhood helped undermine patriarchy and androcentrism from within, since Jesus repudiated the patriarchal qualities of competition, domination, and violence. Rejecting male superiority, he embraced stereotypically "feminine" humble service: peacemaking, long-suffering endurance and a nurturing care for all, especially the weak and oppressed. Had Jesus been a woman this might not have seemed quite so revolutionary.[9] In the end, what is essential is not his maleness or Jewishness, but that he is cosufferer, equalizer, and liberator.[10]

are not. He lives among us through his Spirit. Working through our imagination, the Spirit communicates interior knowledge of Christ and sparks love for him and his way of life. This is a form of consolation in which we experience his call. The cause of Christ attracts and produces friendship. That friendship will carry companions through the hardship and rejection that lies ahead for them.

Their vocation is to live as he did and continue his work. This means reproducing not the details of his life, but his attitudes and way of acting. Employing their talents, they respond creatively to their world as he did to his.[11] As role model and mentor,[12] he reveals to them both his person and his cause. The New Testament discloses the basic contours of that cause for a distant time and place. In the practice of discipleship, shared in community, in action and contemplation, *the Spirit of Christ reveals to Christ's followers what the Reign of God means concretely in their own time and place* (cf. Mark 4:10–11), *and how each one can best participate in it.* Through consolation, the Spirit guides us to flesh out our callings.

This is more a matter of practice than of talk, so enough said.

CONCLUSION

Ignatius says that Christ becomes "model and rule" [344] for those who respond to his call. His Spirit guides them (via consolation) to reproduce his attitudes and way of acting. However, there are many false spirits abroad, as well, and plenty of false turns along the road to sidetrack a committed life. We need to recognize these dangers. Above all, Ignatius stresses the need to understand the way of Christ by which commitment deepens, matures, and produces fruit. This is what the meditation we will consider in the next chapter is about. The "Two Standards" is the pivotal meditation of the Ignatian Exercises, and central to Ignatian spirituality as a whole.

10 The Two Standards

Near the city of Caesarea Philippi, Jesus asks his disciples who people say he is. He gets a variety of answers: Some say John the Baptist, others say one of the prophets of old has risen to life. He then asks the disciples who they think he is. Simon Peter answers, "You are the Messiah, the Son of the living God." This is a turning point in the gospels.

Jesus rejoices at Peter's confession: "Blessed are you, Simon son of Jonah! For flesh and blood has not revealed this to you, but my Father in heaven." Flesh-and-blood humans don't think like this. Only Jesus' Father could have revealed to Peter that this carpenter, now itinerant teacher and healer, is the long-awaited savior. This encourages Jesus to take the group a step farther: "From that time on, Jesus began to show his disciples that he must go to Jerusalem and undergo great suffering at the hands of the elders and chief priests and scribes, and be killed, and on the third day be raised." He will not be the conquering warrior-savior that people long for, and vote for, in every age. His role will be different. As the servant of Yahweh, he will confront evil with the naked weapon of truth—and suffer the terrible consequences.

That is too much for Peter. "Peter took him aside and began to rebuke him, saying, 'God forbid it, Lord! This must never happen to you.'" Apparently, Peter has not understood so well, after all. "Jesus turned and said to Peter, 'Get behind me, Satan! You are a stumbling block to me; for you are setting your mind not on divine things but on human things.'" Peter is thinking like flesh and blood, or worse. Jesus now turns to the disciples and lays things out clearly. Let there be no mistake, "If any want to become my followers, let them deny themselves and take up their cross and follow me. For those who want to save their life will lose it, and those who lose their life for my sake will find it." Jesus will triumph, but not in the way flesh-and-blood thinking supposes. Those who want to share his victory will have to adopt his strategy and pay the price of hardship and rejection. But preparing the disciples includes encouraging them. Peter, James, and John are at least starting to understand. So a few days after this poor showing, Jesus takes them up a mountain where they see his glory. This will strengthen them for what lies ahead.[1]

At the beginning, the disciples accepted Jesus' challenge to change and believe the good news. They have noble intentions, but common-sense thinking still plagues them. Their minds are not yet transformed (*metanoia:* a new mentality [Mark 1:15]).

Like the disciples, we want our lives to count. We hope that years from now we will be able look back and say we spent our time well. Will we follow through? It will be a bumpy ride. Many stall out along the way, or even reverse direction. Every recovering alcoholic knows how easy it is to fall off the wagon. Generosity does not come naturally. Unless we are vigilant, love can turn into its opposite before we notice. The flame flickers, the coals grow cold. Think of all those televangelists, politicians, prelates, community activists, revolutionaries — whole religious communities and social organizations — that started out with the best of intentions but ended up living on faded exploits or mired in scandal.

The prospect of dropping out, burning out, or just petering out obliges us to ask ourselves how we can sustain commitment and avoid pitfalls on the road ahead. For good intentions to bear fruit, we need interior knowledge of flesh-and-blood thinking and how to overcome it. That is the objective of what is arguably Ignatius's most insightful contribution to our understanding of reality, the meditation on Two Standards [136 – 47]. It is the central meditation of the *Spiritual Exercises.*[2]

THE MEDITATION ON TWO STANDARDS

This meditation draws back the veil on the central drama of history, the struggle between good and evil. Christ leads the forces of light under his *standard* (in the old sense of the standard, or flag, that a king would use to lead his army in battle), and the enemy leads the forces of darkness. "Christ calls and desires all persons to come under his standard, and . . . Lucifer in opposition calls them under his" [137]. We live and move within opposing force fields. The powers of egoism pull us backward to slavery unto death, while the divine Spirit draws us forward to freedom and life.

The imagery of the Two Standards calls to mind contemporary fantasies like *Star Trek* and *The Lord of the Rings,* but it clashes with modern sensibilities. While secular society scoffs at transcendent powers, hyper-tolerant liberalism supposes that we can be for life without being against death. By contrast, in the strange apocalyptic vision of the New Testament (and of the Two Standards), Jesus and the Reign of God clash in mortal combat with the prince of this world and his demons. The standards in Ignatius's meditation are the banners that rally the forces of good and evil. They symbolize the strategies of Christ and Satan.

Flesh-and-blood humans easily miss how the great struggle plays out in real life. It would be simpler if "good guys" in white hats faced off against "bad guys" in black hats. But matters are not so simple. The enemy has sown weeds throughout the wheat field of the world, weeds that look like wheat. Every person, action, and institution, every real-world project is morally ambiguous and prone to corruption. Crusades and witch hunts, past and present, al Qaeda, cult suicides, and all the evil done in the name of good bear eloquent witness to how good things can turn demonic.

In this meditation our goal (Ignatius's "what I want") is to learn the deceits of the enemy and learn effective countermeasures to use against them. I "ask for knowledge of the deceits of the evil chief and help to guard myself from them, and knowledge of the true life shown by our supreme and true captain, and grace to imitate him" [139]. What are the two opposing strategies?

First, the enemy "summons innumerable demons . . . scatters them . . . throughout the whole world . . . [and] admonishes them to set up snares and chains" [141–42]. The enemy works everywhere, laying traps. Christ, on the other hand, "chooses so many persons, apostles, disciples, etc., and sends them throughout the whole world, spreading his sacred doctrine among . . . all people" [145]. It sounds like guerrilla warfare or spy vs. spy!

THE APOCALYPTIC VISION

Apocalyptic writing arose in Jewish circles just before and after the time of Christ. The books of Daniel and Revelation and the thirteenth chapter of Mark are classic examples. Apocalyptic visionaries wrote to keep hope alive among the faithful who were suffering persecution. They used exotic imagery (monstrous enemies, supernatural heroes like the "Son of Man") to convey the transcendent meaning of current events. In apocalyptic thinking, God has a design for history as a whole, and our own struggles are part of a cosmic drama in which legions of good and evil spirits clash. Nothing less than the outcome of history is at stake. When the time comes, God will triumph and bring about a new world of justice and peace. In the meantime, the faithful need to decipher how the forces of death and the forces of life are at work in daily events. With this mythical apparatus, apocalyptic thought provided the first framework ever for understanding history as a whole.

Jesus rejected several apocalyptic ideas, however: for example, that God would destroy public sinners and gentile enemies, and that we can come to know the precise time and manner of God's decisive intervention (see Mark 2:17 and 13:32). Four centuries later, Augustine of Hippo recast the apocalyptic vision in his *City of God.* Eleven hundred years after him, Ignatius reappropriated it in the Two Standards. The apocalyptic perspective has a lot to teach us about reality. We need not take the symbols literally in order to take the essential message seriously.

Satan directs his agents "first, to tempt people to covet riches, as he [the enemy] is accustomed to tempt them in most cases, in order that they may more easily come to the vain honor of the world, and then to swollen pride. In this way, the first step is riches, the second honor, the third pride, and from these three steps the enemy leads them to all the other vices" [142].

The strategy is to lead people first to desire riches. Honors follow. But Satan's real objective is "swollen pride." From there, he leads to "all the other vices."

In parallel fashion, Christ charges his collaborators "to seek to help everyone by attracting them, first, to the highest spiritual poverty, and if the divine majesty would be served and wishes to choose them, even to actual poverty; second, to desire insults and contempt because from these two things humility follows. So there will be three steps: first, poverty as opposed to riches; second, insults and contempt as opposed to worldly honor; third, humility as opposed to pride; so that from these three steps they might lead them to all the other virtues" [146].

Christ counterproposes the way of poverty, insults, and humility — and from there to all other virtues. This is the way of Christ as presented in the gospels, the way of humble service leading to the cross. In this meditation, Jesus' followers face the questions he faced when he was tempted in the desert at the beginning of his ministry (Matt. 4:1–11). Would he seek to win people over by offering them bread alone or by ostentatious wonders or by pursuing power as a warrior-Messiah? Or would he empty himself as the servant of all in obedience unto death (Matt. 20:28; Phil. 2:8–9)?

In the Two Standards, we reflect on the contradiction between following him and coveting wealth, with its prestige and power. That would invite Jesus' rebuke of Peter: "Get behind me, Satan!" Can we recognize the way of the cross as the road to life?

RICHES, HONORS, PRIDE; POVERTY, REJECTION, HUMILITY

Ignatius, the practical genius, is sharing what he knows about how commitments unravel, and how they mature. Avarice, honors, and pride pave the typical road to ruin, while poverty, rejection, and humility lead to perseverance and abundant fruit. Let us look more closely.

As a rule (*ut in pluribus,* Ignatius says), the enemy first entices to riches. Greed as the first step to moral decline? Would you have said sex instead? Sex, too, can be a "dangerous good." But, unlike many a Christian moralist, the Bible considers wealth far more dangerous.

"Riches" here means material wealth. "Covetousness" does not mean "disordered desire" for anything whatsoever, such as a long life, health, honor, one's career, and so on (as in the Foundation [23]). Nor is it a generic option for the creature over the Creator. The issue is Mammon, the one idol Jesus mentions in the gospels. "The love of money," says Paul, "is the root of all evils" (1 Tim. 6:10). The first step for undermining commitment—or the first obstacle to its deepening—is coveting possessions.

Wealth brings "honors" even without seeking them.[3] Nothing wrong with wealth or recognition, right? Right. These are good things that can serve the cause. ("Think of what I could do for the poor with a billion dollars!") The point, though, is that the creeping desire for them ensnares us and leads to pride. When pride takes over, the battle is lost.

"Pride" here does not mean healthy self-esteem. Nor is it the generic refusal of the creature to submit to the Creator, that pride (like Adam and Eve's) which Christian theology traditionally considers the basis of all sin. Ignatius is thinking concretely. "Swollen pride" (*crescida soberbia*) refers to arrogance, contempt, selfish ambition, will to power. That is how *hubris* before God plays out in daily life. By bestowing honors on us, society says we are important. "Pride" means believing not just that we are important (we are, after all), but that we are more important than others. Once we catch this disease, we are on the slippery slope to "all other vices" [142].[4]

In short, while the enemy sometimes tempts by other means, the usual strategy (*ut in pluribus*) is to lead to arrogant pride by way of material wealth and prestige. Following commonsense, flesh-and-blood thinking, well-intentioned people pursue this strategy today and end up failing to produce the good they might. Read the newspaper, look around; see if it isn't so. Recall those televangelists, politicians, prelates, activists, communities, and movements that began well but ended up grasping, arrogant, and run amok.

Just recognizing this dynamic doesn't protect us against it. Socrates, Gnostics, and moderns to the contrary, liberation requires more than awareness. On the moral battlefield, we must counterattack in practice.[5] Christ "attracts" followers (he does not browbeat them) to a counterpraxis. Instead of wealth, he proposes, first, "the highest spiritual poverty" to all and "actual poverty" to some (Mark 10:17–31; Luke 14:33; etc.). "Highest spiritual poverty" means interior detachment from material riches and therefore a readiness for material want ("actual poverty"), should God choose us for that. Not everyone is called to share the same degree of material poverty or to work among the poorest. Solidarity with the poor is an objective criterion for our lifestyle, but the particulars depend on our callings.

Second, Christ invites his followers to desire "insults and contempt" rather than "honors"—but, again, only if this better serves God's purpose. We should understand this in the spirit of persecution endured for the "Kingdom"[6] and freedom to endure rejection.

Poverty and persecution are neither desirable in themselves nor infallible means to serve God and neighbor. We could be called to serve in a prestigious job that involves exercising power. But that is not the ordinary way of the Spirit, and we have to be free to embrace the poverty and contempt which following Christ normally entails.

Freedom for poverty and persecution leads, lastly, to humility, the chief weapon against the enemy. From there the Spirit leads to "all other virtues." Again, humility here is not a generic subordination to the Creator, grounding all other virtues. While it includes submission to God, humility means recognizing that I have no greater dignity than anybody else, including the drunk down the street. So I demand no privileges. Humility means identifying with those whom the world deems unimportant. It means solidarity.

Poverty vs. riches, contempt vs. honors, and humility vs. pride are more than private matters between God and me. Poverty vs. riches is a matter of my relationship with the poor. Honors vs. contempt is a question of social status: With whom do I stand? With those whom society honors or with those it holds in contempt? Pride is contempt for others; humility means identifying with the outcast.

Just as the way of the world is individualistic upward mobility, the way of Christ is *downward mobility* leading to solidarity. Upward mobility undermines commitment; downward mobility deepens it, to bear fruit over the long haul.

TO WALK WITH HIM: THE TRIPLE COLLOQUY

The Two Standards meditation begins the preparation for the *election,* or choice, which caps the Second Week of the Exercises and is the climax of the retreat. Ignatius has in mind the choice of a way of life or major life reform in response to Christ's call.

Christ calls everyone to humility via "the highest spiritual poverty" (freedom to share and give away possessions); some, not all, are called to actual material poverty. However, since fear of poverty and rejection can prevent us from hearing and responding, the Two Standards closes with a solemn "triple colloquy," a conversation—first with Mary, then with Jesus, then with the Father—in which we beg to be chosen to walk with Christ in poverty and rejection. I ask

> that I may be received under [Christ's] standard, first, in the most perfect spiritual poverty and also, if... [God] should choose me for it, to no less a degree of actual poverty; and second, in bearing reproaches and insults, that through them I might imitate him more. [147]

We can gauge the importance of this petition from the fact that it is repeated three times in each of the five daily exercises for the rest of the Second Week, that is, from Day Four to as much as Day Twelve!

The triple colloquy helps break down our resistance to poverty and rejection. Its deeper motivation, however, is love. While no sane person would embrace hardship and contempt for themselves, those who have fallen in love with Christ and the poor may well choose to share their poverty and the contempt they receive, out of solidarity.

Some commentators propose a "richer" reading of the Two Standards. They believe "riches" and "honors" can have a wider, nonliteral

THREE TYPES OF PERSONS

The meditation on "Three Types of Persons" [149–56] follows the Two Standards meditation on the same day of the retreat and sharply focuses the issue of riches vs. poverty. The three "types" are really three groups (probably pairs, *binarios* in Spanish) of entrepreneurs, each of whom has acquired the fabulous sum of ten thousand ducats. Although they have not acquired the money dishonestly (which would oblige them to renounce it), neither did they acquire it with the purest of motives. Now they realize that they are unduly attached to their wealth and that this is an impediment to discovering and doing God's will. Troubled in conscience, they want to free themselves of their attachment to the wealth [cf. 150, 153–55]. What should they do?

The parable presents the three ways people typically respond in such a situation. The first group wants to "clean up their act," but they never get around to it. They procrastinate and die before taking effective action [153]. The second group goes farther. They, too, want to overcome their excessive attachment to the money. They are even willing to take practical steps. But they cling to one nonnegotiable condition: they will take measures as long as they do not actually have to give up the money [154]. They want to "make a deal" with God, like the employer who contributes to the church rather than pay his workers a living wage. Only the third group goes to the heart of the matter. Not that they simply give the money away. It is not completely clear that they should do

application: "In the wider sense, *riches* and *honour* can be anything at all that meets the inherent human need for identity, security, esteem, love." That is, "riches" could be anything that I might cling to unduly, like my time or my friends. Similarly, "actual poverty," that. But they will not know what they should do until they get free internally to hear God's call and respond to it. Therefore, the third group strives for indifference to the wealth they possess. That is the key lesson of the parable of the Three Types. Those in the third group place their wealth in psychological escrow. They place themselves in God's hands and strive to conduct themselves with this wealth with complete interior freedom. *Then* they discern what they should do with this money to bring about the greatest overall good.

What does it mean to strive for indifference, to neither desire nor repudiate the wealth out of hand [155]? The answer is given implicitly in the colloquy of the Two Standards meditation, just discussed here, which is repeated for the Three Types [156]. It is given explicitly in a note appended to the Three Types, which reads: "When we feel an inclination or a repugnance against actual poverty, when we are not indifferent to poverty or riches, it is very profitable . . . to ask . . . that the Lord choose [us] for actual poverty and to desire, ask and beg for this, only provided it be for the service and praise of the divine goodness." [157]

The parable of the Three Types is not about indifference in general (as many commentators say) but specifically *the freedom to give up riches.* Ignatius's note says that begging for actual poverty is a great help toward this freedom. (This, by the way, confirms that the meaning of "riches" in the enemy standard is material wealth.)

"humiliation," and "contempt" "are to be understood in an extended as well as in a literal sense."[7]

I cannot agree. All these words can have a wider meaning, but not in this crucial meditation. The meaning of "riches, honors, and pride" and "poverty, insults, and humility" determines what it means to be received under the standard of Christ, or to "be placed with the Son." This is the heart of Ignatian spirituality.[8] My insistence on the concrete (and social) meaning of the key terms in the Two Standards is not motivated by "Ignatian fundamentalism," however. The point is rather that Ignatius is faithfully and creatively communicating the gospel message, the good news, for today:[9] To be placed with the Son is to be placed where he said he would be found: among the hungry, the naked, the sick, and imprisoned (Matt. 25:31–46). It is to opt for the poor. Only in this way will "thy Kingdom come," the Kingdom of life in abundance, new social relations, with no more poverty, hunger, or tears (cf. Luke 6:20–26).

I believe there is a sound intuition behind commentators' desire to expand the key concepts of the Two Standards, namely, the recognition that we should not apply the two strategies universally and uncritically. Covetousness, prestige, and arrogance really do make the world go around; they are what sabotage commitment. But are they the chief temptations of everybody, without exception? Of the downtrodden as well as the powerful? Shall we propose poverty and contempt to poor and abused people? Humility and obedience have long been used to keep second-class citizens "in their place." Feminists argue that arrogant pride is more the capital vice of men than of women and other victims.[10] Some believe that *acedia,* or excessive timidity ("sloth"), is more often the capital vice of women and other oppressed groups, and prescribe self-esteem and assertiveness as its antidotes.

Ignatius, too, recognized that different temptations beset people who are prone to self-doubt. We will revisit these important themes later.

In any case, the message of the Two Standards has lost none of its relevance for today. Covetousness plays a central role in consumer society. The "pride" of the Two Standards is precisely "patriarchal" arrogance, contempt, and ambition. Riches-honors-pride does describe how our patriarchal capitalist world operates. The enemy strategy translates into the individualistic *upward mobility* which traps so many of our contemporaries, women and men alike, social losers as well as winners.

The Two Standards speaks to our society, and to my middle-class "tribe," in particular. While the gospels say a great deal about rich and poor, which were the most important social classes in Jesus' day, they say little directly about those in between. The Two Standards' inspired interpretation of the gospel message throws a bright light over the rocky moral terrain of today's large middle classes. It reveals the ambiguity and danger of their situation and offers a solution: Christ calls us to humility and solidarity via a double freedom, the readiness to renounce everything, and even to embrace material poverty, and freedom from the fear of rejection to which members of the lonely middle-class crowd are so vulnerable.

CONCLUSION

The Two Standards meditation outlines two strategies which are not just for individuals. As the apocalyptic imagery suggests, it refers to social projects. Satan is enthroned in Babylon, "a *world* constructed from sin and by sin"[11] (cf. Rev. 18:2, 9–17). Christ occupies the region around Jerusalem, "the holy city...God's dwelling among humans" (Rev. 21:2–3) [cf. 138]. In the Book of Revelation "Babylon" is code for the Roman Empire, which resists God's project, and Jerusalem stands for God's Reign. Just as Revelation depicts the Babylon project and the Reign of God for the first-century Mediterranean world, we need to do the same for our own. What do the Babylon project and the Jerusalem project look like today?

11 Downward Mobility

> *If I washed your feet — I who am teacher and lord — then you must wash each other's feet.* (John 13:12–14)

The Two Standards meditation sketches the main lines of the struggle between that "old person" we have been and the "new person" we are trying to become. The tempting logic of riches-prestige-arrogance stalls personal transformation, or even turns it around. Poverty-contempt-humility deepens the process and leads to abundant fruit.

This personal drama is part of the wider conflict between a "Babylon Project" (the anti-reign) and a "Jerusalem Project" (the Reign of God). Although their contours depend on social conditions that vary from age to age and from place to place, in these times of globalization we can point out general features that prevail almost everywhere.

THE WAY OF THE WORLD: UPWARD MOBILITY

The Babylon Project is the way of the world. While the world is good and "God so loved the world that he sent his only son" to save it (John 3:16), here I mean the world that resists salvation (cf. John 1:11). Although its logic is usually camouflaged, at times the disguise is paper-thin, as in the following letter which a friend of mine received from a leading credit card company:

> Dear ______:
>
> Recently I invited you to apply for the **** Card. . . . I believe you've earned this invitation. You've worked hard and have been recognized for your efforts. And nothing is more satisfying than achieving your own personal goals.
>
> Now it's time for you to carry the card that symbolizes your achievement — the **** Card.

> Only a select group will ever carry the **** Card. So it instantly identifies you as someone special—one who expects an added measure of courtesy and personal attention. And with the **** Card, you enjoy an impressive degree of convenience, financial flexibility and service....
>
> The **** Card says more about you than anything you can buy with it. I think it's time you joined the select group who carry it.
>
> Sincerely,

The letter suggests that holders of the **** Card are superior to lesser mortals! Sustaining such a crazy notion requires a whole *world* of institutional and cultural support. To understand the logic of that world, we begin, once again, with insecurity.

We are insecure by constitution. We fear pain and rejection. We fear the collapse of meaning. Ultimately, we fear death. Contemporary society aggravates our fear and insecurity. We worry about crime, environmental disaster, and nuclear and industrial accident.[1] September 11, 2001, marked the globalization of insecurity: a sensation of physical insecurity has now spread to people who once felt safe.

Whether rich, poor, or in between, we are all subject to the caprice of markets. Capitalism weakens traditional bonds, so that we also feel more alone than our forebears did in stable rural communities and tight-knit neighborhoods. Individualism reigns. I don't mean egoism, but rather that people tend to confront their needs as individuals, pursuing goals and projects for themselves and their immediate dependents. Without wider social support, both individuals and families then sink into crisis.[2]

Insecurity reaches to our sense of self. Since we are socially mobile (up, down, and sideways), we no longer identify with traditional roles, or with our occupations. All that can change from year to year. Meanwhile, pluralism discredits traditional sources of meaning: custom, religion, and ideologies. Doubts plague us. We take a long time to figure out who we are and what we believe.[3]

Our responses to all this insecurity are fraught with ambiguity. A senior citizen takes out an insurance policy; a farmer struggles for solvency; a young man goes off to college; an entrepreneur scrambles for power at the top; a weary searcher joins a fundamentalistic religion.

In traditional societies with little social mobility, the typical security strategy was to keep your head down and snuggle up to a powerful protector (or be a powerful protector yourself). In modern societies, the most common strategy is upward social mobility. A powerful symbol, "upward mobility" evokes a range of images, feelings, and values. Today, even in the poorest countries, images seen in the media, stories told by traveling relatives, and items seen in shop windows beguile everyone with the hope that upward mobility might someday make their dream come true.[4]

In the United States, upward mobility is the road to success, the American dream of a college education, a home in the suburbs, and a two-car garage. It means hard work and initiative but also rugged individualism, the rat race, and the devil take the hindmost—with "the hindmost" turning out to be disproportionately people of color.

Upward mobility can be a real good, or a god. "Yuppiedom" worships at its shrine. Besides selfish social climbing, upward mobility can mean the pursuit of something good, often for decent motives, that wreaks unintended havoc and corrupts over time. This is the story of Steinbeck's *The Pearl,* where a poor family comes to ruin after discovering a valuable pearl. Upward mobility can mean economic security for refugees and their children; and escaping poverty is good. But it can turn into an escape *from the poor themselves.* Which is it? Which will it be in the long run? We can have bread without justice; attachment to possessions detaches us from one another.

Today the riches, honors, and pride of the Two Standards translates into individualistic upward mobility. The personal drama of upward mobility is in turn embedded in wider social processes. It is part of a social project whose general features, described below, increasingly characterize social life around the world, even in the poorest countries.[5] From the beginning we see that "riches" and "honors" are more than personal temptations. They perform vital social functions.

The following elements characterize the Babylon Project today.

Covetousness

The most straightforward road to security is by pursuing wealth. Capitalism aggravates the universal desire to possess and rewards covetousness more generously than earlier societies in which social position depended more on birth.

René Girard argues that our desires are stimulated and shaped by social rivalry (*mimesis*):[6] First, I desire more or less consciously to be like a certain person, X. The more I perceive that X desires something, the more I desire it for myself. That can lead X to desire it even more, fueling a mutual desire that easily leads to violence, especially when X stands between me and what I want. Girard helps us understand how rivals' desire for oil, or even a basketball, leads to violence; why marketing strategists propose models or celebrities (like X) for us to emulate, making us feel inadequate and creating artificial needs; how advertising turns commodities into "sacred objects" that promise relief—and even happiness itself.

Status symbols

We have a deep need to belong, to feel that we are valuable and our lives are worthwhile.[7] We can take none of this for granted today.

Our society mediates meaning and a sense of self. It tells us who we are and where we fit. From our first years, we interiorize its criteria as the price of belonging. Parents, school, church, the media, etc. communicate what it means to be a good girl, a good boy, and an acceptable adult (as well as a bad girl, etc.). Society assigns us roles, roles which represent institutions and their requirements. Society recognizes us, with approval or disapproval ("honors" or "dishonor"). This socialization process shapes our personalities and communicates values. While we exercise some freedom in this, a society will tolerate only so much dissent. In short, our identity, self-esteem, and values depend decisively on social relations and institutions.[8]

Our personal worth is registered by status symbols. These credentials can be innate and enduring (race, gender, social class) or acquired and mostly temporary (a fancy car, a good job, schooling, credit cards).

The social ladder

In the logic of the world, society is structured as a hierarchy, as rungs on a ladder. Some people are more important than others. It is not just that some (say, surgeons) perform more important functions than others, or that some exercise authority. Rather, some are more human than others — more valuable as persons.[9]

By the dominant yardstick, important people wear smart suits and drive late-model cars; they have university degrees, bank accounts, and lucrative jobs. Unimportant people are poor inner-city youth, the rural unemployed, the severely handicapped, and the faceless masses of poor countries.

Arrogant pride

On the social ladder, we look up to some and down on others. The ladder model fosters arrogant pride and contempt for "inferiors" — foreigners, addicts, or uneducated people. This goes hand in hand with resentment of our "betters" and a measure of self-contempt. The pain of inferior status leads "underdogs" to construct alternative totem poles, redefining success and virtue.

The idea that some are important while others don't count explains how public policy and institutions work. "Unimportant" people are nameless and two-dimensional for "important" people who do not identify with them and feel no obligation to do unto them as they would have others do unto themselves. In sexual relations, labor relations, and foreign relations, they treat them more as means than as real persons with moral claims. Discrimination, on the one hand, and privilege, on the other, just seem natural. Just as pride leads individuals to "all other vices" [142], the logic of the ladder leads society to every kind of injustice. If some are more important than others, then, when push comes to shove, anything can be justified.

The outcast and the paragon

The more people there are below us on the social ladder (and the fewer above us), the more valuable we are. And, just as every ladder has a bottom rung, the social ladder depends on labeling some as outcasts. The outcast is the measure of inhumanity: the mentally ill person, the homosexual, the ugly prostitute, the person with AIDS, the homeless alcoholic. In parallel fashion, the paragon at the top is the measure of the human: the movie star, the president, the CEO, the pope, depending on priorities.

Upward mobility

The principal life strategy is "upward mobility" toward the goal of "success." While some can never rise high enough on the slippery ladder, others can rest content with a modicum of security. But no individual can change the rules of the game. Even when they act with good will, upwardly mobile individuals participate in wider, ambiguous processes.

Competition

The logic of the ladder fuels the kind of competition that undermines trust and community. From my slippery rung, I perceive the climber below me as a threat.

The pyramid

This logic produces institutions and societies in the form of a pyramid. (The ladder, a metaphor of social relations, runs up through the pyramid, a political metaphor.) By "pyramid" here I mean institutions and societies where a few at the top decide for the majority without having to answer to them. Pyramids exclude people from participation in decisions that vitally affect them. In the pyramid, authority and power, which are necessary in social life, are exercised as domination, to contain weaker groups and keep them dependent, ignorant, and divided. The logic of the pyramid characterizes most local, national, and international relations.

Fear, mistrust, and coercion

This pyramid logic generates corruption and provokes hostile reactions but, above all, a climate of fear, mistrust and coercion. Today elites hide behind elaborate security systems in gated communities. Governments increase surveillance and police and military budgets; they provoke arms races and wars for hegemonic control.

INSTITUTIONALIZING INEQUALITY

The United States is the most unequal of industrialized societies. The richest 1 percent of Americans owns 40 percent of the nation's wealth, which is more than what is owned by the bottom 95 percent.[10]

Sociologist Immanuel Wallerstein explains how injustice can reign amid affluence in the democratic United States:

> We think of a despotic system as one in which one man, or a very few at the top, can rule over and exploit all the others. But in fact, a very few at the top are limited in their political capacity to extract too much from the bottom; nor do they need all that much to sustain themselves very comfortably indeed. But, as we expand the size of this group at the top, as we make this group at the top more equal in their political rights vis-à-vis each other, it becomes possible to extract more from the bottom; indeed more is required to feed the needs of those at the top. A political structure with complete liberty for the top half can be the most oppressive form conceivable

Cover-up

Systematic unfairness and corruption require systematic cover-up — which is partly engineered and partly taken for granted as "common sense." However, it is harder to sustain public lies in the Information Age, as we see, for example, in the Bush government's conduct of the "war on terrorism." Superior force may have to assert itself with greater cynicism in the future.

Contemporary limits to economic growth have turned up the moral temperature on upward mobility. The post–World War II economic boom is long over. Since the 1970s the world economy has grown for the bottom half. And in many ways, it can be the most stable. Perhaps a country half free, half slave can long endure.

The very possibility of individual upward mobility, which the United States as a country has pioneered and institutionalized, and which the rest of the world has been borrowing, is one of the most efficacious instruments in maintaining the society as half slave, half free. Upward mobility justifies the reality of social polarization. It minimizes the unrest by removing many potential leaders of protest from the bottom half while holding out the mirage of potential promotion to those left behind. It transforms the search for betterment into competition with others. And whenever one stratum has more or less moved up, there is always another to enter at the bottom.[11]

In a liberal society, education is crucial to advancement. Yet, public education is financed in the United States on the basis of local property taxes which are abysmal in poor communities and abundant in affluent communities.

slowly in the rich North and stalled in most countries of the poor South (with important exceptions in East Asia). This pattern will probably continue.[12] The new informational economy and extreme "free"-market policies combine to enrich comparatively few and to connect a great many to new opportunities. But they exclude many more—hundreds of millions—from access to information and decent employment and living conditions. Entire regions, like most of Sub-Saharan Africa, are cut off from the global economy and stuck in crisis, as are the majorities in poor countries and U.S. ghettoes. Poverty has been growing in all regions for three decades, with even sharper rises occurring in rates of extreme poverty. The gap between rich and poor continues to widen within countries and between nations, producing a stigmatized and sometimes criminalized underclass. The welfare state and social spending shrink, as all nations compete in global markets without the institutional framework that is necessary to safeguard the weak and insure a global common good. As it becomes harder to conceal these realities, civility declines, reliance on force increases, and violence, criminality, and barbarism spread on a world scale.[13]

As paths for social climbing narrow and upward mobility turns into a more ruthless game of hardball, we are awakening to the disquieting fact that it is impossible for everyone, or even the majority, to enjoy the affluent lifestyle of the world's middle classes. The planet's ecosystems could never sustain it. To pursue that lifestyle, at least as a collective project, violates Kant's categorical imperative that criteria for behavior must be applicable in principle to everyone.[14]

There has to be a better way.

THE WAY OF CHRIST: DOWNWARD MOBILITY

> *Let the same mind be in you that was in Christ Jesus, who though he was in the form of God, did not regard equality with God as something to be exploited, but emptied himself, taking the form of a slave, being born in human likeness. And being found in human form, he humbled himself and became obedient to the point of death – even death on a cross. Therefore God also highly exalted him and gave him a name that is above every name.*
>
> (Phil. 2:5 – 11)

In 1994 Janine Geske was elected to a ten-year term as a Wisconsin Supreme Court justice. Four years later, the *Milwaukee Journal-Sentinel* reported that the "widely known, widely respected justice" had decided to resign. A wife and mother of two, Geske was forty-nine years old and making more than $100,000 a year. She said her decision had not come easily, and that "it will be difficult for some lawyers and judges to understand." But "prestige and stature and money are not what drives me. I want to do more. . . . After seventeen years as a judge, the time has come for me to change directions."

The Geskes had recently spent a week living among the poor in the Dominican Republic. The hospitality of Janine Geske's hosts moved her deeply. "I could see daylight through the boards that made up the walls," she said. "I thought of my crowded closets, drawers, attic, basement and garage back home. Why did I need all that stuff? Why is my life so complicated, busy, and noisy?" Geske had asked herself. "Are my children being raised in an environment that is better than this quiet, simple, faith-filled place? Would I be as generous and kind to a stranger as this impoverished family is to me?"

While on a retreat after returning home, Geske made a list of the reasons why she should remain on the Supreme Court. The list included money and power. "Those things are not what I want to live my life for," she decided.[15] Geske opted for downward mobility, the contemporary translation of the standard of Christ: poverty, contempt, humility. This personal strategy, too, is part a wider social project with the following general features.

Faith

To seek security through control of our surroundings dehumanizes us and destroys our environment. The alternative strategy is faith, by which we abandon ourselves to God's care. Faith allows us to let things go and share what we have.

Indifference to honors

Human dignity depends simply on being human, not on social status. From the perspective of faith, life itself and our talents are unmerited gifts. Our dignity and our standing before God do not depend on our merits but on God's goodness. The good news of divine acceptance provides a solid sense of security (Rom. 8:38–39). It allows us to be indifferent to "honors" [23], which Paul considered "dung" (Phil. 3:8), and to insults. It exposes the fallacious logic of the social ladder. If we are accepted by God, who presides over the universe, can we count for less because we are black or handicapped or don't wear designer jeans?

Recognizing others' humanity; sharing

A sense of being accepted ourselves enables us to recognize the humanity of our neighbor, especially the outcast. That shakes the foundations of a world divided into important and unimportant people.

Christ addresses us through the outcast, enticing us [cf. 146] to share their poverty and rejection and to recognize the crucified outcast (not the celebrity paragons) as the measure of humanity: *Ecce homo!* (John 19:5).

In the gospels, Jesus' disciples don't understand. They discuss who will be the most important when Jesus comes into power. He solemnly assures them that being important means becoming unimportant like a child (Matt. 18:1–4). His followers are not the big ones, but the "little ones" (Matt. 10:42; 18:3, 10–14), whom the world regards with contempt (1 Cor. 1:26–27). They are the poor in spirit, the afflicted (Matt. 5:3–4), the last who will be first (Matt. 19:30), the humble who will be exalted (Matt. 23:11–12; cf. Luke 1:48, 52). They "have the mind of Christ," the servant of all (Phil. 2:6–7; cf. 2 Cor. 8:9).

Humility as solidarity

Solidarity is the social meaning of humility [cf. 167]. Just as humility leads individuals to all other virtues [146], humility as solidarity is the foundation of a just society.

In short, the standard of Christ today is "downward mobility." That means entering the world of the poor, assuming their cause, and, to some degree, their condition.

Solidarity shapes our lifestyle, which will depend on each one's vocation. Solidarity doesn't necessarily mean destitution. It has nothing to do with denying our training or neglecting our talents. Special obligations, for example, to family and benefactors, carry weight in deliberating about lifestyle. We should beware of dogmatizing about having a car or a computer, about whether to save for old age or where to educate our children. These are legitimate matters for discernment, but not for one-size-fits-all formulas.[16]

At the same time, the objective criterion of our "poverty" is solidarity with the poor. We will feel uncomfortable with superfluities when poor friends lack essentials. Attachment to them will detach us from luxuries, and even necessities. As the New Testament and Christian tradition tells us, possessions are resources entrusted to us, to be administered for the good of all, especially those in need. This logic extends to other resources. What about pursuing higher education in a world of hunger? If we have that opportunity, then studying means storing up cultural capital to be administered later on behalf of those who need us.

How much should we have? Better to reframe the question: Do we feel at home among the poor? Do they feel comfortable in our homes? Or do our furnishings and possessions make them feel like unimportant people?

Solidarity leads to sharing the obscurity, misunderstanding, and contempt experienced by the poor. Assuming their cause will most likely bring the world's ridicule and fury down on our heads. We might even feel left out if our friends suffer these things and we do not.

Communities of equals

The solution to our global social crisis is not that the poor become rich, which is neither feasible nor desirable, but that the rich join with the poor. The only solution is communities of equals, resisting pyramids of inequity (see Luke 22:25–26). While some economic differences are legitimate, discrimination and misery are not. In communities of equals, personal talents, instead of advancing some at others' expense, are stewarded for the benefit of all. Authority is a service for the common good.

Cooperation

Cooperation replaces cutthroat competition. While visiting an elementary school in a slum outside Lima, I was puzzled to see all the little desks pushed together and teachers encouraging students to cheat! The school principal patiently explained to the dumb gringo that the kids were helping each other find the answers! "We want to overcome poverty," she said, "but if we are going to move up, we will all move up together."

THE CENTURY OF SOLIDARITY

Today, we have no clear road map to a more humane society and no precise blueprint for it. That is probably a blessing. But how can we advance toward it? While politics remains important, these days few look to governments, political parties or even liberation movements to solve the problem of poverty or save the environment. At the same time, in many parts of the world we are witnessing the burgeoning of citizens' groups pushing for change from the bottom up and across the base of societies. Groups of struggling neighbors, indigenous people, women, ethnic and sexual minorities, consumers and immigrants, environmental groups, human rights organizations, unions, small and medium-size businesses, cooperatives and communal banks are sowing the seeds of a new social order. Many of these groups stress democratic participation, transparency, and accountability in their internal organization.

This effervescence in civil society is a principal sign of hope. However, whether in Chicago or Zambia, their micro-initiatives are up against macro-obstacles. In Central America, where I live, if you openly challenge companies that are polluting the river, you could be found floating in the river the next morning. The same goes for challenging official crime and corruption. Therefore, human rights activists make friends with Human Rights Watch. Environmental activists ally with Greenpeace. Forced to compete with big business, cooperatives link up locally and internationally. So do women, indigenous peoples, and unions. Local communities forge ties with sister communities and sister parishes in the United States and Europe to work for local development. Without these allies, the local groups have little chance against those who control the market and the means of violence.

Even with allies, these groups look like small fish in a pond of sharks. Titanic competitors dominate the international scene: transnational capital, the G7 governments, international finance and trade institutions (the International Monetary Fund, the World Trade Organization) with their political and economic power, and the ultimate backup of military force. Yet there are potent signs of hope at the international level, as well. To mention just two examples: a coalition of more than thirteen hundred NGOs pushed through the global Land Mine Treaty in record time and won the 1997 Nobel Peace Prize. The Jubilee 2000 coalition pressured the G7 countries to concede debt relief to the most indebted poor countries. International civil society is growing and challenging global power.

The implications are clear. To combat world poverty and environmental decay, we need to make this the Century of Solidarity, especially international solidarity. As elites extend their power through globalized markets, finance, and communications, the response can only be to globalize the practice of love. We need to enlist the Internet, e-mail, and discount air fares in the cause. But more than anything else, we need "new human beings" who identify with the poor majority of the planet — including people in rich countries who know about trade, finance, and human rights law and can help address the complex causes of misery. Many such people are stepping forward, especially from colleges and universities and from the churches, with their unique potential to connect people across borders and a wealth of experience on the ground.[17]

There are plenty of grounds for hope. And there is plenty of work to do.

Communities of "new human beings" and humane relations must exercise *prophetic witness* to unmask the great cover-up. They must be places from which to work for a more hospitable world—for a society where, as the Zapatistas say, "everyone has a place" and where, as Peter Maurin used to say, "it is easier for people to be good."

CONCLUSION

These are times of global social crisis in which many people feel insecure and alone. Our reflections lead to the conclusion that we find security in community. If we seek first the Reign of God and its justice, our security needs will be met (cf. Matt. 6:33). Both security and community arise from faith and from the praxis of solidarity that replaces unjust relations and institutions with just ones. To be genuine and avoid condescension, solidarity must be humility-in-practice. Like the gospel, Ignatius assigns humility a central role in our lives. For only in its soil can love take root, grow and bear fruit. To be authentic, however, humility must be solidarity. We turn now to reflect further on that and after that to unmask counterfeit versions of humility.

Humility and Solidarity 12

As they left the council, the disciples rejoiced that they were considered worthy to suffer dishonor for the sake of the name.[1]

(Acts 5:41)

From humility, says Ignatius, the Spirit leads "to all the other virtues." Humility flowers into solidarity, identifying with others to the point of sharing their suffering.

- When Archbishop Oscar Romero received death threats, the Salvadoran government offered him protection. He refused because the poor did not enjoy the same protection.[2] Better to walk with them.
- For months my co-worker Margarita suffered through her baby's illness. She kept vigil by his crib, unable to bear the thought of him suffering alone. Margarita told me that she would gladly have changed places with her baby, and I believe her.
- Twice a week a student brought sandwiches to homeless people downtown and gradually won the trust of a homeless man named Dave. Dave told her the life story no one else had had the patience to hear. She was amazed to discover the real person, just like her, under the grimy clothes and disheveled hair. Taking her hot shower and picturing Dave out there in the cold, she felt an uncomfortable twinge at the distance between them, and a desire to share his journey more closely.
- Friends of mine traveled to New York immediately after the September 11 attacks to be with suffering New Yorkers. Others later went to Baghdad and risked their lives to accompany Iraqis during the U.S. invasion.

This is the logic of love. Our heart goes out to those who suffer—the way Jesus was moved by the leper, the crowds, and the widow of

Nain — and we long to join them. Comfort and respectability are good things. But it is preferable to walk with the poor than without them. And sharing their hardship and rejection helps free us from fear.

THREE KINDS OF HUMILITY

Ignatius describes three stages of maturity as "Three Kinds of Humility" [165 – 67], though we could as easily say three stages of love.[3] He says the first is "necessary for salvation": "I so lower and humble myself" that, for all the world, even to save my life, I would never deliberately violate my conscience in a serious matter [165].

The second kind of humility is in the single-minded availability of the Foundation: "I do not desire or feel myself strongly attached to having wealth rather than poverty, or honor rather than dishonor, or a long life rather than a short one" [23]. So, not for the whole world or to save my life would I deliberately violate my conscience in any way [cf. 166]. Beyond avoiding evil, I habitually desire to do what is best. More than mere obedience, the first two kinds of humility are degrees of friendship with God.

The third form of humility presupposes the first two. Ignatius writes:

> when the options equally further the praise and glory of God, in order to imitate Christ our Lord better and to be more like him here and now, I desire and choose poverty with Christ poor rather than wealth; contempt with Christ laden with it rather than honors. Even further, I desire to be regarded as a useless fool for Christ who before me was regarded as such, rather than as a wise or prudent person in this world. [167][4]

This third kind of humility coincides with Christ's standard [146] in desiring "actual poverty" and rejection. The second, too, includes the indifference to wealth ("spiritual poverty" [146]) of Christ's standard and indifference to honors. Love comes to full flower in the third: one has the mind of Christ and desires to walk with him (cf. Phil. 2:5). Francis of Assisi called this "perfect joy."

The third kind of humility is a bias for downward mobility. Charles de Foucauld, who lived and died among the nomadic peoples of the northern Sahara, expressed this poetically a century ago:

> Our master was despised; the servant ought not be honored.
> The master was poor; the servant ought not be rich.
> The master lived by the work of his hands; the servant ought not live off his own rent.
> The master walked on foot; the servant ought not ride horseback.
> The master surrounded himself with the little ones, the poor, the workers; the servant ought not associate with the great lords.
> The master was calumniated; the servant ought not be praised.
> The master was poorly dressed, poorly fed, poorly sheltered; the servant ought not roam about well-dressed, well-fed and well-established.
> The master worked and tired himself; the servant ought not look for repose.
> The master wished to appear small; the servant ought not wish to appear great.[5]

Ignatius does not commend poverty and insults for their own sake. He commends a preference for them, to counter the lure of riches and honors that lead to "swollen pride." Since serving God and neighbor brings hardship and rejection, we must be free to embrace them. Asking for them helps us escape the gravitational field of narcissism.[6]

At the same time, although they are not worthy ends in themselves, poverty and rejection can be fruitful means, since they are privileged "places" for God's action.

> But we have this treasure in clay jars, so that it may be made clear that this extraordinary power belongs to God and does not come from us.... For while we live we are always being given up to death for Jesus' sake, so that the life of Jesus may be made visible in our mortal flesh. So death is at work in us, but life in you.... We are treated... as sorrowful, yet always rejoicing; as poor, yet making many rich. (2 Cor. 4:7–12; 6:8–10)

Christ told Paul, "My grace is sufficient for you, for power is made perfect in weakness." "So," says Paul, "I will boast all the more gladly of my weaknesses, so that the power of Christ may dwell in me... for whenever I am weak, then I am strong" (2 Cor. 12:8–10).

Even so, poverty and contempt are neither universally fruitful, nor an ideal for all. Resources to which the poor have little access can serve God's Reign. So can social recognition. Paul even had to "boast" like a fool to defend the mission (cf. 2 Cor. 11–12). In the end, however, the rationale is love—to be like Christ. The logic of love is to think twice before veering from downward mobility. Humility as solidarity is an inertial tendency from which to deviate only when the outside force of the greater good intervenes. "The burden of proof, so to speak, will be on the Holy Spirit to show me that the less poor, less obscure, less humble way is in fact the way God is calling me to follow."[7]

CONCLUSION

The Two Standards, the Three Types of Persons, and the Three Kinds of Humility all prepare for the *election* in the Ignatian retreat. The election is the choice of a way of life or major reform, in response to Christ's call. Only someone who is ready for privation and persecution can "hear" such a call and respond generously. Therefore, Ignatius considered the indifference of the second kind of humility to be the minimal condition for proceeding to the election, while the third kind is the ideal disposition.

The third kind of humility goes beyond "indifference" to actual preference of poverty and rejection! Ignatius recommended humiliations to many of his contemporaries as a helpful means to humility. This sits uneasily today. Although we can stretch to appreciate poverty in solidarity, embracing humiliations is far more problematic. What kind of humility could come from humiliations? We do well to consider humility, true and false, more carefully.

Expanding the Soul 13

No one after lighting a lamp puts it under the bushel basket, but on the lampstand, and it gives light to all in the house. (Matt. 5:15)

Riches, honors and arrogant pride do seem to make the world go around. But is pride everyone's chief nemesis?[1] What about people with low self-esteem? Don't other temptations trouble them more, like lack of confidence? And what about poverty and humiliations? Shall we recommend them to humiliated people? Do *they* need exhortations to humility?

The great challenges of our time—poverty, the environment, war—should inspire humility, but also creativity and bold action. They cry out for large-minded generosity—that is, the *magnanimity* that springs from wholesome self-esteem. Without humility, we elbow others aside. But without magnanimity, we bury our talent in a napkin.

Many have questioned the central emphasis that Christianity has always given to humility and self-sacrifice. In an often-cited article, Valerie Saiving makes the case for women. She takes on the ancient tradition that identifies sin with self-assertive pride and love with self-sacrifice.[2] Saiving argues that, while pride is the primary temptation of men, women's nemesis is "underdevelopment or negation of the self." Measuring themselves by others' criteria, many women fail to develop into the well-defined individuals they could be. Submerging their own agendas in others', they keep the genie of "divine discontent" (Saiving) bottled up inside. They "love too much," responding to immediate needs to the point of living without a clear focus and losing themselves in trivialities. Such individuals are not likely to profit from exhortations to humility. Rather, they should honor their inner authority more—loving, by all means, but in wiser and more fruitful ways.

Saiving argues that differences in biology and early interaction intensify the creative drive of men more than women.[3] Without disputing that, I am struck by how much of the malaise she describes characterizes many oppressed and humiliated people — men as well as women — that I have known over the years. Much of what Saiving says applies to poor people in general, victims of discrimination, handicapped people, and others who have interiorized society's prejudices. They don't all "love too much" or submerge their identity chameleon-like in others' agendas. But many let themselves be persuaded that they don't count for much, that they have little to say and no real mission in life. They stifle their inner voice; they fail to speak and act when they should.

Members of more privileged groups also suffer versions of this malady. Many of us men clip our own wings, or let others clip them. We remain silent and inactive when bold speech and action are called for. We, too, can end up like T. S. Eliot's Prufrock, measuring out our lives with coffee-spoons.[4] All kinds of people take a back seat in life and let hard-chargers drive them where they don't want to go. Self-doubt prevents many of us from taking up new challenges. We avoid risks for fear of failure. Weakness leads us to resent, and disparage, the values of the strong, to carp against authorities rather than engaging them constructively. We sometimes recoil from the messy ambiguity of institutions, preferring to lob in grenades from outside.

A FEARFUL HUMILITY

> *Master, I knew that you were a harsh man,... so I was afraid, and I went and hid your talent in the ground.* (Matt. 25:24–25)

Ignatius recognized that people can douse their inner flame. The enemy *usually* tempts to riches, honors, and pride, but not always. Writing to Teresa Rejadell, Ignatius described a different dynamic. The enemy sometimes leads generous people, like Teresa herself, into a false humility and such a fixation on their moral poverty that they feel abandoned by God.[5] Ignatius told Teresa that people usually experience this subtle assault after fighting off two more straightforward temptations: when someone is reforming her life or facing a costly sacrifice, the enemy sows desolation, bringing to mind how much privation this entails (and leading her to ignore God's consolations). This is a typical situation for the first series of Rules for Discernment. If that tactic fails, the enemy then tempts the person to holier-than-thou vainglory. If both of these direct temptations fail, the enemy then often resorts to the more subtle two-step strategy, which, as we shall see, leads to a state similar to what Valerie Saiving describes.

The two-step temptation works as follows. First, the enemy gets us to deny the good that God works in us—in secular language, to deny something good in ourselves. For example, when we do a good deed or think of a worthwhile project, we suppose it would be presumptuous to attribute that to God's work in us, that is, to speak of good in ourselves. So, we refuse to credit our good works or take our ideas and desires seriously. This is "a false humility, that is, an extreme and vitiated humility." It is actually "a *fear* with the appearance of humility."[6]

From there, the enemy easily leads us a step farther, into the fear that, since we are evil, God has abandoned us. Building on our sensitive moral conscience (perhaps a postconversion conscience), the enemy draws us into imagining, falsely, that we have done wrong, and provokes desolation. Focusing "a too-prolonged gaze at such times on our miseries" leads us to believe "that we are quite separated from [God] and that all that we have done and all that we desire to do is entirely worthless."[7] In this way the enemy undermines our trust in God and our self-esteem.

Fear and discouragement betray the enemy's presence and the counterfeit nature of this "humility." Genuine humility is loving rather than fearful, while false humility shrinks the soul,[8] leading us to think small and lose ourselves in unimportant matters.

How should we respond to these intrigues once we unmask them? Ignatius's advice is revealing: humbling ourselves is the last thing we need. When tempted to arrogant pride, we should humble ourselves; but when tempted like this, we should lift ourselves up, recalling the good that God has worked in us.[9]

These interior dynamics keep good people from acting on their inner authority, which often coincides with the movement of the divine Spirit. Small wonder that in the same letter to Sor Teresa Ignatius discusses the problem of excessive self-doubt in moral matters. The

TEMPTATIONS AND THEIR TIMES

Temptation strikes where we are vulnerable, but we are not all vulnerable in the same places [cf. 327]. What counts as a serious temptation for me will depend on my temperament and maturity. Besides that, the logic of temptation depends on social conditions — more than people supposed in the past.

Our personalities are formed in interaction with society, so that society's values and anti-values take shape in us as virtues and vices.[10] Since our internal weaknesses — moral and psychological — are partly the product of socialization, the logic of temptation depends partly on changing social and cultural conditions.

Ignatius grew up in a late-feudal society where status at birth was the key to wealth and security. Honor was a supreme value and a primary temptation. "In the Ignatian world, . . . with its conception of the human ideal of medieval knighthood, honor was the same as life, and to lose one's honor

enemy tries to make some people see defects where there are none, in order to harass them and even drive them to desperation.

In the *Exercises,* he treats the subject in greater detail[11]: while some people have lax consciences and are insensitive to evil, he says, others are hypersensitive. And just as the bad spirit tries to make the lax conscience still more lax, the evil one pushes those of "delicate" conscience into exaggerated fear of wrongdoing. This drives them to anguish and prevents them from doing good. While God often inspires good people to undertake bold initiatives, the hypersensitive are subject to paralyzing doubts that keep them from translating their inspirations into action. They spontaneously ask themselves questions like, "Am I really seeking my own glory?" "Will this cause scandal?" "Would it be safer to back off, or at least wait?" "Couldn't x, y, or z go wrong?"

was to lose one's life."[12] However, conditions were changing in western Europe at the time and, with them, mores and motivations. The fifteenth-century Spanish classic *La Celestina* records the following observations: "Pleberio does not say that with honor he became rich, but rather that, with his abundant means he acquired honors. . . . Sempronio knows that Celestina's ambition in her business dealings is none other than to 'get rich' and he understands that, impelled as he is by the same ambition, he will have to contend with her."[13]

A new society was developing around the port cities that Ignatius frequented (Barcelona, Genoa, Antwerp, Venice). In this mercantile environment, wealth was displacing birthright as the primary key to status and power. Riches were a powerful temptation on the road to "swollen pride" [142]. In today's capitalist society, too, while honor is less a moral problem than in traditional societies, covetousness is more problematic than ever.

As always, Ignatius prescribes acting against the "disordered inclination." While the lax person should become more sensitive to evil, the scrupulous person should become more "lax," but in a distinctive way. When faced with what appears to be a moral dilemma, he or she should make a reasonable decision and then stay the course, rejecting second thoughts and remaining at peace. Unless there is a clear reason to question their original plans, hypersensitive people should resist doubts and fears and follow through on their first inspiration [cf. 351]. These inspirations are innocent until proven guilty, above all when they arise directly from consolation.[14] Exaggerated self-doubt and fear of doing wrong do not proceed from the good Spirit. Unless checked, they undermine peace and quash fruitful action.

The nightly news confirms that greed, prestige, and arrogant pride has lost none of its destructive power today. But that is not the only threat to a generous life. False humility and excess caution foster sins of omission and block creative action. Tragically, the children of light pursue their goals with less zeal than the children of this age (cf. Luke 16:8).

Temptations depend partly on social dynamics (see the boxed text "Temptations and Their Times"). The social forces that shape and threaten us are not the same today as in premodern times or even thirty years ago. One contemporary malaise, with affinities to false humility and the Saiving syndrome, deserves close attention. I mean *ressentiment,* meaning, roughly, resentment.

RESSENTIMENT

> *Jesus said, "To what then will I compare the people of this generation, and what are they like? They are like children sitting in the marketplace and calling to one another, 'We played the flute for you, and you did not dance; we wailed, and you did not weep.'"* (Luke 7:31–32)

Friedrich Nietzsche (1844–1900), and Max Scheler (1874–1928) after him, borrowed the French word *ressentiment* to label a malady of the human spirit that they believed to be rampant in modern society.[15] Although I think both of them overstated their case, the ressentiment they diagnosed is clearly thriving and spreading in our ultramodern times. Ressentiment is the typical temptation of the underdog, the vanquished, and the political left. No one escapes completely, however. Who, after all, is not in some sense an underdog or a victim today?

We have all felt ressentiment's morbid sting. Like most adolescents, you may have walked the corridors of your high school feeling deflated for not being the most charming and popular of students. In reaction, maybe you came to consider good looks and easy charm as irrelevant, and "dressing up" for others as stupid. Or maybe the history you were studying seemed to you such an incoherent swarm of battles and dates that it eventually drove you to conclude that history was just "dumb."

Consider an adult example or two. You might once have accepted an invitation to the opera, even though opera never appealed you. As the production progressed, the more the audience grew enthralled, the more you felt uneasy, alone, and alienated. You wondered what they all saw in it. You weren't sure whether to consider yourself hopelessly uncultured or to pronounce opera highly overrated and opera buffs a bunch of pretentious snobs. You longed to get home and kick back with a beer and a good film on TV.

Or, if you are an opera buff, you may once have found yourself at a party among rambunctious fans of hunting, twin-carburetor engines, and football stars you'd never heard of. As the party progressed, you began to imagine your fellow partygoers dressed in animal skins and carrying clubs. You wished you were home with a glass of wine and a good book.

"Ressentiment" means resentment, yes, but with nuances. More precisely, ressentiment is the sublimated spirit of revenge, the masked and muted desire to prevail over one's stronger rival. While envy, jealousy, and rivalry can contribute to ressentiment, they are not exactly the same. Ressentiment is a reaction. In ressentiment — literally "re-feeling" — one feels the impotence of frustrating encounters with one's superior rival(s). According to Scheler, one experiences a morbid attraction to return again and again to painful defeats. As ressentiment feeds on the revisited feeling, it grows and develops, producing a painful tension that eventually finds release in the denigration of the rival's values and the exaltation of their opposites. Ressentiment leads frustrated underdogs to invert all that is valuable to their stronger, more attractive, morally superior, more capable or successful competitors. It leads the weak to denigrate strength, the unlettered to belittle letters, and the poor to disparage wealth and power. Ressentiment leads sinners to debunk virtue and the losers to redefine winning. It doesn't only affect the way people think. Above all, ressentiment modifies their spontaneous reaction (attraction, repugnance) to people, practices, and institutions that humiliate them.

Sometimes defeat leads people to react lucidly: to unmask false values and misplaced priorities. Ressentiment is different: it denigrates genuine values, distorting moral perception and judgment. The frustrated desire for revenge recoils on the resentful, poisoning their moral life.

Although present in any age, ressentiment came into its own in modern times, as Nietzsche and Scheler recognized. In traditional society, one's rivals could only be one's peers on a social ladder that was extremely stable. Very few in France could actually envy the king of France in the sense of resenting not being in his place, since they had no chance of being king anyway. In a socially mobile society, however, everyone has more potential rivals. In principle, paupers can hope to change their fate. An inner-city youth might aspire to become the next NBA legend or the next Bill Gates. In this climate we are all more aware and more resentful of successful competitors, especially since, as Scheler pointed out, ressentiment is highly contagious. It spreads quickly through families and communities and can infect entire nations or whole generations.

Nietzsche believed that ressentiment had given birth to Christianity and that Christianity accounted for ressentiment's dominance. He considered Christianity to be the triumph of a "slave morality" which celebrates defeat, weakness, failure, and death while disparaging strength, life, creativity, and success. Christianity exalts what Nietzsche considered the false virtues of humility, altruism, pity, self-control, and long-suffering patience.

Scheler recognized the brilliance of Nietzsche's "discovery." He considered ressentiment to be the wellspring of the value judgments of bourgeois society.[16] However, he rejected Nietzsche's theses that ressentiment accounts for Christianity and that love and humility are sham virtues. Scheler did consider ressentiment a major temptation for Christians, however. While love and humility are the jewels in the Christian moral crown, the corruption of the best is the worst of all, as the old adage has it. In René Girard's incisive words, "Ressentiment is the manner in which the spirit of vengeance survives the impact of Christianity and turns the Gospels to its use."[17]

Nietzsche threw a pail of cold water on those bourgeois romantics who believed that by acting on their spontaneous desires they would make their lives a creative work of art. He announced that these desires were neither spontaneous nor authentic but expressions of a frustrated will to power. Since his time, ressentiment has continued to prosper, as the sometimes silly controversies over political correctness demonstrate. It even thrives in poor countries, as the middle-class ethos spreads with the help of mass media. Ressentiment stalks underdogs of all kinds, as well as their allies on the political left who reject inequality and discrimination.

Of course, privilege and injustice also call forth genuine moral indignation, not just ressentiment. When political constitutions proclaim that "all men (and women) are created equal," people *rightly* resent the denial of their rights. During the last 250 years, successive waves of humanity have awakened to their dignity as persons with the right to think, speak and act for themselves. The *philosophes* of the Enlightenment were followed by laborers, then women, then colonized peoples, poor nations in general, racial minorities, sexual minorities, and lay people in the churches. Now, we even voice moral claims on behalf of the environment. Ressentiment has been part of all this, but not the largest part. Like many of their followers today, Nietzsche and Scheler recognized the awakening to ressentiment, but they failed to appreciate the awakening to dignity. They often confused justified indignation with ressentiment.

It is sheer cynicism to use the ressentiment label to silence the outcry of oppressed people. That is simply ressentiment on the part of the privileged that the masses have dared to claim a place at the table. While Nietzsche and Scheler overstated the resentment of the weak, they understated, and mostly ignored, the ressentiment of the strong (including their own: Nietzsche bitterly resented the weak, and sounds more resentful than they do). Nietzsche and Scheler failed to place the real, pervasive injustice of their day at the center of the canvas on which they painted their picture of the world. Both celebrated the virtues of classical antiquity that accorded powerful and talented men a privileged standing, relegating women and laborers to inferior status. This, too, is will to power, and unwillingness to share it.

In the same way, some wave the ressentiment banner to stifle legitimate protest today. These banner-wavers are, paradoxically, resentful. They resent handicapped people getting better parking places. They resent affirmative action; they resent brown people crossing their borders in search of jobs; they resent uppity women in the church and public life; they resent old people for taking so long to die; they resent gays and lesbians for coming out; they resent the hungry and the homeless for demanding food, work, and shelter. Unlike the underdogs, "important" people do not resent the strength of the strong but the dignity of the weak.

We more commonly attribute ressentiment to the victims themselves, however. Maybe that is why the V-word is falling from favor. Assigning the victim label can be condescending. Appropriating it can foster self-pity. That does no one any good. But it is far worse to deny the reality of victims. And, though we are all victims (and victimizers) to some degree, degrees vary decisively. The rules of the economic and political game are sharply skewed to favor the powerful. That calls for vigorous protest and action, whether some consider it politically correct or not. Neither does being a victim preclude responsible, self-directed action, or vice versa.

At the same time, ressentiment does shadow the underdog. It latches like a parasite onto legitimate protest in the form of reverse prejudice and the denial of real values. Ressentiment finds strong individuals and institutions intimidating and responds with passive aggression. It surfaces in anti-intellectual and antitechnology bias. Ressentiment can see no hope for "whitey's" redemption. It operates in the conviction that women are morally superior to men by nature. Ressentiment is present in an option for the poor that denies the humanity of the rich and disallows the possibility of their conversion. Ressentiment is at work when a poor country's government refuses outside assistance in time of natural disaster and in the rejection of every idea that originates in the rich North for reason of that origin alone. Ressentiment prefers carping and permanent protest to positive proposals. It shuns constructive engagement with adversaries. Ressentiment is at work in an anarchistic fear of institutions – businesses, churches, universities, NGOs, and government – and in the inability to wrestle with their moral ambiguity. Ressentiment would uproot the weeds and risk killing the wheat rather than wade into a field that is sown with both.

Disengaging isn't always ressentiment. Serious commitment can lead to "dropping out" of the rat race. It can lead to alternative schooling, communal living, civil disobedience, persecution, clandestine life, and jail. The history of religious life and monasticism, the radical wing of the Protestant Reformation, and many similar examples confirm the value of disengagement. However, noncooperation can also mask a resentful unwillingness to enter playing fields outside our zone of mastery. The a priori refusal to engage powerful individuals and institutions when that might benefit me or my community disguises a sense of personal inadequacy and the subconscious acceptance of the values overtly scorned.

Finally, ressentiment is hard at work in the denial of the goodness in ourselves — the goodness of our bodies, the values of rest, sexuality, enjoyment, and celebration of the pleasures of life. More radical still is the ressentiment in a false humility that denies our inner authority and leads us to bury our talents. Ressentiment smolders below the surface in oppressed people who more readily doubt themselves than the smooth-talking professionals. It leads them to stifle the impulse to act when they should, to shake off their chains. Ressentiment overlaps with the Saiving syndrome: the neglect of rivals' real values (assertiveness, focused pursuit of objectives in the public arena, and so forth).

DIFFERENT DANGERS

How are false humility, self-negation, and ressentiment related to the enemy standard of riches-honors-pride?

It seems clear that this logic still makes the world go around and probably always will this side of paradise. However, it is not the only threat to a committed life. The force of evil is like water cascading down a hillside. If we successfully block the torrent in the major downhill channel of riches-honors-pride, it will seek alternative routes, especially the underground channels that are harder to detect. Ressentiment is a major downhill alternative. Within patriarchal societies shaped by avarice, prestige, and the arrogant scramble to dominate (the classic enemy standard), when decent people parry the obvious temptations, more subtle traps await them. In the name of "humility" and "equality," they can bury their talents, stifle their initiatives, and/or fall to carping from the sidelines.

Different temptation dynamics are not mutually exclusive. They can coexist and interact. Riches and prestige might dominate me, and I may dominate "less important" people; but I can at the same time bitterly resent stronger rivals. Women suffering from Saiving's complex can yield to greed and arrogant pride as easily as men. Even as someone, like Teresa Rejadell, succumbs to false humility with "peers" and "superiors," she can turn around and smother the initiative of employees, spouse, and children.

At different stages of our lives, we may fall prey to one dynamic more than others. But who ever entirely escapes the lure of greed? Who is safely vaccinated against arrogant pride in all its camouflaged forms?

MAGNANIMITY: THE OTHER SIDE OF THE HUMILITY COIN

> *I pray that, according to the riches of his glory, you may be strengthened in your inner being with power through his Spirit.*
> (Eph. 3:16)

The social ladder and political domination (the "pyramid") describe contemporary societies, and riches-honors-pride has lost none of its pernicious force. So the evangelical call to renunciation of goods and to humility remains as valid as ever. However, the corrosive power of ressentiment and false humility raises questions: is poverty-humiliations-humility a viable strategy today? Shall we commend humility to people who suffer from low self-esteem? What about insults? Ignatius encouraged his contemporaries to welcome humiliation as a privileged means to humility. Are we to recommend humiliations today? If not, what medicine is appropriate for shaky postmodern egos?

Ignatius grew up in a culture in which honor was a supreme value. It was a primary temptation for men, especially, and also for women of "important" social rank. Many of his associates came from aristocratic and professional circles. They had been socialized into a sense of self-importance relative to common folk. He knew from experience how humiliations could serve as occasions to free such people from their conceits and lead them to a more realistic sense of self and solidarity with "little people," that is, to genuine humility.

Our situation is different. In modern societies, where people do not derive their identity from fixed social roles, their personality structure is frequently less stable (or perhaps less rigid) and their sense of dignity is often more fragile. It is true that most middle- and upper-class people half-consciously consider themselves superior to poor people, to those with little formal education, and to foreigners. If they are white, they tend to feel superior compared to people of color and, if men, compared to women. At the same time, modern individualism, pluralism, family breakdown, consumerism, and cutthroat competition generate self-doubt and insecurity.[18] The bags under the eyes of the Doonesbury cartoon characters reflect the anxiety of our middle-class tribe. In this context, humiliations produce more problems than solutions.

Not that my middle-class tribe disdains social recognition. We may be less addicted to honors than the *hidalgos* of Ignatius's day; but we are more hooked on acceptance. We are afraid to disappoint; we need — too much — to please. Middle-class insecurities induce in members of the lonely crowd an exaggerated fear of rejection that clouds our vision and ties our hands. We recoil at the prospect of confronting a stronger personality. We let what others might think limit our actions. Bohemian hairstyles, outfits, and behavior are the rebellion that confirms the rule. Maybe few of us need humiliations; *but most need to get free from the paralyzing fear of rejection.*

Sometimes humiliation can foster authentic humility even now. The Catholic Church has been publicly humiliated by revelations of clergy sex abuse and cover-up. This painful experience could lead to important reform in the Church. The founder of Alcoholics Anonymous, Bill W., valued Ignatius's teaching about humiliations. He knew how they can shake alcoholics from tenacious illusions, help them to "bottom out" and come to their senses. Still, while some addictions may call for such strong medicine, most of our hang-ups will probably respond to milder stuff. In any case, since we cannot heal ourselves by ourselves, Ignatius recommends asking God not only to take away our fears of rejection, but even to send us what we fear most. This prayer can help free us from those fears.

To put the matter positively: our fragile modern egos need what the ancients called *magnanimity* (in Greek, *megalopsychía*). The magnanimous person is, literally, a great-souled individual, an expansive spirit. With appropriate self-esteem and a realistic sense of their talents, great-hearted individuals think big. They refuse to bog down in trivia. Unperturbed by minor grievances, indifferent to the "trinkets" of wealth and status, they are spontaneously generous, even prodigal, the opposite of the stingy, shrunken soul.[19]

Magnanimity is the other side of the humility coin, the antidote to false humility and ressentiment. Together, humility and magnanimity lay the foundation of love, with its indispensable option for the poor. Love for the outcast is not a love of poverty or sickness, masking resentful denigration of health and well-being. According to Scheler, genuine love

> has as its internal point of departure and its motivating force a powerful sentiment of the security, firmness, interior wholeness, and invincible fullness of one's own existence and life; and from all this there arises a clear consciousness of *being able* to give something of one's own being and of one's own abundance. Here love, sacrifice, assistance, the tendency to seek out the most humble and the weakest, is a spontaneous overflow of the forces that accompany happiness and intimate repose.

Genuine love and social protest spring not from bitter impotence but from its opposite. Sacrifice for others is authentic when it is a "free *bestowal* of one's own vital riches" (Scheler). Jesus lavished his interior wealth on all in this way. He recommended carefree "indifference" to food, clothing, and shelter (cf. Luke 12:22–34) not because he denied their value, but because worrying about them eclipses the presence of God working to bring abundant life.[20]

Ignatius was a paragon of magnanimity. According to his *magis* principle, we should always choose what is more conducive to God's reign [cf. 23], what is more universal and divine.[21] His reflection on the Call of the King contrasts magnanimity with small-mindedness [94–98].

We have many examples of magnanimity to inspire us. Drawing on her inner strength, Catherine of Siena urged the pope to return from Avignon to Rome and made her protest public. Gandhi's serene self-assurance enabled him to appreciate the humanity of his British adversaries as much as he detested the injustice of colonial rule. From prison Nelson Mandela dealt with South Africa's apartheid regime in a similar spirit. Magnanimity enabled Rosa Parks to hold her ground at the front of the bus in Montgomery, Alabama. It enabled little Tessie to help God desegregate New Orleans public schools. Normally self-effacing Archbishop Oscar Romero proclaimed the truth each Sunday in the cathedral of San Salvador, fully aware that he was inciting mortal enemies.

Each of us, too, is called to make history in our own way, to speak and act with boldness (*parrhesia*), as the early Christians did. For "God did not give us a spirit of cowardice" (2 Tim. 1:7). We need to take initiatives while taking others' initiatives into account, neither bullying the weak nor cowering before the strong. Many need encouragement to speak and act. Encouragement sometimes means affirming appropriate anger and challenging fearful silence, inaction, and self-effacement when the situation calls for their opposites.

Cultivating magnanimity should leave fewer guilty bystanders on history's sidelines. Spreading poverty, violence, and cynicism are more than enough to induce desolation and shrink our souls. The challenges we confront surely ought to inspire humility—but the authentic humility that leads to bold, creative action.

CONCLUSION

While riches, honors, and arrogant pride remain the most common danger to a committed life, we can also bog down in false humility, self-negation, and *ressentiment*. Although poverty, contempt, and humility remain the sure path to mature commitment, we need magnanimity for humility to be genuine.

Magnanimity helps us appreciate the ironies of life. When daily disappointments and injustices lose their power to crush our self-esteem, or even ruin our day, a robust sense of humor can grow. That, too, is a major asset for persevering over the long haul. If so, a life of persistent service will combine three strengths:

- *humility:* a sense of our own limits and of the dignity of the outcast;
- *magnanimity:* an appreciation of our own dignity and a sense of inner fullness;
- *a sense of humor:* an appreciation of the ironies of life, especially our own.

We have been reflecting on the vocation to a life of service, especially after the pattern of Christ. We must now consider more closely how to make wise choices as part of a committed life. The first challenge is to think of discernment outside the box of moral minimums. For as we have seen, the children of this age pursue their goals with greater zeal than the children of light (cf. Luke 16:8). That will not do for the twenty-first century. We must transcend the morality of obedience to law, to live the full freedom of those children of light.

DISCERNING AND DECIDING

In practice, a vocation to service boils down to making good decisions and acting on them. The themes we have been considering—in The Call, Two Standards, and other reflections—are designed to foster an outlook on life that enables us to make wise choices, especially important vocational choices. Wise decision making is not chiefly a matter of obeying rules or measuring up to abstract ideals, however, but of following the lead of the Spirit (chapter 14). The Spirit guides principally by means of consolation (chapter 15). However, consolation is neither infallible nor the only touchstone for discernment. For a more complete picture, we will study the three procedures for decision making that Ignatius presents in the *Spiritual Exercises* (chapter 16). Finally, discerning in daily life calls for a still more comprehensive set of criteria that together make up a way of proceeding that can nurture ongoing growth in practical wisdom (chapter 17).

14 Life in the Spirit

And this is my prayer, that your love may overflow more and more with knowledge and full insight to help you to determine what is best. (Phil. 1:9–10)

How much time and income should the Harrises devote to the Coalition against Homelessness? Should Carmen marry Ben? What expressions of affection are appropriate at this stage of their relationship? Should Chris enter the seminary or novitiate? Should our group practice civil disobedience to protest the war?

Making wise decisions is the most important skill in life. It requires sizing up situations and determining the best course of action. This is discernment, a hallmark of Ignatian spirituality. Over a lifetime, we learn this art well or poorly. According to Ignatius's Foundation [23], all our thoughts, words, and actions should be directed toward the single goal of God's Reign. In the best of cases, we struggle all our lives to integrate our complex selves into single-minded service. The Spirit transforms us, resolving inner contradictions and sharpening our moral perception. In the end, beyond techniques and criteria, discernment is a matter of character and sensitivity, of becoming the person we should be.

THE RICH MORAL LIFE

Discernment is not about choosing between right and wrong. We don't discern whether to kill innocent people, or whether to cheat someone out of a job, but only among morally legitimate alternatives [see 170]. However, when sincere people are unsure about moral issues, as many are today, they must discern right from wrong. It might not be clear to you, for example, whether it is right to deceive a person in a given situation, to sue, to go out on strike in a hospital, or to smoke. You might be in doubt about using force to defend your family or community or about working for a corporation that contaminates the environment. You might sincerely be uncertain about the morality of contraception, therapeutic sterilization, or divorce and remarriage.[1]

Churches and ethical traditions offer clear norms on these matters. However, if you do not identify with those churches or cannot now in good conscience embrace some of those norms, then you must discern, earnestly and honestly.

Even if you do embrace a moral tradition, religious or secular, no set of principles, no matter how complex, can determine right and wrong in every situation. Whole areas of our moral life are constitutively ambiguous, especially in situations where norms (and values) clash among themselves. Moral norms cannot substitute for practical wisdom (*phronesis:* "prudence") and discernment.[2] Life is too rich for that.

Most of us oversimplify things, imagining that morality is like a sheep corral, with the commandments fencing off the outer darkness of error and sin. We think of moral norms as mostly negative prohibitions — Thou shalt not stray outside the fence! — while inside the fence we can do pretty much as we please.

There is a kernel of truth to this. When the rich young man asked what he had to do to inherit eternal life, Jesus responded by citing the commandments forbidding harm to one's neighbor. But when the rich young man replied that he had always observed these prohibitions, Jesus challenged him to take a step farther. Looking on him with love, Jesus said "You lack one thing" and invited the youth to renounce his possessions and follow him (cf. Mark 10:21). Eternal life requires more than observing the standard prohibitions.

Sheep-corral thinking undervalues positive demands to feed the hungry, clothe the naked, defend the weak, turn the other cheek, walk the extra mile, and lend freely to the poor (cf. Matt. 25:31–46; 5:38–48), which most people regard as "counsels" of moral heroism that cannot be required of everyone. By contrast, Jesus challenges the young man to follow him in making love the measure of morality. Love, *agape* in Greek, means treating your neighbor as you want to be treated. That is the whole moral law (Matt. 7:12). While we can specify the "floor" (the minimum) below which love never falls — Do not murder; do not commit adultery; and so on — love has no maximum, no "ceiling."[3] According to the Foundation, our vocation is to choose "that which is *more* conducive to the goal for which we are created" [23].[4] When love becomes the measure of morality, the sky opens above us, a wide-open space of possible actions.

But beyond the moral minimum, a curious thing happens. The demands of love grow boundless as we awaken to concentric circles of human need, environmental crisis, and death-dealing policies — especially today, when we are exposed to suffering and cruelty on a global scale by the communications revolution and burgeoning travel. This turns up the moral temperature in our time. As Daniel Berrigan says, the price of being human has gone up.

Infinite needs and demands lead to frustration, guilt trips, Messiah complexes, and crash landings — unless we have internalized the good news that we are forgiven before we clean up our act and that love will someday, somehow, triumph because God is laboring through us, and despite us. This good news, this gospel, transforms harsh demands into the sweet yet challenging requirements of love. But though our response will fall short daily, our hope and inner peace are secure, thanks to the good news, independent of our performance or measurable success. As Anne Patrick says, we must allow high moral demands "to play over a ground alto of God's healing and empowering and justice-making love for us all."[5]

The good news turns the wide-open space beyond moral minimums into the space of freedom and gratuity, where we follow neither the flesh nor abstract ideals, but the Spirit (Rom. 8:1–10). In this space, we need to discern *which* hungry people to feed, *which* sick people to visit and when, *which* homeless to house, whether to visit the prison or not, in *which* causes or campaigns we will participate, and *how much* time and resources we should devote to any such effort.

Even apart from our weakness, responding to all the urgent needs that press upon us is physically impossible. No individual can do it. Mother Teresa couldn't. Archbishop Romero couldn't. Not even Jesus could: he, too, was human. He walked among the "many invalids — blind, lame, and paralyzed" at the pool of Bethzatha and selected one individual, crippled for thirty-eight years, to cure him (John 5). Jesus had discerned what was required of him at the moment, and that did not include responding to every sick individual lying around the pool.

So even though feeding the hungry, housing the homeless, and defending the weak are strict moral demands and not optional acts of "charity," we are not obliged to feed and house every hungry and homeless person within reach. Feeding Ed, who is hungry, might not be demanded (a) of Evelyn (b) today. How Evelyn should conduct herself today depends on other factors as well, including the need to care for her sick mother and the possibility that Meals on Wheels could visit Ed. To live by compassion in a world of infinite needs, we must weigh alternatives—discerning, deciding, and commending to God what we cannot achieve ourselves.[6]

In addition to choosing how to respond to urgent needs, we face many other choices among legitimate alternatives. Should Carmen marry Ben or not? Should Dave join a political movement? Should Theresa leave the insurance company and work for low-income housing? Should the Smiths adopt Ricardo? Should Gloria attend medical school? All these kinds of decisions—between what would be good and what might be better—require discernment. That is a specialty of Ignatian spirituality. Discernment is about creative generosity.

CREATIVE GENEROSITY

If we live by the Spirit, let us also be guided by the Spirit.
(Gal. 5:25)

Though love seeks the most appropriate response, it is not perfectionist.[7] The ideal option in the abstract is not always the best in practice. The abstract ideal might be to travel to a poor country and serve the poorest there, but that may not be the best for you or me right now. The real best course of action depends on circumstances, which include the one who is choosing. Should Esther stay in Seattle or move the household to Toronto? The best thing for all concerned might be for Esther to remain in Seattle, whereas, faced with similar circumstances, Leslie would do better to move the household to Toronto. In the wide-open space beyond minimums, the requirements of love are often personalized. The objectively best option can depend, decisively, on the subject who is opting.

How should the DeMarco family respond to hunger? Would it be better to take sandwiches down to the railroad tracks at night, work in the church soup kitchen, spend three weeks next summer in Haiti, contribute to Save the Children, or some combination of these? Should I contribute five dollars to the campaign against hunger, or five thousand? How much of my income should I dedicate to good causes and people in need? How much time? While one may suppose that God has preferences in such cases (God's will), God generally does not provide us with a precise dollar figure, or a precise number of hours per week!

When Paul took up his collection for the destitute Christians in Judea, he left the amount up to the creative generosity of the Corinthians (see 2 Cor. 8–9). He did indicate objective criteria: give according to what each one has, and the end result should be a certain equality between givers and receivers. But beyond that, Paul, and we might suppose God, left the contribution to each one's creative generosity. "Each of you must give as you have made up your mind, not reluctantly or under compulsion, for God loves a cheerful giver" (2 Cor. 9:7). While the gift is important, so is the motive. God is no fool. Reluctant giving today augurs poorly for tomorrow. God wants those who live by the Spirit to do what they are convinced is best.[8] For "those who are spiritual discern all things, and they are themselves subject to no one else's scrutiny. 'For who has known the mind of the Lord so as to instruct him?' But we have the mind of Christ" (1 Cor. 2:15–16). Love, which shares in divine creativity, is profligate, daring, imaginative. Lucky for us, since nothing less can meet the world's needs.

CONCLUSION

How do we decide whether to participate in a hospital strike, or how to respond to homelessness, or whether to marry Ben? On what basis? By what criteria? It is tempting just to muddle through or to act just

LAW AND SPIRIT

We are not justified (forgiven, made just) by keeping the moral law, but by God's grace. And "we are not under law but under grace" (Rom. 6:14) — that is, in our behavior the Spirit, not moral laws, must be our principal guide (Gal. 5:25). What place, then, do moral norms have for us?

Paul says "The law is not laid down for the just but for the lawless and disobedient" (1 Tim. 1:8–11). The force of law is necessary to wake up unrepentant murderers, warmongers, kidnappers and torturers and to defend their victims. The situation is otherwise for those who know they are forgiven sinners. Instead of looking to laws, they respond to the needs around them, following the Spirit (cf. Gal. 5; Rom. 8). To stagnate in pure obedience to laws, authorities, or abstract ideals and fail to assume responsible freedom is a form of self-indulgent narcissism (see Heb. 6:1–2). Nevertheless, as we see in Jesus' dealings with the rich young man, norms can serve to remind and to orient us.

in response to pressure. Yet our vocation and people's needs call for more. While minor matters don't require time-consuming discernment, important ones often do. When the press of events obliges us to decide quickly, we need to have our priorities in order. We need criteria and strategies to navigate the wide-open space beyond the moral minimum.

Norms have a part in this, but not the most important part. Authentic freedom is about responding to reality under the guidance of the Spirit. There are three dimensions, or "poles," of moral experience to which we must attend: *reality* itself, the world outside us; *norms,* which signal what is at stake in a given situation; and the action of the *Spirit* on our interior life. As we mature beyond moral minimums, we follow the Spirit more than we are guided by norms or abstract ideals in responding to the world. For Christians, Christ is the norm of norms, and his Spirit guides them.

Christian theology has long neglected the Holy Spirit in the moral life. Ignatius recognized the Spirit's action in his and others' experience, although, as we shall see, he did not always refer to the Spirit explicitly.

The Spirit guides especially through consolation. Recognizing consolation, following its lead, and avoiding the traps that can accompany it are essential for responsible living. That is the subject of the second series of Rules for Discernment, which we will explore in chapter 15.

More Rules for Discernment  15

Beloved, do not believe every spirit, but test the spirits to see whether they are from God; for many false prophets have gone out into the world. *(1 John 4:1)*

The Spirit guides via consolation. Consolation, you will recall, is more than comfort for the sorrowful. By "consolation," Ignatius means "inner peace, spiritual joy, hope, faith, love, tears, and elevation of mind, all of which are gifts of the Holy Spirit."[1]

The call to a life of service comes in the form of consolation, which faith perceives as the call of Christ. Something "clicks" inside: we say to ourselves, "Yes, this is who I was meant to be!" It is something like the thrill parents have when, seeing their baby for the first time, they awaken to their vocation as parents. It is analogous to what Michelangelo must have felt when he stood back from the completed sculpture of Moses. This is not a once-and-for-all experience, however. God guides people day by day through the consolation of the Spirit—provided they are internally free, that is, provided that, despite their weakness, they want to live by compassion, no matter what the cost. Supposing this "indifference," consolation is a critical touchstone for discerning such questions as whether we should move into a poor neighborhood or stay where we are, whether we should enter the ministry, whether to marry Carmen, or what kind of expression is appropriate in an intimate relationship. As Ignatius says, "This consolation points out and opens up the way we are to follow."[2]

It is therefore crucial to be able to recognize consolation, follow its lead, and avoid traps in doing so. That is the subject of Ignatius's second set of Rules (really, criteria) for discerning interior movements.

The Rules of the first series are addressed mainly to people struggling to reform their lives. Like smokers trying to quit, they experience a backward pull toward their old ways, as well as a fear of the future. This is desolation: sadness and turmoil, repugnance toward religious practice and the service of others, and attraction to selfish indulgence. At other times, they feel drawn forward with exhilaration toward a new way of life. That is consolation.

The first series of Rules deals chiefly with desolation, which is our major problem in a time of reform. The second series deals chiefly with consolation and the deceptions that can accompany it. While consolation is a sure guide when struggling to reform, those who are more internally free must proceed with discretion. For though it is characteristic of God to give consolation, the "enemy," too, can inspire consolation in order to lead us astray. And even when God gives consolation, it frequently happens that some of the plans and ideas that follow in its wake may turn out to be dangerous and misleading.

For example, people who claim religious motivation launch crusades and terror campaigns; they enforce authoritarian regimens, engage in masochistic austerities, and proclaim salvation diets; they utter loony oracles. Are they simply crazy? Or did many of them actually experience consolation in the past and, through self-deception and false reasoning, conclude that God was sanctioning their strange behavior? President George W. Bush claims Christian motivation in waging his "war against terror." Maybe he has had experiences of consolation. Does that mean God is inspiring his ideas and plans? No. All through history, inspired charismatics have wandered down blind allies into destructive behavior.

On the other hand, people may discredit consolation and fail to act on it due to false humility, as we have seen. How many social reforms or church renewals have aborted or petered out because revolutionaries and reformers failed to tend the flame of generous zeal that once burned in them? How many have ignored the inner call to act and, through failure of nerve or misplaced inhibition settled for crying out "Lord, Lord!"? Why do so many prophetic dreams fail to produce the good fruit they once promised?

The second series of Rules aims to help us recognize the action of the Spirit in our lives as well as to unmask and parry temptations to indulge in indiscreet zeal, on the one hand, or misplaced inhibition, on the other.

At the same time, Ignatius cautions us that this set of Rules is not for people who are wrestling with powerful direct temptations. They may not speak to their experience and could even do them harm [see 9].

THE RULES: ALL THAT GLITTERS IS NOT GOLD

Do not despise the words of prophets, but test everything; hold fast to what is good; abstain from every form of evil.

(1 Thess. 5:20–22)

In explaining these Rules, I will follow the order of *Spiritual Exercises* [328–36].

1. It is characteristic of the Holy Spirit to move us to "true joy and spiritual delight, taking away all sadness and turmoil induced by the enemy." It is characteristic of the enemy "to work against this kind of joy and spiritual consolation, introducing false reasons, subtleties, and persistent fallacies" [329]. (Notice that God *gives* consolation and only *permits* desolation. God does not send desolation.[3] While slacking off can bring on desolation [322], we should not attribute desolation—sadness, discouragement, guilt—directly to God, as people often do.)

That is the general principle. In fact, matters are more complicated. The remaining rules explain that the enemy also induces consolation and manipulates it.

2. Only God can produce "consolation without prior cause." This is because "it is proper for the Creator" alone—as proprietor—to touch the soul directly, "drawing it wholly into love of God." In this case, that subterranean river within us overflows into our conscious life of its own accord. Consolation with no prior cause means joy and peace unprovoked by any creature or any activity on our part.

Of more immediate interest is consolation with prior cause. "Cause" here simply means our mental and volitional acts and their objects [cf. 330]. All the spiritual exercises of the Ignatian retreat (the meditations, contemplations, etc.) are acts of this kind, designed to occasion ("cause") consolation. We ask for consolation in the prayers (sorrow for sin, love of Christ, joy and peace, etc. [see 55, 104, 203, 221]) and do what we can – contemplating, meditating, concentrating, and so on – to prepare ourselves to receive it.[4] A beautiful sunset, a conversation, an inspiring passage in a book, recalling a heroic person – all "objects" of knowledge and will – can also inspire consolation. In these cases, the "prior cause" taps into that subterranean river and causes it to overflow into consciousness.

3. Consolation with cause might come either from God or from the evil spirit. Both God and the enemy can use an idea, a sunset, a Bible passage, a memory, or a conversation to elicit consolation.[5] As the saying goes, "The devil can quote scripture." The enemy does not induce a phony imitation but the real article, consolation.[6] But, while God gives consolation only for good, the enemy induces consolation only to cause harm. How does this happen?

4. It is characteristic of the enemy to assume the guise of an "angel of light" (2 Cor. 11:14), inspiring "good and holy thoughts," and then, little by little, draw us to harm or less good. The enemy "piggybacks" on consolation and the thoughts that arise from it to lead us astray. Suppose, for example, that you really should study. However, when confronted with real needs that perhaps someone else should respond to, you feel inspired and drawn (by consolation) to respond to them; and in doing so you neglect to study.[7]

This kind of temptation is different from the straightforward temptations that arise out of desolation (see the first series of Rules). Instead of stirring up fear of hardship and rejection, here the enemy "introduc[es] false reasons, subtleties, and persistent fallacies" [329; cf. 315]. Direct temptations also involve deception and false promises ("You can't possibly keep this up!" "You need money [or more sex or chocolate] to be happy!"), but they are easily recognized as temptations. While overt temptations can pose a serious threat to people who are shaky in their commitment, they are little threat to veterans who have fought these battles in the past. Their dangerous temptations are more subtle and indirect. The enemy, frequently by means of consolation, inspires thoughts and actions that, though good in themselves, set off a process that gradually leads to ruin, or less good. We have already considered two examples: drawn to wealth for the sake of legitimate security, we can eventually lose our moral bearings. False humility, which appears virtuous enough, leads us to deny the good in ourselves or even to despair of God's love.

Deceptive consolation draws generous people into indiscreet commitment, displacing higher priorities. "The community campaign has to come first this year; my wife and kids will have to take a back seat." We can become so absorbed in job, studies, family, community work, church work or devotional practices, or so wedded to the letter of the law – all real values – that we neglect important responsibilities, health, recreation, prayer, or emotional equilibrium. We feel moved by God. And we might be – at first. The disorder creeps in only over time. At some point the experience turns sour. Our choices might involve great sacrifice. Nevertheless, we are probably responding to a secret compulsion, a disordered love.

Temptations are tailor-made to our weaknesses [cf. 327]. The first series of Rules considers direct temptations that target our moral weaknesses. The second series considers indirect temptations that target our *moral strengths* and our *psychological weaknesses.*[8] My tendency to overwork can slide into exaggerated zeal leading to exhaustion, resentment, and throwing in the towel. If I am withdrawn by nature, I may be tempted to exaggerate contemplation and neglect necessary action. If I am impetuous, I may be tempted to rash action in the name of urgent charity. The enemy tempts pragmatists to betray their ideals in the name of "realism" and "efficiency," and idealists to impose unrealistic measures that are inappropriate to the situation.

The enemy leads us to overextend the range of our virtues and favorite values: virtues like industriousness, spontaneity, humility, patience, religious devotion, generosity, compassion; and values like patriotism, freedom, justice, tradition, order, family, efficiency. All of these can be exaggerated and misapplied. Overextending values, misapplying valid principles, and exaggerating particular virtues is the essence of tragedy. The remedy is wisdom, or discretion, a favorite Ignatian theme. It means knowing how to prioritize values and virtues and how to apply principles under complex circumstances.

At the beginning of his conversion, Ignatius was consoled for hours by the thought of doing difficult things for God, as the saints had before him. He later commented that at the time he was still "blind";

CONSOLATION AND ITS CAUSES

Ignatius's brief remarks about consolation without prior cause have generated truckloads of mutually conflicting commentaries. The interpretation I offer seems to me to square best with Ignatius's text, experience, and sound theology. It also helps me make sense of the joy of the poor.

The limit case of consolation without prior cause throws light on the way all genuine consolation is *disproportionate* to its apparent causes. Praying or reading scripture might "cause" consolation, but the consolation will be disproportionate to the effort expended. It will seem to arise from nowhere. This disproportion reflects the gratuitousness that characterizes God's activity.

A "cause" of consolation is a "prior feeling or thought concerning some object by means of which such consolation might come through acts of understanding and will" [330]. In other words, we choose, ask for, or try to understand something, an "object," and this occasions consolation. Depending on our perspective, we can refer to the "acts" of willing or knowing or their objects as the cause of consolation.

Suppose, for example, that while praying over the story of Jesus welcoming the children, it occurs to you to help out in an orphanage. You express to God your desire to do that, or you "move your will" by deciding to do it. The "object" here is Jesus receiving the children, which you visualize in your imagination. You think and choose (intellect and will); you are moved by what you contemplate and drawn toward what you propose. In the process, joy comes over you of such a kind that, if you reflect on it, your own efforts seem incapable of having brought it about by themselves.

Or: you enjoy a meal with friends; you take in a beautiful landscape; you hear news of a natural disaster; you consider a plan of action. These experiences can occasion a peace, a joy, or a sense of sympathetic sorrow which is disproportionate to the apparent causes. This dessert dish cannot produce such joy all by itself. Or: given the rotten situation in which I find myself, it is hard to explain why I still believe and still hope, why I love my neighbor, and even my enemy [cf. 316].

The Spanish Jesuit theologian Francisco Suárez (1548–1617) considers this disproportion the key to consolation without prior cause. He rejects a literal interpretation of "without prior cause," because that would make the experience strictly miraculous, which is not what Ignatius has in mind.[9] What distinguishes consolation without prior cause is that it appears suddenly and without apparent antecedents that could account for it. This is what happens when we understand things suddenly, or understand a truth that is beyond our capacities or prior experience. An unbeliever might suddenly and without systematic reflection come to understand that God is Creator. Or an uneducated believer might suddenly understand the Trinity in a profound way. Suárez also points to disproportionate practical judgments.[10] This calls to mind Franz Jaegerstaetter, the Austrian farmer with an elementary education who was executed in 1943 for refusing to enlist in the Nazi army. Against the opposition of his family, his neighbors, and the local clergy, Jaegerstaetter stood fast serenely throughout his ordeal until his death, utterly convinced he was morally right.[11]

Suárez considers disproportionate movements of affect and will to be even surer evidence of divine influence. We can be morally certain that the Spirit is at work when we are attracted "more forcefully than the [attracting] object itself, all alone, could or is wont to" attract us, especially when we are attracted to sublime things and counter to our natural inclinations.[12]

I see no good reason to suppose, as some do, that consolation with cause necessarily differs in character or intensity from consolation without cause — apart from its unexpectedness. Nor do I see much reason to suppose that the latter is exceptionally rare, or limited to people who practice lengthy prayer. I think many busy parents and workers, and many poor people, with comparatively little time for formal prayer, experience it.

he was not "observing interior things." He had no understanding of that "discretion which regulates and moderates [the] virtues." Beginner that he was, he was responding to abstract ideals "without observing any other particular circumstance."[13] His indiscreet fervor led to health problems that reduced his ability to help others. Later, he wrote many letters urging moderation for zealous souls who were in danger of undermining their health and their service to others.

The enemy takes advantage of our psychological weaknesses, whether clinical or garden-variety: our impulsiveness or excessive caution, laxity or perfectionism, idealism or cynicism, exaggerated pessimism or optimism, our lack of self-esteem or our exaggerated need for approval. Devoted parents want to help their child overcome a drug problem. However, their usual kindness and tolerance don't work in this situation, while their exaggerated fear of "losing" their child and "failing" as parents prevents them from practicing the "tough love" their child really needs. Similar fears and skewed desires lead into codependence or other traps when we try to help others in trouble.

5. How can we overcome temptations like these? The first thing we need to do is to unmask the enemy. We must attend closely to how our thoughts progress during and after consolation. If the beginning, middle, and end of our thought-progression is sound and leads toward what is good, that is a clear sign of the divine Spirit. But if our thoughts lead to something evil or distracting or less good than what we previously set about to do, that is a clear sign, too: enemy at work! It is also a clear sign of the evil spirit when we are led from inner peace to anxiety and turmoil.

6. Once we have detected the "serpent's tail," we must retrace the progression of our thoughts and notice how we moved from good thoughts to bad, or to less good or to desolation. Identifying the pattern helps prevent recurrence.

7. The key to discovering the pattern is the disturbance which the enemy characteristically causes. The disturbance arises in the thought-progression that consolation sets in motion. We get the vague feeling that there is a "stranger in the house."[14] For "in those who are advancing from good to better, [the Holy Spirit] touches such persons sweetly, lightly, and gently, like a drop of water which enters a sponge; and the

evil spirit touches them sharply and with noise and disturbance, as when a drop of water falls on a stone." Vice versa for those going from bad to worse. It all depends on whether the "spirit" in question is going with the grain, that is, the general direction of the person, or against it [335].[15]

8. Finally, even in the case of consolation without prior cause, which can come only from God, one must distinguish carefully between the original consolation and its afterglow. According to Ignatius, it "frequently" happens in this afterglow period that other thoughts, attractions, and practical proposals arise, not directly from God, but from our own inclinations or mental habits. Or they might come from the enemy. We need to examine closely the ideas and plans that arise in this time when it is so easy to suppose that every idea is inspired by God.

SOCIALIZING THE RULES

Although the Rules refer to movements in individuals, they also apply to groups. The founder of a religious community may have experienced divine inspiration, but that is no guarantee that the community will continue to follow God's lead. Subtle and insidious forces can latch on like parasites to genuine religious experience and turn religious movements and organizations complacent, or even demonic.

A political or social movement (a union, a human rights movement, etc.) can begin with lofty ideals, even divine influence, but that is no guarantee that it will maintain its original thrust. Little by little it can be penetrated by the spirit of ambition and even corruption and betrayal. No religious community, no revolutionary movement or popular organization, no philosophical or cultural movement escapes this peril. The most sinister danger is not the obvious one of backsliding but that of exaggerating the virtues of the organization or movement in such a way as to neglect complementary truths and values.

The same principles apply to cultures as a whole. Not only each person but also each people has its typical virtues, its strong points, and its characteristic vices and temptations. The typical vices are easy to detect. What requires vigilance is the way our virtues and values can lead to destruction. A community may prize the value of family — or efficiency, or personal freedom, or humility, or law and order — in such a way as to neglect the complementary virtue and the complementary truth. Without vigilance, discretion, and discernment, family values will insulate us from wider social responsibility; efficiency of means will close off discussion about ends; appeals to personal freedom will end up sabotaging the common good; false humility will undermine initiative and boldness; law and order will cover for repression; strict justice will suffocate gratuity.

CONCLUSION

How do we decide about whether to participate in a hospital strike, or how to respond to homelessness, or whether to marry Ben, or to enter religious life or ministry? On what basis? By what criteria? In matters like these, in the wide-open space beyond moral minimums, we follow the Spirit. The Spirit guides by consolation, but not by consolation alone. Nor is consolation infallible.

In the *Spiritual Exercises,* Ignatius presents three ways to discover God's will when facing a major life decision, or "election." These procedures, which presuppose the Spirit's active guidance, can also help us make more ordinary decisions in daily life. We now turn to examine them.

Three Ways to Make Decisions  16

Lord, what would you have me do?
(Acts 9:6)

In the open field of creative generosity, beyond moral minimums, the Spirit is our principal guide, and discernment is a kind of dancing with God. An active partner in this dance, the Spirit labors to unite our freedom to God's own, to help us respond to the world. Like all dances, this one has steps. In the Spiritual Exercises, Ignatius proposes three sets of "steps," three ways to determine where the Spirit is leading. They are an invaluable help for making wise vocational choices, and less weighty ones, as well.

According to Ignatius and the early directors of the Exercises, these procedures only "work" for people who have arrived at sufficient internal freedom ("indifference"), that is, for those who have the "boldness to let themselves be led" wherever the Spirit may lead.[1] Lack of availability apparently prevents God from getting through to us in the way the Ignatian methods envision. It is even more desirable to have reached the third kind of humility,[2] for when we are inclined to the standard of Christ, fear of privation and rejection are less likely to block God's communication.

Given the danger of self-deception when using these Ignatian procedures, it is highly recommended to share this process with an experienced guide.

THREE "TIMES" FOR MAKING DECISIONS

While they were worshiping the Lord and fasting, the Holy Spirit said, "Set apart for me Barnabas and Saul for the work to which I have called them." (Acts 13:2)

The first way in which God guides people is by directly moving their will; the second, by moving their feelings; and the third, by guiding

GOD'S PURPOSE

For Ignatius, discernment is *seeking and finding the will of God.* (He ends almost all of his letters with the desire "that we may know [*sentir,* perceive] and completely fulfill" God's will, or an equivalent expression.) In this he follows Jesus who said he had come "not to do my own will, but the will of the one who sent me" (John 6:38). Christ's disciples seek only God's will (see John 4:34; 5:30; 8:29; 14:31; Matt. 7:21; 26:39; Rom. 12:2; Eph. 4:10; 5:10, 15–17; Col. 1:9–12; Heb. 13:20–21; etc.). They pray, "Your kingdom come, your will be done!"

The idea of conforming to God's will can grate on contemporary sensibilities. At first, it may look like obedience to an absolute authority who, to make matters worse, plays the game of Guess-What-I'm-Demanding-Now!

While God-language always falls short of what it points to, standard talk of God's will, even in the Bible, compounds the problem. It is tempting to try an end run around this concept. However, I don't think we can do justice to discernment without it.

Rightly understood, "God's will" refers principally to God's purpose of abundant life (rather than to norms or practical details). God invites us to plug in to an ongoing enterprise, instead of undertaking whatever good works might occur to us as self-employed freelancers.

But God is not capricious. God is exclusively ("full time") about the business of overcoming harm and maximizing good in the universe. Since that excludes some kinds of behavior and enjoins others, at least in general terms, moral norms can express God's will. However, we should clarify. Actions are not bad because God forbids them or good because God requires them. Rather, God forbids some things only because they are harmful and enjoins others only because they are beneficial.

However, norms are not the chief indicator of God's will. Since God works through us, God wills that we be able to size up a situation and respond appropriately. Paul therefore exhorts the Christians in Rome to "discern what is the will of God — *what is good and acceptable and perfect*" (Rom. 12:2). In the end, that means you must "love and do what you will," as Augustine said. Discernment is necessary because it is not always clear what love calls for.

More than requiring us to do this or that particular thing, therefore, God wills us to be guided by the life-giving Spirit — rather than by inner compulsion or external law. Detecting and following God's purpose is therefore our freedom. God's will is that deepest and best will which emerges from our center, even though, as I said earlier, we are frequently somewhere else! God calls us home to live out our vocation. The communication of God's will is actually God's *self*-communication, the indwelling action of the Spirit who produces in us the kind of freedom we see Jesus exercising in the gospels. Seeking only his Father's will, he acts with serene self-assurance in the face of pressures, traps, and threats.

Seeking and finding God's purpose is a matter of detecting the lead of the Spirit and collaborating with God (cf. 1 Cor. 6:1) who, according to Ignatius, labors to communicate with us in a deeply intimate way — through the promptings of the Spirit, especially via consolation.

their reason (*Spiritual Exercises* [175–88]). Each of these modalities corresponds to a procedure for our making a decision, and each procedure is appropriate for a particular state of soul, or "time." Using one procedure rather than another depends on one's interior mood—on whether one is in the "first time," the "second time," or the "third time."

The experience of the "first time" [175]. The first "procedure" is really an experience which obviates the need for methodical discernment. The "first time," says Ignatius, "is when God our Lord so moves and attracts the will that, without doubting or being able to doubt, the devout person follows what is proposed, just as St. Paul and St. Matthew did in following Christ our Lord" ([175]; cf. Acts 9; Matt. 9:9).

Is this a case of direct divine revelation? Infused mystical knowledge? An extreme case which Ignatius includes more for systematic than for practical reasons?[3] According to Ignatius, it is essentially a movement of the will.[4] The intellect follows. He gives no indication that he considers this experience quasi-miraculous or exceptionally rare (as many have supposed).[5]

Ignatius himself recounts one such experience. After arising one morning at Manresa, he experienced a vision of meat. He had resolved not to eat meat. However, on this occasion, having felt no previous desire to eat meat, his will was wholly moved to resume the practice of eating meat. Neither at the time nor reviewing the matter later could he doubt that this was what he should do.[6]

Jules Toner recounts the more recent testimony of a certain "Malia." Malia had never considered entering religious life. Yet on the last day of a retreat for high school seniors she was suddenly moved to choose religious life with an irrevocable conviction. Visiting the chapel, "As she began to kneel down she experienced a powerful shock—like a lightning bolt that went straight through her from head to feet. She felt her whole being lifted up in a surging 'yes!' She had no control over it.... There were no images, no words, no arguments, no doubts, no reasoning process to make. It was decided – period! She knelt there a few seconds absorbing the impact. There was a sense of great peace and joy and direction." Malia's decision was tested by initial parental opposition, a difficult novitiate, and trials through the years.

However, throughout, the memory of her retreat experience sustained her conviction that God had chosen her for that way of life.[7]

Making decisions in the "second time" [176]. Apart from the "first time," the preferred situation[8] for making decisions is "when one receives abundant clarity and knowledge through the experience of consolations and desolations and through the experience of the discernment of various spirits" [176]. This is the "second time."

Consolation and desolation give rise to inclinations toward and away from action, and to thoughts about action. According to Daniel Gil, when Ignatius "speaks to us of consolation, he always refers to feelings accompanied by an inclination, an orientation, with inspirations or thoughts which emerge from it and make it intelligible."[9]

Ignatius says one "should observe, when one finds oneself in consolation, to which alternative God moves him or her, and likewise in desolation."[10] Where does consolation incline me? To Seattle or Toronto? To marry Ben? To adopt Ricardo? Toward the ministry? To oppose the death penalty? To speak, or remain silent? And to what does the desolation attract me (and from what does it repel me)? The Rules for Discernment tell us that, "just as in consolation the good spirit guides and counsels us more, so too in desolation the evil spirit does" [318]. Desolation draws us to "low and earthly" things [317], and spontaneous thoughts arise about less generous courses of action. Therefore, when in desolation we should not reverse an important decision. Consolation, on the other hand, begets magnanimous thoughts and inclines toward generous action. The Spirit of Christ moves us to follow him. During the election time, the person making the Spiritual Exercises is contemplating the life of Christ, begging to love him more deeply in order to follow him more closely.

Consolation (and desolation) set imagination and thought in motion, so that images, thoughts, and consolation (or desolation) reinforce each other, inclining the person toward (or away from) action. However, what is essential in the "second time" are not the thoughts and images themselves but the movement of the feelings and will.[11]

In Ignatius's view, God communicates to people *directly* in consolation [15]. Although no "cause" is necessary for this, nonetheless prayer and other "spiritual exercises" can open the way for consolation. Facing major decisions — like whether to marry Ben, enter the ministry, or adopt Ricardo — can also provoke consolation and desolation, as well as anguish and struggle. Events in the world — a work of art, a sunset, a poem, a "random act of kindness," a scripture passage, even a senseless crime or some "sign of the times" on the evening news — can also trigger consolation that moves us toward action, even in the bustle of daily life.[12]

However, consolation in the "second time" rarely draws us uniformly and unambiguously toward a single practical alternative. In consolation, the Holy Spirit guides us "more" [318] but not infallibly. The "enemy," too, can induce consolation to gradually turn good intentions to evil or less good. Therefore, one or two interior movements are usually insufficient to determine where the Spirit would lead us. The second time requires "a great deal of [*asaz*] clarity and knowledge" gathered through repeated experiences of interior movements. What counts are patterns of experience.[13] How much light, how much experience of consolation is sufficient for coming to a decision depends on the gravity of the matter and the time available. "However, in Ignatius's own discernment, one thing appears to be the 'clincher' for him," writes Toner. It is a "sense of security in having made a good discernment and found God's will; freedom from anxiety about opposing God's will.... In short, it is an untroubled assurance that he has done all he ought to do."[14]

Making decisions in the "third time" [177–88]. Although consolation and desolation are normal when making an important decision, they are not inevitable. And when they occur, they may fail to produce "abundant clarity." In such cases, Ignatius recommends two ways (*modos*) to make decisions in the "third time." The third time is a time of tranquility, and the two submethods for this time depend on reasoning. A time of tranquility is a time of inner peace, not necessarily profound peace, but without strong consolations and desolations or the kind of agitations — anger, fear, worry, depression, fatigue — that inhibit clear reasoning and sound judgment.[15]

Discernment through reasoning is especially appropriate for communal decision making. For while we cannot expect subjective experiences of consolation and desolation to coincide, members of the group can appeal to the same objective data in searching together for the most reasonable thing to do.[16]

The first way to decide in a time of tranquility is to list the pros and cons of various alternatives and weigh them. The second way involves three thought-experiments, or exercises of the imagination.

In the first way, you (or the members of your group) first recall the Foundation: all decisions should be directed to the service of God's Reign. You should therefore strive to overcome the bias that clouds judgment [179].

The next step is to ask God to move your will toward the best alternative and to help you to use your reason to discover and choose it [180]. Next, consider and weigh the pros and cons for each alternative, observing where reason, not the senses, most inclines [181–82]. Finally, offer this alternative to God and ask for confirmation [183] (see below).

What counts for "pros and cons" in using this submethod will depend on the matter at hand. Ignatius provides excellent (though general) examples in the *Constitutions* where he specifies criteria for works that Jesuits should undertake. Adapted slightly, the criteria are as follows: *other factors being equal,* we should choose to work (1) where there is greater or more urgent need, (2) where more fruit is to be expected (for example where more people will benefit), (3) where we have a debt of gratitude, (4) where the beneficiaries of our service will in turn help others (the multiplier effect), (5) where the enemy has "sown weeds" that could undermine our efforts in the future, (6) where both spiritual *and* material benefits can be expected, (7) where we are more equipped to meet the need and others are less apt to do so. In addition, *all other things being equal,* we should choose to work (8) where there is greater safety rather than danger, (9) where good can be achieved more easily and quickly, and (10) where works will endure and continue to bear fruit.[17]

The second way to make a decision in the "third time" is a kind of "final resort,"during the election process of the retreat,[18] for when the other methods provide no clear indication of God's intention. It also is based on reasoning. It involves three thought-experiments, three mental "cold showers" designed to overcome cowardice and pusillanimity in order to think straight and choose the most beneficial course, no matter what the cost. The three exercises help ensure that the ultimate motive for the final decision will be the love that "descends from above" [184].[19]

The first experiment is to consider a person you have never known or seen before and ask yourself what you would counsel that person to choose in this situation – supposing you wished only the best for that person and that the choice should be for the greatest good. Then follow the same advice that you would give [185].

The second thought-experiment is to imagine yourself on your death bed and consider what you will then wish to have chosen. Choose what will give you peace and satisfaction when your last day on earth arrives [186].

The third experiment is to consider what you will wish to have chosen when, after death, you meet Christ, who loved you to the end, to give an account of your stewardship to him [187].

Ignatius applies these procedures in his Rules for Almsgiving [337–44], frequently repeating the language of the thought-experiments word for word and emphasizing the following of Christ in austerity [344].[20] That is, he recommends this method for deciding what to contribute to others in need and how to steward our resources.

In the third time, at least, discernment does not end with the sense that we have done all that is necessary and have therefore found the best option (the "clincher"). After that decision, Ignatius recommends offering it to God in prayer and seeking *confirmation* [183, 188]. Psychologically, this is easy to understand. Suppose that Carmen and Ben have been talking about getting married. Carmen has been wavering. Finally, the evidence seems to be in for her, and she opts for marriage. Now that she has crossed that bridge, the implications of her decision begin to sink in. The decision helps to flush out any subconscious reservations and to appreciate more fully what she is getting herself into! It either becomes clear to Carmen that she made the right decision or that marrying Ben is not the best option, at least for now. The experience of confirmation (or refutation) is like that. It can take many forms. While it may come in the form of consolation, it can also consist in "new reasons, awareness of greater force in the reasons already had, intensification of the movement of the will . . . , and a sense of assurance that the discerner has done all that could reasonably be done and that God's will has been found."[21] Positive results are not essential to confirmation or sound discernment. Apparent failure is no guarantee that we have made a wrong turn — as Jesus' own death on the cross makes clear.[22]

The relationship of the three methods of decision making. The experience of the "first time" is sufficient all by itself for coming to a decision about an important matter.[23] But what about the methods of the second and third "times"? Is each sufficient in itself, or should they be combined? Is one method superior to the others?

These issues have stirred lively debate, for more is at stake here than one might suppose at first. Ignatius clearly gave the second method, of consolations and desolations, priority over reasoning in the third time. However, soon after his death his interpreters began to react against the so-called *alumbrados,* or enlightened ones, mainly in Spain, a loosely defined movement whose participants fancied themselves enlightened by the Holy Spirit. They appealed to immediate experience of God independently of church institutions. In reaction, early interpreters of Ignatius emphasized the dangers of private revelations. The reaction not only stressed the safeguards of obedience to church authority (as Ignatius himself had), but also the preeminence of reason in discernment. In this way, contrary to Ignatius's teaching, the rational method for the time of tranquility came to be considered a safer and more secure path than the second-time method based on affective movements. The preference for the way of reason over the way of affect became enshrined in the Jesuits' Official Directory of 1599, which thereafter guided the presentation of the Ignatian Exercises.[24]

Suspicion of the second method and fear of unbridled "enthusiasm" — "Spiritphobia," as Tad Dunne aptly calls it[25] — persisted into the twentieth century in retreat work and in Catholic pastoral practice generally. Fortunately, recent studies have helped to rehabilitate the second method. Karl Rahner has been instrumental in this restoration, and Harvey Egan has developed Rahner's insights systematically. Rahner's and Egan's general position (they disagree on some points) can be summarized as follows: the second method, that of assessing consolations and desolations, is more reliable for finding God's will than the method based on reason for the third time. The first-time method is a rare limit case of the second, and the third-time method is a derivative form of the second. Whereas the second is sufficient by itself for making major decisions, the third is not; it is, rather, confirmatory of the second, since in the third time we are guided solely by our natural powers. In short, sifting consolations and desolations is the ideal method of discernment; reasoning employed in the third time is ancillary.[26]

The work of the Holy Spirit – the Spirit that filled Jesus and all genuine prophets – has been chronically undervalued in Western Christianity, and Western culture has frequently denied the disclosive power of affectivity. Against this background, the rehabilitation of the second method is certainly welcome. Ignatius considered it more reliable than the way of reason. But does that make the way of reason purely accessory? No. Ignatius considered each of the three methods to be autonomous and reliable in its own right. He presented them as "Three Times in Each of Which [*en cada uno dellos*] a Sound and Good Election Can Be Made" [175]. The sometimes-devalued way of reason is adequate, by itself, for discovering God's purpose. When we use the method of reason, God does not simply leave us to our own devices. Rather, God frees our reasoning from prejudice and assists our memory and intellect in weighing the evidence[27] – grace perfecting nature, as the scholastics said. It is not that pristine feelings are preferable to corrupt reason, or pristine reason to corrupt feelings. It is a question of different but legitimate routes to the best course of action, depending on one's subjective state.

The second and third methods can be used in tandem.[28] Depending on the gravity of the matter and time available, it is desirable that the method of reason confirm the second method – and vice versa. This might even be necessary to arrive at the sense that we have done all we could to come to the best possible decision.

DISCOVERING GOD'S PURPOSE

> *We have not ceased praying for you and asking that you may be filled with the knowledge of God's will in all spiritual wisdom and understanding.* (Col. 1:9)

Having done all he could, Ignatius felt certain he had found God's will. On what basis could he make such a claim? Can we say the same if we follow these methods? Ignatius's certainty was not based on a theory of the powers of the human intellect, nor on the infallibility of consolations or other data of experience. His assurance rested, ultimately, on his belief that God is supremely good and requires only that we do our best to determine the most beneficial course of action. God would have to be malevolent or capricious to require something of us and then frustrate us after we had tried our best to do it. In the end, Ignatius's certitude rested on "faith in God's gift of the Holy Spirit."[29] His experience convinced him that God is more eager to communicate what is good for us than we are to discover and embrace it.

From this it follows that this kind of certainty of having found God's will is not reserved to a spiritual elite. We, too, can have that assurance if we are ready to be led by God ("indifferent") and to do all we can to discover the best decision.[30] That is a powerful stimulus to persevere in the face of obstacles. It enabled Robert Coles's little friend, Tessie, to confront jeering segregationists in New Orleans.

Nevertheless, certainty of doing God's will is circumscribed in several ways that must be kept in mind if we are to avoid self-deception and fanaticism. For one thing, we only arrive at moral certitude, not absolute certitude, about God's purpose. Moral certitude sees darkly, as in a mirror (compare 1 Cor. 2:15–16 and 13:12), and remains open to revision. The Ignatian procedures allow us to discover God's will *for now.* The best course of action depends on circumstances, and circumstances change. As new information comes to light, we must be ready to recognize that what had been the best option may no longer be best. Toner puts it more sharply: the Ignatian procedures permit us to discover only what we should *try* to do.[31] They do not guarantee the results of our efforts. You may decide to go to work in Africa, say, and then get too sick to go. This does not mean you made a wrong

BEHIND THE THREE "TIMES"

If the Ignatian procedures for making decisions respond to the action of the unfathomable divine Mystery on us, they nonetheless reflect a straightforward logic. We can appreciate this by observing that our interior life consists of three intermingling realities: volition, affect, and intelligence (the last including memory, imagination, reasoning, understanding, and judgment). In the first time for decision making, God moves the *will;* in the second, the *feelings;* in the third, God collaborates with our *reasoning*. God's action is more apparent in the first time, less so in the second, and least in the third. *We* are more active in the third, less in the second, least in the first.

The will, or volition, is a kind of "rudder" which steers the whole person, whereas feelings move a part of us and often conflict among themselves. Since it moves the whole, we locate volition at the personal center and sometimes even speak of the will as if it were the whole. Following Aristotle, the scholastics defined the will as "rational appetite." That is, volition partakes of both affect and rationality. We might imagine the will as the vertex of a "V," with feelings and intellect as its two arms. God moves the whole person by

decision. The decision was apparently right when you made it. Our efforts may appear to fail. But, as Jesus' apparent failure shows, that does not mean we were mistaken about what God asked of us. Moreover, since we can be certain only about what we should *try* to accomplish, we won't pursue success (as we envision it) at any cost. We will do our best and leave the results in God's hands. Ignatius, who channeled all his energies into founding and organizing the Society of Jesus, once said that he would need only fifteen minutes to adjust if the Society were suppressed.[32]

touching the will directly in the first time. God moves the feelings directly in the second time, and moves the intellect—if less perceptably—in the third.

When "seeking the divine will," it is best to leave "the Creator and Lord himself to communicate himself to his devout soul, embracing it... deal[ing] directly [*inmediate*] with the creature and the creature with its Creator and Lord" [15]. Ignatius means that God deals with people directly, at least in the first two methods for election. (This immediacy does not preclude all mediation. God's immediate action is always mediated, inasmuch as we always experience that action in ourselves, that is, in and through our bodies, our affectivity — including our unconscious — our imagination, our intelligence, our will, etc.)

Compared with the first two "times," Ignatius supposed a less perceptible divine agency in the third time. Nonetheless, he says that in a time of tranquillity I should ask God to move my will and "put into my mind" what I should do [180]. Elsewhere, too, he attributes thoughts to the good and the evil spirit [32; cf. 17, 336, 351], remarking that such thoughts seem to come from "outside" us [32], apparently meaning that they arise spontaneously, independently of our will and effort.[33]

Finally, personal discernment only discovers what *I* should do (or try to do)—not what Maria or Joe should do. (Communal discernment is another matter.) This frees me from the need to coerce others in the name of my crusade—and from frustration when they fail to sign up for it.

CONCLUSION

Ignatius explains these three ways to make decisions in the *Spiritual Exercises* chiefly to help people make wise vocational choices—about marriage, ministry, religious life, or career change. We can discern highly personal matters like these while setting aside consideration of much of our social context. By contrast, discerning action-problems, such as whether to open a school, and where, or whether to engage in civil disobedience next week, require detailed knowledge of the social environment.

The Ignatian procedures we have been examining target the chief obstacles to a life of generous service, namely, fear of hardship ("poverty") and fear of rejection ("insults"). However, these fears are not the only impediments to discernment. Psychological blocks, bias, and limited experience can also prevent us from discovering what we should do, discovering God's purpose. While they may not invalidate discernment in a retreat, we need to address them in the longer term.

The Ignatian procedures take us as we are here and now, as we have matured up to this point, and given the information available to us. While they can help us discover what God asks of us here and now, still, the immaturity, ignorance, and unconscious prejudice that remain in us — limitations that we cannot overcome on the spot — circumscribe what God can reasonably ask of us here and now. We cannot respond to hunger in our town if we are unaware of it.

All this indicates the need for a more complete set of criteria for discernment — to discern complex issues in daily life, to overcome lack of awareness and bias, and to foster ongoing growth in moral sensitivity and practical wisdom.

The Way of Truth and Life  17

Then you will understand righteousness and justice
and equity, every good path;
For wisdom will come into your heart,
and knowledge will be pleasant to your soul.
(Prov. 2: 9–10)

The *Spiritual Exercises* proposes three different ways to make vocational decisions: first, when God directly moves the will; second, through weighing consolations and desolations; and, third, through reasoning. These procedures can also help us decide practical matters in daily life, like how to deal with a drug problem in the household or workplace, whether to open a school, or whether to boycott a company that is polluting the river. Unlike vocational discernment, this kind requires gathering information, sometimes lots of it—about personal histories and drugs, about the feasibility of opening a school on the North Side, about the practices of the polluting company and their effects, and so on. When deciding technical issues, acquiring information can be decisive. Think of the challenge of balancing development plans with environmental costs or designing a peace strategy for feuding groups. Still, while gathering data may be difficult, the challenge it poses to discernment is straightforward.

Limited experience and lack of awareness pose a different kind of challenge to discernment. Many decent people are unaware of the scope of structural poverty in the world; the dimensions of our environmental crisis; the scale of violence against women, child abuse, and abortion in our societies; inhumane sweatshop conditions at home and abroad; the danger of proliferation of weapons of mass destruction; and the pervasiveness of racism and patriarchy.

To some degree, we all lack awareness of issues like these. How can we expect to arrest poverty, spreading violence, and environmental

BIAS

With our different backgrounds, we have a hard time agreeing on issues today, and a harder time taking common action. Decent people debate free trade, the death penalty, premarital relations, the ordination of women, immigration policy, and abortion. Even when we know the facts, we can disagree about their significance and how to respond to them. We can argue endlessly, even coherently, without resolving the issues. Why? Not only because we have different conscious assumptions, but also because of the largely unconscious assumptions that underlie our thinking. I mean the anthropological, cosmological, and moral myths and presuppositions that constitute the horizon of each person's world, the "grid" within which we interpret and evaluate data. Marx, Freud, Nietzsche, Gadamer, sociologists of knowledge, and feminists have all labored to map this substratum of our conscious and rational life. Most prescribe more reason and conscious awareness as the solution. While that is certainly necessary, is it enough?

"Postmoderns" tell us that our basic assumptions rest ultimately on value-commitments, including religious commitments, that are in the final analysis irrational. From this they conclude that our worldviews are mutually incommensurable and that we have no rational way to arbitrate among them. Therefore, we should not expect value-laden debates to arrive at any "correct" conclusions.

While there is some truth to this, it lets us off the hook too easily, insofar as our basic assumptions are unexamined and based on limited and partial experience and unfounded prejudice.

Our cultural formation (by family, school, church, and the media), our location, experience, and past choices circumscribe our imagination and intelligence. Along with many benefits, we also inherit the biases and blind spots of our social class, race, age group, sex, religion, and nation. As a result, problems escape our notice and some questions fail to arise. To that extent, discovering truth and discerning for action depend on unmasking the unconscious ignorance, falsehoods, and half-truths that stand between us and reality. It seems even Jesus faced this challenge. Like other Jews, he apparently expected to find little faith outside of Israel. The pushy woman from Syrophoenicia had to convince him otherwise (cf. Matt. 15:21–28). Fortunately, Jesus was open to enlightenment from all quarters.

We can't be blamed for the ignorance and prejudice that we have simply inherited, any more than Jesus could. Unfortunately, unlike him, we cling to our prejudices and resist enlightenment. Why? Intelligence is guided by interest. We have a stake in our basic assumptions. They are rooted in the structure of our desires, which were shaped by interaction with our early family environment and social institutions. They are embedded, in the end, in our identity, so that to question them is to question our notion of who we are and to shake the foundations of our world.

Clear perception therefore demands cognitive hygiene. That requires more than pure reason and conscious awareness, as important as they are. It also requires untangling the habits of our heart and ordering our commitments. And since our deepest assumptions and commitments are rooted in our identity, cognitive liberation depends on personal transformation (conversion).

Like few others, Ignatius of Loyola understood that affectivity and commitment, which are central to the problem, are also crucial to the solution. Consolation — the rush of the Spirit — leads into the light, provided we collaborate via the praxis of love that can order our disordered loves.

degradation, unless more decent people become aware of how bad things are?

Here and now we all must discern as best we can, according to our lights. But in the longer term we need to address the way "our lights" are limited.[1] That challenge is compounded by the bias we all inherit from our families and communities, which causes us to resist information that would reconfigure our world. We can design retreats and workshops around issues like poverty, race, or the environment. But we need more. The problem is deep and the task ongoing. Good discernment requires continuing growth in moral sensitivity, that is, in our ability to grasp what is at stake in a given situation. (This is especially important when we must make decisions "on the fly." We don't have much time to respond to a winter eviction, a hurricane, or a mugger. Our instincts must be honed and our priorities in order.) For this we need a regular discipline that can help expand our horizon and deepen sensitivity. It should be part of a life-long search for truth and practical wisdom.

Searching for truth and the right thing to do is no easy task in these pluralistic times, as we know. With help from fellow-travelers, my own searching and struggling over the years has led me to identify several elements which I believe must be part of our search if it is to be honest and authentic. (Authenticity remains one of the few criteria that practically everyone can salute today.) Together, these "touchstones" make up a discipline, or way of proceeding. Although we could argue for most of them on strictly rational grounds, Christian faith helps us see their unity and coherence more clearly.

The ten touchstones seek to take into account all the ways truth comes to us in experience. This means giving due attention to the three poles of experience: the world around us, our inner life, and the cultural word about the world. That will lead us to conclude that discovering the truth and sound discernment depend, first, on facing reality, especially the reality of the victims; second, on personal transformation and discerning interior movements; and, third, on identifying with a community that can sustain an alternative vision and praxis.

TEN TOUCHSTONES FOR DISCERNMENT[2]

1. Reason and Science

To understand reality and act well, we must use our heads. We must observe, read, remember, question, interpret, think, and dialogue. In short, we must reason. And we have to do so systematically. We need the sciences—philosophy, psychology, the social sciences and all the other disciplines.[3]

Yet reason by itself is not enough. Reality is reasonable, but we are naive if we suppose that reason alone can take us to it. Because reality is vast and complex, and because of our biases, getting at the truth requires reason integrally considered—that is, reason enriched by experience, practice, imagination, and affectivity; reason rooted in personal transformation; reason drawing, critically and creatively, on wisdom-traditions.

2. Personal Transformation

Since life is a moral drama, understanding it requires moral empathy and depends, in the end, on the kind of people we are.[4] For this reason, understanding and discernment demand personal transformation. Otherwise, we walk in darkness.[5] That is why Jesus heals the blind and the deaf at strategic points in the gospels. "Be transformed by the renewing of your minds," writes Paul, "so that you may discern what is the will of God—what is good and acceptable and perfect" (Rom. 12:2).[6] With conversion comes cognitive liberation. We open up to the world, awakening to new things and seeing old things in a new light.

3. Experience and Praxis

What we see depends on where we stand. Entering new worlds and engaging people who are different broadens our horizon. Suffering people, especially victims of injustice, have unusual power to do this.

Action—praxis—sharpens (or dulls) our perception. The best place to analyze a basketball game might be on the sidelines. But we only understand the game of life by participating.

Action affects understanding the way decisions do. Earlier we saw how making a decision leads to confirmation of discernment. It shakes out ambiguities and helps us see issues more clearly. St. Augustine's decision to believe, based on solid but inconclusive evidence, freed him from the hell of skepticism. *Crede ut intellegas,* he repeatedly urged others, "Believe that you might understand."[7] Risky but reasonable decisions enlighten.

In the same way, action helps us understand. The Big Book of Alcoholics Anonymous says that we don't so much need to think ourselves into a new way of acting; we need to act ourselves into a new way of thinking. Through action we penetrate reality, and reality penetrates us. Praxis raises questions; it forces us to think things through—and to change.

Not every action brings us closer to the truth, however. To know the truth, we must do the truth: "Those who do what is true come to the light" (John 3:21; cf. 1 John 1:6 and John 7:17). It is the person who practices compassion who sees straight. *Ama ut intellegas:* Love that you may understand.

When linked to compassion, religious practice and contemplation, which is part of reason integrally considered, also sharpen perception and sensibility.[8] We carry out discernment within the rhythm of action-contemplation-action.

4. *Love and Discipleship*

Conversion opens us to the value of all life and, especially, to recognize our neighbor as another self. This makes love the supreme norm of action. For Christians, that means following Christ who said, "Love one another *as I have loved you*" (John 15:12).

5. *Discerning Interior Movements*

As Pascal said, the heart has reasons the mind knows not. Consolation typically moves us toward greater self-transcendence. Desolation often discloses resistance to self-transcendence. The converted heart (not just any heart and not just any inclination) tends toward what is true and good.[9]

Just as the father of lies is behind desolation, the Spirit of truth is behind consolation (John 8:44; 14:17). Desolation gives rise to images and concepts that narrow our horizon and distort reality. Consolation gives rise to images and concepts that expand our horizon and liberate us from bias. Some examples, based on people's experience, can illustrate this.

All conscious experience is interpreted experience. So, when we feel lonely, a spontaneous interpretation usually accompanies the experience. Not only do I feel alone; an interpretive "word" wells up within me: "I am lonely" or "I am alone." It is important to distinguish the feeling from the interpretation. Sometimes another "word" arises to challenge the first: "You are *not* alone." If we are prepared to welcome this new word, it can transform the way we interpret our situation and even how we feel.

For "lonely," we could substitute "guilty." I might spontaneously interpret guilt feelings as: "I am guilty," or even "I am no good." Then, recalling someone who accepts me warts and all, or recalling God's grace (perhaps the image of the good shepherd), can make the world change colors.

Consider another example. At times, we all experience sexual desire compounded by loneliness and the normal frustrations of life. In that situation (whether we are married, celibate, or temporarily single), the thought spontaneously arises that a life of responsible chastity is beyond our powers. The sensation takes on greater force in desolation. Only later, when our mood changes and we are more at peace, can we recognize that we have been implicitly interpreting our sexuality according to the "volcano" model. We felt like a volcano under pressure; as though time would only increase that pressure until we "erupt" in emotional crisis or some outrageous indiscretion. We may only become reflexively aware of this image because, with our change of mood, another complementary image has spontaneously emerged (with consolation), namely, the image that our sexual feelings are more like the weather: storms come, sometimes violent ones, but they also pass in favor of calm and sunny periods. The new image helps us see that the volcano model is only a half-truth which, when accepted as the whole truth, turns into an anxiety-producing, self-fulfilling prophesy. The new image, however, when tested, turns out to be liberating and helpful in stormy times.

Consider, finally, what happens when we engage people rejected by society — homeless people, people in jail, the poor. The clash of injustice and human dignity commonly provokes consolation and desolation. (I sense this happens frequently, for example, with northern visitors to Central America and similar places.) These interior movements give rise to subversive thoughts and images — a circle of friends, a banquet, a wedding party — that clash with the social ladder and political pyramid. They undermine the root prejudice that some people are important and others are not. They help us to see the world with new eyes and prime us to spy out the lies behind official policy and commonsense discourse. Such encounters are privileged moments for consolation to enlighten us.

In these examples, a "word" (often an image) accompanies consolation, unmasking the distortions that discourage, sadden, and discriminate. Paul Ricoeur says that the symbol gives rise to thought,[10] to which we can add: consolation gives rise to liberating symbols.

6. Conscientization

The last example, of encounters with victims, illustrates what conscientization is: an awakening to social reality, especially to its cruelty but also to its promise.

Christians profess belief in original sin, personal sin, habitual sin, and structural sin. And yet we rarely consider the cognitive consequences: original, personal, habitual, and systemic distortion, especially in its two most deadly forms, (1) the cover-up of injustice and (2) the "original prejudice" that some people are important and others (most) don't count. Because of distortion, discovering the truth about the world is not a simple matter of pushing back the frontiers of ignorance. It requires unmasking the more or less deliberate lies that suffuse everyday discourse and cloud people's minds. This is conscientization, which is part of reason integrally considered. The key questions for conscientization are: Who suffers? Why? Who profits? Who has control? To whom are they accountable? How do these policies and institutions affect the weak?

Conscientization exposes injustice, its causes and its institutional logic. But whether we are oppressors or oppressed, we resist having our world dismantled. Therefore, conscientization, like psychotherapy and conversion, requires time, effort, and mediators.[11]

Conscientization undermines dominant ideologies. Ideology itself is not evil, however, even though it has a bad reputation due to dogmatic abuse, but due also to anti-intellectual bias and short-sighted pragmatism. We all need to develop, with varying degrees of scientific depth, an ideology, in the sense of a coherent view of our social reality, permanently open to revision. We can't change a world we don't understand.[12]

Conscientization poses challenges for discernment. Fresh awareness can make us uncomfortable with our situation, for example, about owning more than we need; or about having assets tied to polluting industries, sweatshops, or arms sales; or about barbarities committed by our government. While our new awareness might not oblige us to a particular action, we may still feel morally challenged, or invited to take action of some kind.

Ignatius's meditation on "Three Types of Persons" [149–56] speaks to this situation.[13] In his parable three pairs of entrepreneurs awaken to a new moral perspective on their situation and want to order their affairs. What they should do is not yet clear, however. The moral of Ignatius's exercise is that they should not act precipitately but rather strive for indifference, trying to overcome any "disordered attachments" that could prevent them from acting as they should when that becomes clear. This is good counsel for when we awaken to the injustice that surrounds and entangles us.

7. Utopian Imagination[14]

The world is in worse trouble than we usually think, but it is also a more wonderful place than we realize. It is pregnant with possibilities for peace and community. Few things paralyze us like the short-sighted "realism" that expects no surprises in history. Locked into the apparent possibilities of the present, *realpolitik* cannot move beyond the "war on terror," nuclear deterrents, razor wire, and free-market anarchy. It is clear-sighted about selfishness but blind to human goodness and, especially, to divine grace.

As the animal endowed with imagination, we have a right to dream. And, since the possibilities for good are not always obvious, we have a duty to dream. Utopian imagination is also part of reason integrally considered. It asks, What kind of people do we want to be? What kind of society? What kind of church? What kind of economy do we want? What kind of government?

How do we distinguish responsible dreaming from escapist fantasy and the idealism that leads to bitter disillusionment? Genuine prophetic visions like those of Isaiah and Jesus show us. They spring from the authentic consolation that is rooted in suffering and liberating action.[15] They produce hope, like Martin Luther King's dream, which we can expect to inspire action until the day when the children of former slaves will sit down at table with the children of former slave owners—as King prophesied.

8. Community

We search with others, not in isolation. We don't start from scratch, but draw, critically and creatively, from treasuries of wisdom.

Each of us has spent only a short time on the planet. Much more remains in the dark than the patch of reality we have illuminated up to now, and we owe most of that light to others.

Personal autonomy is important in our search for what is true and right. We need to get free from the tyranny of external authority, legalism, and slavery to superegos and ids. But personal autonomy has nothing to do with self-sufficiency. While our sole obligation is to do our best to find out what is right and true, "part of doing one's best, even the greatest part for some, may mean seeking advice from those more learned, experienced, and gifted."[16] Our individualistic culture generates a climate of moral relativism and a naïve sense of our own self-sufficiency: you have your truth—and your morality—and I have mine. But this is a sure-fire formula for sabotaging social agendas. It abandons society to its own inertia, which means, in practice, its most powerful and least scrupulous members.

We can only escape from this hypertolerant swamp if we recognize our need for a moral community that can support and challenge us in our search for truth and the right thing to do. Not every community will do for this, only those that draw on a deep tradition of practical wisdom. That is what churches are for. What they should do for us is nourish an experience of transcendence, a shared praxis, and an alternative vision; and help us sustain that alternative in a hostile environment and communicate it to others. The first Christians faced just this challenge: to conserve and transmit their experience of Jesus and his vision. The Christian church was the answer to that need.

9. Tradition

Communities that offer comprehensive guidance for living are bearers of traditions of wisdom. They draw from the well of centuries, even millennia, of experience and reflection. Wisdom-traditions are indispensable for living well. In fact, we cannot escape them. We cannot wipe the cultural slate clean and start out "fresh," as if culture were something outside us. Cultural traditions shape us and are part of us. We don't just have culture; we *are* culture. We search for truth in dialogue with traditions in which we stand, or "swim." As Daniel Berrigan says, we can't go anywhere unless we're coming from somewhere.

Since traditions embody prejudice as well as truth, to remain life-giving they must adapt to changing circumstances and correct distortions that accrue like barnacles over time. The biblical traditions stand out in their demand for prophetic self-critique and purification.[17]

While some traditions enlighten more than others, all traditions can benefit from dialogue that fosters mutual correction and enrichment, and an ecumenical social agenda.

The point to stress in liberal, individualistic societies is that, unless we identify critically and creatively with a tradition-bearing community, we flounder about, shaped as much by market forces and mass media as by anything else. Or, in adolescent rebellion against deeper traditions, we end up in the shallow waters of astrology, fundamentalisms, or the religion of the month.

10. Authority

Although nothing is easier to abuse than authority, that shouldn't blind us to its importance. Every wisdom-bearing community needs

TOUCHSTONES AND TRANSCENDENTAL PRECEPTS

Bernard Lonergan's cognitive theory provides a good framework for the ten-step path, provided we make two adjustments. According to Lonergan, knowing involves four interconnected activities: experience, understanding, judgment, and response. The last of these includes evaluating a situation morally, discerning, deciding, and acting. The four activities generate four imperatives, or "transcendental precepts," in the search for truth: first, be attentive to reality. Second, be intelligent: that is, think and understand. Third, be reasonable, that is, distinguish between the genuine insights that correspond to reality and all those bright ideas that do not. Finally, be responsible. By complying with the four imperatives, the search for truth engages the whole person in a process of self-transcendence or "conversion"—intellectual, moral, and religious—leading to greater authenticity. This cognitive theory takes distorting prejudice seriously and proposes a way to overcome it.[18]

While I think the ten-touchstone program squares with Lonergan's theory, it introduces two modifications. First, it connects the two ends of Lonergan's chain, experience and action, in a complex first step (see touchstone number 3, above, "Experience and Praxis"; the first and second touchstones are general and introductory). Tying the two ends of the chain gives us a heuristic circle, or rather a spiral, which progressively discloses more of reality and leads to what Lonergan

to define its borders and conserve and develop its treasury of wisdom. The appropriate exercise of representative authority in such a community deserves respect. This is indispensable for discernment in the church.

calls a "higher viewpoint." The spiral should lead of itself to the cognitively crucial encounter with the victim. However, since many factors can impede that encounter, we must incorporate the reality of the victim explicitly into the heuristic circle (in the same step 3). That is the second modification. When it comes to understanding our situation and its moral implications, it is not enough to be attentive to experience in general. We must experience the impact of the *victims* on us and attend to their experience. That leads us to the heart of life's moral drama.

In a provocative essay, Gil Bailie tries to diagnose the crumbling of Western philosophy, which we witness today in the thought of deconstructionists like Jacques Derrida. Appealing to René Girard's analysis of culture, Bailie understands Western philosophy as an attempt to explain reality abstractly while ignoring the violence that lies at the foundation of all societies. By trying to explain reality while ignoring the victim, Western philosophy, for all its progress, has chased its tail for twenty-five centuries and has entered into a radical crisis, along with most of our social institutions, now that we are no longer able to hide this foundational violence.[19]

As Paul said to the Christians at Corinth (cf. 1 Cor. 1–2), the key to understanding reality is the cross — the cross of Christ and the other crosses to which Christ points us. Only from the foot of the cross can we see straight. When we avoid the crosses of history, our wisdom turns to folly.

Does authority undermine personal autonomy? Actually, it should foster it. When we need our teeth or our car fixed, we consult authorities. We have similar needs in our search for truth and the right thing to do.

We submit to authority not for its own sake, but because we believe it points us in the right direction—just as we follow a doctor's instructions because we believe that will help to heal us. Conscience does not kneel before authorities but before the truth. It does not seek what is approved or permitted but what is right and good. This can lead to conflict, but the community needs prophets in order to be faithful.

In real communities, disagreements are unavoidable. We all pay for the benefits of a tradition-bearing community, and sometimes the price is unjust; but we cannot eliminate all injustice this side of paradise. It is better to stay and struggle than to hand over the store to those who have made a preferential option for prestige or for the status quo.

THE THREE POLES OF DISCERNMENT

It seems to me that all ten touchstones must be part of our search for truth and regular growth in practical wisdom. This is a matter of giving due attention to the three poles of experience: the self, the world, and culture.

Every experience has a subjective side, namely, myself, the one who experiences, and an objective side, which is the world beyond me consisting of other people, institutions, and the non-human environment.

That world also embraces culture, including all the means by which we interpret reality: the symbols and languages we use to make sense of the world. Culture also includes the values, virtues, and norms that govern behavior. Even though we carry culture within us, we mostly find it "out there" in the world.

In short, the three poles of experience are the subjective pole (i.e., myself) and the two objective poles (i.e., concrete reality and the word, or *logos,* about reality). Although these poles of experience overlap and interpenetrate, each is clearly distinguishable.[20] Each is a source of truth and a necessary touchstone for discernment. A trinitarian correspondence may help: we must take into account the truth of the Creator of the world, of the Son who is the Word and of the Spirit within us.

If we fail to respond to concrete reality, we are irresponsible narcissists. If we ignore deep traditions of wisdom, we suffer from delusions of self-sufficiency. If we neglect conversion, we walk in darkness; if we neglect the data of our inner life and our inner authority, we stagnate in heteronomy (ruled from outside) and abrogate adult responsibility.[21]

There are ten touchstones (and maybe more), since each pole is complex, and so are the relations among them. My interior life is a complex mix of affect, understanding, and will. Concrete reality is obviously complex and so, too, is the cultural word, which includes every kind of human word, as well as the Word of God, that is, both reason and revelation.

The subjective pole is the place of conversion, interior movements (consolation and desolation), utopian imagination, and reason. Objective reality is the locus of experience and praxis, conscientization and community. The pole of culture provides interpretation of reality and moral principles — love, discipleship, the sciences, tradition, and authority.[22]

It simplifies matters to identify the *nucleus* of each pole. The central element of concrete reality is the *victim,* or *outcast,* since the central drama is oppression/liberation, injustice/love, sin/grace. (The centrality of the Good Samaritan in Luke and the final judgment in Matthew reflects that.) Personal transformation is the central drama of our interior life; it enables us to live by following consolation's lead. As for the cultural word: interpretative criteria, norms, and values all cluster around the recognition of each person as another self. The Golden Rule is the heart of ethics. For Christians this norm takes on flesh in the *person of Christ,* the key Word interpreting all words and norms. Guided by the Spirit, Christians respond to the world as Christ responded to his world in love.

CONCLUSION

I believe these "touchstones," or something like them, are necessary if we are to search for the truth with coherence and discern as we should.

Today intelligent, committed people disagree about reality and morality. Most recognize that no one philosophical system can account for everything. Nor can we ground an adequate moral system apart from religious or quasi-religious beliefs that divide us. That tempts us to sink into a hypertolerant individualism that cuts off enriching dialogue and hands over the world to the most powerful and ruthless. If we take the needs of the world seriously and if we take our own dignity seriously, then we will help each other search for truth more authentically and act more coherently. We will question questionable opinions and behavior.

The ten touchstones do not make up a philosophical or theological system but a path, a discipline, to guide the search for what is true and right. Don't we need something like this to navigate the turbulent waters of our time?

In the Spiritual Exercises, as retreatants contemplate the life of Christ, they "elect" to follow him in a particular way, or to reform their lives as disciples. They then enter the Third Week in which they contemplate the suffering and death of Christ in order to be shaped by his Spirit, sealed in their commitment, and strengthened against hardship and persecution. Identifying with the suffering Christ will draw them to other crosses in the world around them.

PASSION AND COMPASSION

Contemplating the suffering and death of Christ intensifies our union with him. It should also draw us to know and love the crucified people of today.

18 The Grace of Compassion

As Jesus came near and saw the city, he wept over it, saying, "If you, even you, had only recognized on this day the things that make for peace!" (Luke 19:41–42)

We can imagine Jesus weeping over Jerusalem even today—and also over Ramallah, São Paulo, Kisangani, and Southwest Baltimore. Grieving over the passion of people today humanizes us. It is sharing in God's own grief.

On Friday nights in the Bronx, we used to drag our tired selves to John's place after the last neighborhood or parish meeting. Surrounded by burnt-out buildings, Neil, Angel, Kathy, Mili, John, Louise, Gerry, Joe, and I would read from the New Testament. With the Cross-Bronx Expressway roaring in the background, we turned over the week's events: families unhinged by drugs, a building saved from demolition. One night we absorbed the tragedy of Jesse Small. She had been carried out of her building frozen stiff after the landlord had refused to fix the boiler. Our sessions were free-flowing: some silence, shared reflection, then beer and pretzels. There was plenty to grieve over, and also plenty to laugh about. We would leave around midnight, feeling renewed. Few experiences have refreshed and consoled me like those Friday nights at Shakespeare Avenue and Featherbed Lane.

In the Third Week of the Exercises and similar moments of our lives, we ask for that kind of consolation. Grieving is a sober and serious affair, but not always a depressing one: "It is also consolation," says Ignatius, "when one sheds tears which move to love of the Lord, either out of sorrow for sins, or for the passion of Christ our Lord" [316]. We sometimes experience this kind of sorrow when we accompany a family that has lost a loved one. In that situation, we don't want to be anywhere else in the world. We might also experience it while grieving over genocide in Rwanda or homelessness in Chicago. Grieving over the crosses of the world (not over a broken electric toothbrush!) gathers our fragmented selves, centers and heals us. When we share the sorrow of the crucified of the earth, we are no longer alone. This, too, is part of our vocation. We were made to share each other's burdens.

While in college, years before the Bronx, I struggled with faith. Did God exist? Were moral principles arbitrary? Are we humans just one more animal like the rest? Is there hope for this world? These questions, swirling in my head, provoked the deep crisis I have already mentioned. I didn't know what to believe in. I was searching for myself and for a future.

One day four years later and still struggling, I stumbled across the news report of the brutal murder of a child. It was an account like so many, but especially pathetic. As I took in the tragedy, grief swept over me, body and spirit. As I abandoned myself to this grief, my scattered and anxious energies collected themselves to focus on the calamity of a tender life snuffed out. For two days I experienced, in sorrow over that murder, a time of centering. Maybe I didn't ordinarily allow things to "get to me" like this. Maybe this time my own crisis set me up. As the tragedy of this child worked on me, I began to feel less alone and more at peace. The bittersweet experience opened a new stage in my journey, driving home to me what is really important in life and where the center of gravity of the universe lies. It led me, slowly, to a new vision and sense of purpose. It taught me that I could trust that kind of consolation to lead into the light.

Suffering dehumanizes those who inflict it. But it need not dehumanize all who endure it or those who let it move them. Just as our joy is incomplete until we share it with others, suffering is more tolerable when we bear each other's burdens. Although that doesn't take away the pain, it helps. Above all, it generates hope and love in those who share others' suffering and in those who find their suffering is shared by others who care. In Latin America we sing:

> *Sólo le pido a Dios*
> *Que la guerra no me deje indiferente....*
> *Que la miseria no me deje indiferente.*
> All I ask of God is this:
> That war not leave me unmoved....
> That misery not leave me unmoved.

It is only natural to experience repugnance before suffering. But to feel nothing? God deliver us from that!

In the last century, humanity suffered the horrors of genocide in Armenia, the gulags, the Holocaust, saturation bombings, Hiroshima and Nagasaki, the killing fields of Cambodia, massacres in Central America, and genocide in Rwanda. The new century has begun with more of the same: war across equatorial Africa, terrorism, barbarism in Israel, Palestine, Afghanistan, Iraq, and Colombia. Meanwhile, the silent holocaust of the poor continues. This is all part of the long procession of humanity marching through history, trailing blood in the dust. Each of us entered this procession at birth. None of us grasps its full dimensions. We dare not stand apart from this march, alone with hearts unmoved. We grow into our humanity by entering fully into it and allowing it to fashion us, as Etty Hillesum says, into a "balm for all wounds."[1]

That is the meaning of the grace of compassion.

A BALM FOR ALL WOUNDS

Etty Hillesum was killed in Auschwitz at the age of twenty-nine. In the years before her death, she underwent a remarkable transformation that equipped her to minister to fellow Jewish deportees in Holland. On life in the Westerbork camp, from which Jews were sent to Auschwitz, Etty wrote in December 1942:

> The human suffering that we have seen during the last six months, and still see daily, is more than anyone can be expected to comprehend in half a year. No wonder we hear on all sides every day, in every pitch of voice, "We don't want to think, we don't want to feel, we want to forget as soon as possible." It seems to me that this is a very great danger.
>
> True, things happen here that in the past our reason would not have judged possible. . . . But if we abandon the hard facts that we are forced to face, if we give them no shelter in our heads and hearts, do not allow them to settle and change into impulses through which we can grow and from which we can draw meaning—then we are not a viable generation. (p. 250)

Still in Holland one year before her death, she wrote:

> It is possible to suffer with dignity and without. I mean: most of us in the West don't understand the art of suffering and experience a thousand fears instead. We cease to be alive, being full of fear, bitterness, hatred, and despair. God knows, it's only too easy to understand why. But... I am in Poland every day, on the battlefields, if that's what one can call them. I often see visions of poisonous green smoke; I am with the hungry, with the ill-treated and the dying, every day, but I am also with the jasmine and with that piece of sky beyond my window; there is room for everything in a single life.... I sometimes bow my head under the great burden that weighs down on me, but even as I bow my head I also feel the need, almost mechanically, to fold my hands. And so I can sit for hours and know everything and bear everything and grow stronger in the bearing of it, and at the same time feel sure that life is beautiful and worth living and meaningful. Despite everything. (pp. 152–53)

In March 1941, Etty wrote in her diary of our need to open a space for this reality in our hearts:

> And finally: ought we not, from time to time, open ourselves up to cosmic sadness? One day I shall surely be able to say to Ilse Blumenthal, "Yes, life is beautiful, and I value it anew at the end of every day, even though I know that the sons of mothers, and you are one such mother, are being murdered in concentration camps. And you must be able to bear your sorrow; even if it seems to crush you, you will be able to stand up again, for human beings are so strong, and your sorrow must become an integral part of yourself, part of your body and your soul, you mustn't run away from it, but bear it like an adult. Do not relieve your feelings through hatred, do not seek to be avenged on all German mothers, for they, too, sorrow at this very moment for their slain and murdered sons. Give your sorrow all the space and shelter in yourself that is its due, for if everyone bears his grief honestly and courageously, the sorrow that now fills the world will abate. But

> if you do not clear a decent shelter for your sorrow, and instead reserve most of the space inside you for hatred and thoughts of revenge—from which new sorrows will be born for others—then sorrow will never cease in this world and will multiply. And if you have given sorrow the space its gentle origins demand, then you may truly say: life is beautiful and so rich. So beautiful and so rich that it makes you want to believe in God." (pp. 96–97)

Although Hillesum was not a Christian, the gospels profoundly influenced her transformation. Living the paradox of shared suffering, she found herself in "a strange state of mournful contentment" (p. 288), like the apostle Paul, who wrote to the Christians at Corinth that his hope in them was unshaken, "for we know that as you share in our sufferings, so also you share in our consolation" (2 Cor. 1:7).

CONCLUSION

We do not desire any more pain in the world. We simply want, and need, to share the pain that is there, in order to lighten the load for all of us. We want to be more and more a part of humanity's march, with its suffering, its hope, and its joy. For unless we share the suffering of the world, its beauty cannot heal us and solidarity cannot fill our void.

The grace of the Third Week is to share God's grief over our wounded world. We see this divine pain and grief most plainly in Jesus' suffering and death. We ask to empathize with him. The focus is not on pain but on *being with* the one who suffers. For two thousand years, contemplating his passion has helped his followers bear others' burdens. It has helped them overcome their fears and strengthened them for the trials that all who respond to suffering must face.

The Solidarity of God 19

God proves his love for us in that while we still were sinners Christ died for us. (Rom. 5:8)

Contemplating Christ's passion – from the Last Supper to the sepulcher – helps us know him better, love him more deeply and follow him more closely [104]. It should also move us to respond to the crucified people of today and strengthen us against hardship. To this end, what Ignatius recommends us to seek in contemplating Christ's suffering is "sorrow with Christ in sorrow, a broken heart with Christ brokenhearted, tears and interior suffering on account of the great suffering that Christ endured for me" [203]. This is a *schola affectus,* an exercise that softens and strengthens the heart.

Ignatius proposes contemplating Christ's passion the way we contemplate other events of his life, entering into the story in our imagination, as though taking a minor part in the drama.[1]

First, we select a section of the gospel story of the passion (for example Jesus in the garden, his arrest, Jesus before Pilate, the crucifixion, etc.). As in the other contemplations of Christ's life, we (1) pay attention to the participants in the drama, (2) listen to what they are saying, and (3) observe their actions, allowing all this to move us. For the passion of Christ, Ignatius suggests three more perspectives from which to contemplate: (4) "consider what Christ suffers,"[2] (5) "consider how the divinity hides itself," and (6) "consider how Christ suffers all this for my sins" [192–97]. We reflect on the six points as the narrative moves us. (The order for these points is not fixed.) Finally, we respond, conversing with God and with Christ, expressing our feelings and thoughts and asking for help, perhaps to make progress or in taking action [199]. Ignatius expects that this contemplation will generate an empathy with Christ that will have a practical effect in our lives.

FOR LOVE OF US

He loved me and gave himself up for me.
(Gal. 2:20)

What does it mean to say that Christ suffered for love of us and for our sins? [193, 197, 203] The catechism response is that he died for our eternal happiness, to save us from ruin, and, above all, to win our love. Plumbing the meaning of this is a gift that comes less through reasoning than through contemplation and ritual. Those who live and suffer like Christ surely understand best. Some perceive its meaning through the cadence of a gospel spiritual: "Were you there when they crucified my Lord?" Others glimpse it during the way of the cross procession or by comparing a martyr like Oscar Romero to Christ. Nevertheless, even though rational explication is of limited value in this matter, it will help to offer some brief reflections in order to clear the path of unnecessary obstacles and orient contemplation and reflection.

Though suffering is neither good nor desirable, *love* that suffers inspires and humanizes like few other things. That is why we contemplate Christ's passion. His death crowned a life of love (Heb. 10:5–10). He proclaimed the good news of God's love for all, especially for the poor and sinners, an end to poverty, hunger, and exclusion (Luke 6:20–26). (This immense goodness of God is God's "glory.") Although the powerful perceived this as a threat, Jesus persisted in announcing that the last would be first and the first last, since God exalts the lowly and humbles the exalted.

For this cause — for the glory of God and trampled humanity — he gave his life freely. The motive was love, including love of his enemies. He did not commit suicide, but when his hour came he did not flee. "No one takes [my life] from me, but I lay it down of my own accord" (John 10:17–18; cf. 12:27–28; 18:11; Heb. 12:2).

To the eyes of faith, Christ's passion expresses God's own love.

> God's love was revealed among us in this way: God sent his only Son into the world so that we might live through him. In this is love, not that we loved God but that he loved us and sent his

> Son to be the atoning sacrifice for our sins.... So we have known and believe the love that God has for us. (1 John 4:9–10, 16)

In light of God's immense love, what could John's letter — and Ignatius — mean by affirming that Jesus died *for our sins* [cf. 193, 197]? Did God the Father send Jesus to die as a scapegoat to placate the divine anger? If so, God's "glory" is called into question.

The New Testament says that Jesus *"bore our sins* in his body on the cross" (1 Pet. 2:24; cf. 2 Cor. 5:21; Rom. 8:3). Although the usual interpretation is that he alone bore our sins, the passages do not say that. All human beings bore the weight of these sins before Jesus came; and we continue to bear them now, as the news attests night after night. The source of humanity's great suffering is greed and contempt, idolatry of power and violence, addiction, culpable blindness, refusal to welcome the stranger or to forgive. This egoism is what aggravates accidental suffering,[3] it is what makes humanity's procession so tragic. We all share, though unevenly, the burden of the sins of our race.

The New Testament presupposes this universal human burden when it reports that Jesus, *too,* chose to suffer the consequences of sin. He joined our bloody procession, and, although he was innocent, like us he suffered the legacy of sin, even to death. God did not send him to die in our stead as a scapegoat to placate the divine anger. The New Testament recasts traditional sacrificial language and transforms its meaning. When it says that Jesus died as a sacrifice for sin,[4] that means that in him God has drawn near and joined humanity's procession, shouldering the consequences of our moral failings like the rest of us. The point is God's solidarity and love. At the Jordan River, Jesus takes his place among those whom John is baptizing for repentance of their sins. The Father ("a voice from heaven") and the Spirit ("like a dove") sanction this act of solidarity with sinful, suffering humanity (Matt. 3:13–17).

Paul uses another provocative metaphor to illustrate the same good news. He says that Jesus fell under the condemnation of the Law (Gal. 3:13). What does he mean? The Law of Moses points the finger at sin and condemns the sinner. Paul says that Jesus himself, though innocent, suffered the condemnation due to sin. He joined the human race and endured the consequences of its sin like everybody else. Does that mean that he died to pay our debt to a vengeful God? No. It means that, instead of exacting the Law's just condemnation of sinners, God preferred to join with sinners and share with them the burden of sin. This is what so amazed Paul. "Rarely will anyone die for a righteous person.... But God proves his love for us in that while we were sinners Christ died for us" (Rom. 5:7–8). By drawing near in this way, God makes the divine power (the Spirit) available to human beings, to free them from the power of sin and the Law.

While to some this is myth and madness, to others it is the supreme expression of love and changes the color of the universe: he died for me, for my sins. And though he died once and for all, the drama continues today. We are everywhere in it, crucified and crucifying. As popular devotion has always recognized, we are in some sense accomplices of those who drove the nails — and of those who drive them today (cf. Heb. 6:6). We are also crucified. Christ's passion continues, especially in those who suffer for doing good. In this dying (and rising) the divinity is hidden — and revealed.

THE DIVINITY CONCEALS ITSELF

He had no form or majesty that we should look at him,
nothing in his appearance that we should desire him.
(Isa. 53:2)

Ignatius recommends (point 5) that we "consider how the divinity conceals itself" [196]. Jesus could have asked his Father to send legions of angels to rescue him (Matt. 26:53). But there are no angelic battles, no miraculous rescue, nothing to disguise the brutal torture and execution. Precisely by hiding itself, however, the divinity reveals its greater splendor. It reveals God's complete solidarity with our weakness and suffering.

It had been that way all along. He had been born in a stable; he lived and labored obscurely for thirty years. He refused to turn stones into bread or to draw crowds by spectacle (Matt. 4:1–11; cf. John 7:3–6). When healing the sick, he drew them apart to avoid display, forbidding them to publicize their cure (Mark 1:43–44; 3:12; etc.). There would be no "signs from heaven" (Mark 8:11–12; etc.) to validate him. If people could not recognize God working in this ordinary way, they would never recognize God at all. Neither conventional nor miraculous displays of power can reveal the "glory" of a God who wishes to join humanity's procession as one more pilgrim.

Jesus' crucifixion and death reveal his glory and his Father's, says John (John 8:28; 17:1; etc.). In Mark's Gospel, Jesus is recognized as Son of God on the cross: "Now, when the centurion...saw that in this way he breathed his last, he said, 'Truly this man was God's son!' " (Mark 15:39). Expecting a different kind of Messiah, the chief priests and scribes call out, "Let the Messiah, the King of Israel, come down from the cross now, so that we may see and believe" (15:32). We can sympathize with them. Wouldn't we prefer a Messiah who could come down from the cross to one who cried out, "My God, my God, why have you abandoned me?" Wouldn't we prefer a God who would take him down?

The New Testament inverts our expectations. While Jews demand miracles, and Greeks convincing proof, Paul announces only Christ crucified, the power and the wisdom of God (1 Cor. 1:22–24). An ignominious death becomes, arguably, the most powerful symbol of all time. The executed prophet becomes the most influential figure in history. By hiding itself, the divinity reveals its glory.

Oscar Romero was killed in 1980 for the same reasons and in much the same way as Jesus. Although his death seemed senseless at the time, today it seems anything but senseless. Romero has become a point of reference for what it means to be Christian and human, and what it means to be church.

Jesus—and Romero—practiced a credible love. A solidary and credible love is effective.[5] It inspires faith, hope, and love. It produces life. The strongest obstacle to goodness is not brute force or cinder blocks but hearts that are cold and unmoved. Only a love that draws near in costly solidarity can transform that obstacle. The gospel announces that God has drawn near in just this way.

In Jesus on the cross, divinity shines forth. To say that God was in Jesus on the cross should not so much change our idea of Jesus; it should change our idea of God. As the church has always taught, Jesus hanging on the cross discloses God best. He does this only because he was so human. Only God could be so human (L. Boff). Miracles are frosting on the cake and could distract us from this good news.

In Latin America, the poor speak of *Diosito,* our "little God." They speak of *Jesusito* and *Papá Dios.* Diminutives and terms of endearment express belief in a God who draws near, understands, forgives – a "little God," little like them, for whom the world shows contempt. This is the *Deus menor,* the lesser God. Because God walks among us and shares our sufferings, this *Deus menor* is greater still, *Deus semper maior.*[6] By sharing our weakness, God is more wonderful and more powerful still, and challenges our ideas of divinity and of power.

Christ's passion teaches us where to find God hiding today. Elie Wiesel recounts a horrible execution at the Auschwitz death camp. "He was still alive when I passed in front of him. His tongue was still red, his eyes were not yet glazed," Wiesel recalls. "Behind me, I heard [a] man asking: 'Where is God now?' And I heard a voice within me answer him: 'Where is he? Here He is – He is hanging here on this gallows.'"[7]

Wiesel is a Jew, and Christians understand. God suffers in the victims of injustice. We say that Christ's passion did not end in 27 A.D. He continues to suffer today:

> "Lord, when was it that we saw you hungry . . . or thirsty . . . a stranger . . . or naked . . . sick or in prison . . . ?" And the king will answer them, "Truly I tell you, just as you did it to one of the least of my brothers and sisters, you did it to me." (Matt. 25:35 – 39)

> He fell to the ground and heard a voice saying to him "Saul, Saul, why do you persecute me?" He asked, "Who are you, Lord?" The reply came, "I am Jesus, whom you are persecuting." (Acts 9:4 – 5)

> I have been crucified with Christ, and it is now no longer I who live, but it is Christ who lives in me. (Gal. 2:19 – 20)

> In my flesh I am completing what is lacking in Christ's afflictions for the sake of his body, that is, the church. (Col. 1:24)

Christ suffers today in his followers, including those who, without explicit faith, reproduce his love and pay the price. His passion continues, first, in those who are persecuted, as he was, for the good news and in defense of human dignity. But must we not also recognize him, present in different degrees, in all who suffer,[8] including the sick and sinners who reject him? Christ, "the same today" (Heb. 13:8), draws near to all of them, as he did two thousand years ago. Though not all identify with him, he identifies with them.

CONCLUSION

Contemplating the passion draws us closer to Christ and deeper into the procession of suffering humanity. "Since God has loved us so much, we also ought to love one another" (1 John 4:9–11; see [197]). We discover the divinity hidden in weakness today. We share God's grief over humanity and our wounded earth. We locate our own suffering in a larger context. Finally, we are strengthened for the persecution that befalls all who take the gospel, and life itself, seriously.

20 Blessed Are the Persecuted

We also boast of our sufferings, knowing that suffering produces endurance, and endurance produces character, and character produces hope, and hope does not disappoint us, because God's love has been poured into our hearts through the Holy Spirit that has been given to us. (Rom. 5:3–5)

They say no good deed goes unpunished. While life is not so perverse as that, those who are determined to do what is right should prepare to pay a price, especially if they side with the poor in God's name.[1] "When I give food to the poor, they call me a saint," said Bishop Helder Câmara of Brazil; "when I ask why the poor have no food, they call me a Communist."

- An African American opens her colleague's eyes to racism in the workplace. The white colleague finds that raising this issue provokes hostility from co-workers.
- Pete is a lawyer. All during January, the city-owned building next door has gone without heat because of a broken boiler. When he accompanies the tenants to municipal offices, Pete is dismayed at the officials' complacency in the face of bronchitis and pneumonia. As he speaks up on the tenants' behalf, he finds the same contempt directed at himself.
- Maria protests against abortion and finds herself eating lunch alone.[2]

While Jesus proclaimed peace, he was frequently embroiled in conflict. The good news sparked division (Luke 12:49–53; 16:16–17). He insisted on unmasking bad-news doctrines and practices that twisted the truth of divine mercy and human dignity. He could have asked the sick to come back the next day to avoid a scene over curing on the Sabbath. But Jesus wanted to make a scene: "Stand forth in their midst!" (Mark 3:3). Little wonder that his message aroused opposition.

He told his followers to expect the same (Matt. 10:24; John 15:20; Mark 10:30); and down through the centuries, when they have been faithful, they have suffered persecution. For "all who want to live a godly life in Christ Jesus will be persecuted" (2 Tim 3:12; cf. 1 Thess. 3:3–4; 1 Pet. 2:21). Of course, not all hostility toward the church deserves to be labeled persecution, since infidelity and scandalous behavior can also provoke hostile reactions.

In recent decades, Christians have endured calumny, threats, espionage, break-ins, theft, exile, prison, beatings, torture, and death for their faith. Christians suffered bitterly under Communist regimes and, especially in Latin America, under capitalist ones. Latin America stands out for the way Christians, along with others, have suffered for defending the poor, especially after the Catholic bishops assumed that commitment at the Medellín Conference in 1968.

Worldwide, Christians are recovering their roots. From the time of Constantine, when the church allied with secular power, the mainline churches often lost sight of the centrality of prophetic witness and consequent persecution to their calling. Now that most Christians live in poor countries, the church of the poor South challenges Christians elsewhere to break their alliance with the powerful and cast their lot with the outcasts, as Jesus did. For those who wish to speak of God today, standing with the victims is the price of credibility. From now on the authentic church will be a persecuted church.

We therefore need a spirituality for times of persecution. I suggest it include the following elements.[3]

First, a spirituality of persecution will remind us that persecution is *inevitable* when defending truth and human dignity. Since we are schooled to think that conflict is bad, we tend to avoid or suppress it. But defending what is right always brings conflict. Following Christ means taking up the cross of costly witness daily. If we experience no opposition, we should ask why. "Woe to you when all speak well of you, for that is what their ancestors did to the false prophets" (Luke 6:26).

Second, this spirituality will help *prepare* us for persecution. "For which of you, intending to build a tower, does not first sit down and estimate the cost, to see whether he has enough to complete it?" (Luke 14:29). This is not so much a challenge to measure our strength as an invitation to recognize our weakness and abandon ourselves in faith to God's care. The psalms express this faith and freedom:

> O Lord, how many are my foes!
> Many are rising against me;
> many are saying to me
> "There is no help for you in God."
>
> But you, O Lord, are a shield around me,
> my glory, and the one who lifts up my head.
> I cry aloud to the Lord,
> and he answers me from his holy hill.
>
> I lie down and sleep;
> I wake again, for the Lord sustains me.
> I am not afraid of ten thousands of people
> who have set themselves against me all around.
>
> Rise up, O Lord!
> Deliver me, O my God! (Ps 3)

The gospels invite us to a radical faith. When the boat is sinking and his disciples panic, Jesus scolds them, "Why are you afraid, you of little faith?" (Matt. 8:26). He later warns them not to fear persecution: "Even the hairs of your head are all counted. So do not be afraid" (Matt. 10:26–31). They shouldn't worry about what to say when dragged before the authorities, "for it is not you who speak, but the Spirit of your Father speaking through you" (Matt. 10:20).[4] Preparing for persecution does not mean worrying about it but learning not to worry.

Third, this attitude rests on *God's power,* which is "made perfect in weakness." Paul writes, "I will boast all the more gladly of my weaknesses, so that the power of Christ may dwell in me. Therefore I am content with weaknesses, insults, hardships, persecutions, and calumnies for the sake of Christ; for whenever I am weak, then I am strong" (2 Cor. 12:9–10). God's power was manifest in Paul's sufferings: "Death is at work in us, but life in you" (2 Cor. 4:12). Just as divinity revealed itself by hiding itself in Jesus' passion, God's glory shines forth in his persecuted followers.

Fourth, persecution for justice's sake produces *consolation* – joy, clarity of vision, and confirmation. Jesus tells the disciples to "rejoice ... and leap for joy" when they are persecuted (Luke 6:23). Paul writes that God "consoles us in all our affliction" (2 Cor. 1:4).[5]

Archbishop Oscar Romero rejoiced that the church was persecuted for standing with the poor: "I rejoice, brothers and sisters, that our church is persecuted precisely for its preferential option for the poor and for trying to become incarnate in the interests of the poor." And again,

> Christians ought always to foster in their hearts the fullness of joy. Try it, brothers and sisters. I have tried it time and again, yes, and in the bitterest hours of the worst circumstances, when calumny and persecution was at its wildest. I have felt the gladness of grafting myself onto Christ, my Friend, and have tasted the sweetness that the joys of this world cannot give.[6]

Testimony like this reflects the *clarity of vision* that persecution often brings. Many prisoners of conscience have testified that jail time helped them see things more clearly.

Persecution thus confirms our commitment. It shows that the idols of wealth and power are threatened. The persecuted may even sense that they are sharing in the great tribulation that heralds God's victory. "This must take place.... This is but the beginning of the birth pangs" (Mark 13:78; cf. vv. 9–13). Persecution means that the anti-reign is being overcome and the Reign of God is at hand (2 Thess. 1:4–5; Acts 14:22; 1 Pet. 4:16–17).

Fifth, consolation in persecution inspires *boldness*. Teresa Pérez, an ever-joyful catechist and grandmother from Los Sitios, a town in rural El Salvador, illustrates this. The first anniversary of the 1989 killings at the UCA (Central American University) included a celebration in Los

Sítios, where one of the martyrs, Ignacio Martín-Baró, had worked. During the Mass, Teresa reminded the congregation that many had left the parish after Nacho's death. (For several weeks the army had used the chapel where we were celebrating as a barracks.) "Well, I say," she continued, "if death finds us here serving the church, let's welcome it!"

Many poor people exhibit Teresa's kind of courage. Her Mayan ancestors wrote in their epic *Popol Vuh:*

> They tore off our fruit,
> they cut our branches,
> they burned our trunks,
> but they could never kill our roots.

Suffering produces endurance, endurance produces character, character produces hope (cf. Rom. 5:3–4; 1 Thess. 1:4), and that produces the love that "casts out fear" (1 John 4:18).

Sixth, a spirituality of persecution will teach us to *love our enemies* (Matt. 5:43). Blessing our persecutors keeps bitterness at bay and overcomes evil with good (cf. Rom. 12:14, 21).[7]

Seventh, enduring persecution and loving our enemies require *creativity.* A spirituality of persecution will help us become "wise like snakes and guileless like doves" (Matt. 10:16).[8] Both Jesus and Paul employed a wide range of tactics in dealing with adversaries. Depending on the situation, Jesus went into hiding, overturned tables, publicly excoriated his foes, flushed them out with revealing questions, waited serenely to be arrested, and kept silent. Paul denounced, threatened, cajoled, fled, cleverly pitted Pharisees against Sadducees (Acts 23), and appealed to the emperor.

Today we may need to use novel forms of communication, improvisation, drama, humor, or even creative trickery, like Miguel Pro, martyred in Mexico in 1927.

Finally, persecution generates *solidarity* among its victims and with their allies. It unites groups, churches and peoples in action. A spirituality of persecution must be a communal spirituality that enables us to support one another in trial.

CONCLUSION

Contemplation of Christ's passion and death is a *schola affectus* that leads to deeper union with him—in knowledge, love, and practice [cf. 104]. It draws us to our crucified neighbors and fortifies us to face opposition.

When we contemplate his suffering and, above all, his victory, it becomes clearer that union with him is real, not just felt. These contemplations lead into the heart of the Christian message: Christ's followers participate in the "paschal mystery" of his suffering, death, and resurrection. That is the deepest meaning of their lives. United to him in his death and resurrection (Col. 2:12), they are now the Body of Christ. They continue his presence in history. In the Eucharist, when they eat his body and drink his blood (1 Cor. 10:16–17), they become what they eat, as Augustine said. Even as they share his sufferings, they experience the power of his resurrection (cf. Phil. 3:10–11; 1 Pet. 4:12–19; Eph. 3:13).

The Pauline letters use words beginning with the prefix *syn* (with), which Paul and his followers probably coined themselves. Christ's disciples "suffer with" him, are "crucified with" him, "die with" him, are "buried with" him; they are "glorified with" him, "raised up with" him, "live with" him, are "seated with him" at God's right hand and "reign with" him.[9] This is because the Spirit of Christ dwells in them. The indwelling of the Holy Spirit is what Christ's resurrection means for them. That is the substance of the Fourth and final week of the Spiritual Exercises.

RESURRECTION

Where do we find hope today? Part 5 invites readers to examine their experience in the light of Christ's victory over death, which signals the beginning of a new world (chapter 21). Christ rises in those who live as he did; his Spirit in-spires them to liberating action (chapter 22). The same Spirit enables us to find God in all things, working to bring about a new creation. God's self-gift moves us to respond with grateful love and service (chapter 23).

21 Resurrection and the Spirit

> *Blessed be the God and Father of our Lord Jesus Christ! By his great mercy he has given us a new birth into a living hope through the resurrection of Jesus Christ from the dead, and into an inheritance that is imperishable, undefiled, and unfading.... Although you have not seen him, you love him; and even though you do not see him now, you believe in him and rejoice with an indescribable and glorious joy, for you are receiving the outcome of your faith, the salvation of your souls.* (1 Pet. 1:3–9)

When an abandoned woman who is the mother of three small children laughs on her worst day ever, is she being dishonest? Or is her joy deeper than her pain? Might she know in her heart that life is worth it, despite everything? Among the poor, a fiesta is always appropriate. Is that escapism or something else? Homeless men, battered women, the young man with AIDS—they can't always explain their smile. Are they crazy? Or is smiling in hard times an act of faith with a basis in reality? When poor folks struggle against the odds with good humor, they cannot always tell you why. Sometimes they can only sing, "Deep in my heart, I do believe, we shall overcome some day." They are not as foolish as they may look to observers in newsrooms and boardrooms. They *shall* overcome some day.

Rejoicing always, despite everything, is a requirement of faith—and a sign of faith (cf. Phil. 4:4–5). Faith denies evil and death the last word. That changes everything, even now.

CONTEMPLATION OF THE RISEN CHRIST

Christian faith affirms that in Jesus' resurrection good triumphed over evil and death and that we share that victory even now. The Fourth

Week of the Spiritual Exercises invites us to contemplate his appearances to the disciples after he rose from death. (See the narratives in the last chapters of the gospels and the first chapter of the Acts of the Apostles.)

Like the contemplations of Christ's passion, these also seek to foster union with him. At the beginning of each exercise, we ask to know him more intimately, to love him more deeply, to follow him more closely [104] — this time in his victory. We ask "to rejoice and be intensely glad because of the great glory and joy of Christ our Lord" [221]. As always, the grace requested guides the prayer.

As in earlier contemplations, we vividly imagine the scene — for example, Jesus' appearance to Mary Magdalene before the tomb (John 20) — (1) observing the people involved, (2) listening to their words, and (3) noting their actions — allowing the drama to move us and reflecting in whatever way is fruitful. Ignatius suggests two additional points: consider (4) how the divinity, hidden during the passion, now manifests itself to those who believe in Christ and (5) how Christ consoles the disciples "as friends are accustomed to console each other." See [222–24]. We converse with Christ or God (and Mary). We use these suggested points in the order and to the extent that they contribute to the "grace" asked for.

That is the nucleus of the Fourth Week. It is more a matter of practice than of study. However, as before, it will be helpful to clarify, briefly, what "resurrection" means for Christ and for us, to clear away unnecessary obstacles, and point the way toward a fruitful understanding of this reality, including its social significance.

RESURRECTION

What do these narratives of encounters with the risen Jesus tell us about Christ and his new existence? What does his resurrection mean for his followers and for the world?

In these appearances, Christ's new existence is both continuous and discontinuous with his earlier existence.[1] On the one hand, this is the same Jesus present among his disciples as before. He is not a disembodied ghost. He eats and drinks with them and shows them his wounds (Luke 24:39–43; John 20:20). Therefore, the first communities announced: "Jesus is alive" — but not as a disembodied soul, as Plato (and maybe most believers) would construe the hope of immortality.

On the other hand, Jesus is not present exactly as before. He is not a revived corpse, like Lazarus come back from the tomb. Some of the disciples find him hard to recognize. His humanity pulses with divine life. So the early witnesses also proclaim, "Jesus is Lord!"; he has been exalted to God's right hand, as Psalm 110 foretold.

This discontinuity-in-continuity is also a reversal of his defeat. Resurrection reverses death, and vindication reverses condemnation: God has raised up precisely the condemned and crucified one (cf. Acts 2:36; etc.). "This is the stone which was rejected by you builders, but which has become the cornerstone" (Acts 3:11).

However, this is more than a personal triumph. Jesus' victory over death announces a turning point in the history of creation and God's dealings with humanity. For devout Jews of the time, resurrection signified the coming of God's Reign, the final defeat of evil. So, for the disciples, Jesus' resurrection was the beginning of a more general resurrection (cf. Matt. 27:51–53). Like the Reign of God which it signifies, resurrection is a collective salvation. Jesus is the "firstborn of many brothers and sisters" (Rom. 8:29).[2] The disciples rejoice in his new presence not only for his sake, but also because a new world is dawning for them in which poverty and death have been vanquished.

However, in Jesus' day the promise of resurrection did not mean immortality for *all* believers, as we tend to understand it today. In the preceding centuries, hope in resurrection had developed in response to the murder of so many Jews who remained steadfastly faithful to God in the face of persecution. (See, for example, the eloquent testimonies of 2 Maccabees 7 and Wisdom 2–3.) So resurrection meant that God would vindicate innocent victims, especially those who had been killed for their faithfulness. The hope of resurrection was not the fruit of a generic personal longing for immortality (as understandable as that may be), but a hunger and thirst for the justice of God on behalf of innocent victims.

Against this background, Jesus' resurrection vindicates the kind of life he lived and the kind of death he died. God did not raise up just any dead person but precisely a crucified prophet, a "just one" (*saddiq* in Hebrew). The hope of resurrection is first for innocent victims, especially those who live as Jesus did and suffer for it. However, it is not only for them. Just as God's forgiveness does not depend on our integrity, but on God's compassion (grace), and just as God sides with the poor not because they are good, but because God is good, we can affirm something similar about the resurrection. It is not a matter of merit but of the gratuitous goodness of God. Like God's Kingdom, of which it is a principal sign, the resurrection is especially for history's victims. Though they are sinners, God will reverse the injustice they have suffered.[3]

Of course, the church and the New Testament writers quickly came to understand Jesus' resurrection as a symbol of hope for all. This is perfectly legitimate, just as it is legitimate to say that the Reign of God is offered to all, not just to the poor. Nevertheless, both Kingdom and resurrection lose a central dimension of their meaning when we forget that God comes as king to liberate the poor (Luke 6:20) and resurrect the victims of injustice.

CHRIST RISES IN HIS DISCIPLES: THE LORD IS THE SPIRIT

The first Christians continued to experience Jesus present in prophetic utterance, in healings, and in the freedom to live as sisters and brothers, bearing witness under trial. The New Testament reports how they understood this new existence. According to Paul, Christians share in Jesus' victory. They have died to the world, as he did. Its egoism no longer controls them. They now live with Christ's own life.[4] "You have put off the old person [*anthropos*] with its practices and put on the new person" (Col. 3:9–10; cf. Eph. 4:22–24). "Born again" from above, they are a "new creation."[5] A process is underway in and among them. They must strive each day to allow God to make them what they already are, and so grow to full maturity.[6] The New Testament explains the transformation in two words: Holy Spirit.

SPIRIT IN DISGUISE?

On first inspection, the Holy Spirit seems to play a minor role in the *Spiritual Exercises.* The Spirit is mentioned explicitly only in six places, [263, 273, 304, 307, 312, and 365]. All but one of these paragraphs simply transcribe a biblical reference. In the Rules for Discernment, Ignatius refers only to the "good spirit" [314, 318, 336; cf. 32]. There is no contemplation of Pentecost in the *Exercises.* The latest post-resurrection subject for contemplation is Jesus' ascension to heaven [226, 312].

Surely one reason for this apparent absence is that the dynamic of the retreat centers around friendship with Christ. Another is that sometimes Ignatius fails to identify the work of Spirit or refers to the Spirit only obliquely.

I mentioned earlier how church authorities in Ignatius's day were highly suspicious of people who claimed to be inspired by the Holy Spirit. Ignatius himself was detained more than once on suspicion of belonging to the "illuminist" (*alumbrado*) movement, whose mostly unlettered participants appealed to immediate experience of God independently of the church hierarchy.

The *alumbrados* met in closed conventicles. Many believed in the impossibility of serious sin among the enlightened. With the Protestant Reformation underway, the very word

With Jesus' physical departure, the disciples experienced a new divine presence, the Holy Spirit. Jesus' Spirit had burst the confines of his body destroyed on the cross and now filled those who believed in him.[7]

That is, Christ rises in his followers: "The Lord is the Spirit" (2 Cor. 3:17; cf. 1 Cor. 15:45). The community of disciples is now the Body of Christ: "Now you [pl.] are the body of Christ and individually members "spiritual" evoked among authorities memories of the revolutionary "spiritual" fraternities of the late Middle Ages. A brief mention of the "unction of the Holy Spirit" in the Prologue to the Latin translation of the *Exercises* ran afoul of censors even after the manual had received papal approval. Ignatius recalled the climate of suspicion in his autobiographical reflections (see *Autobiog* 65).

Another probable reason for the lack of explicit reference to the Spirit in the *Exercises* is that Ignatius compiled the manual before studying theology, when he lacked the tools to express more adequately his experience of God. His later writings (mostly letters and other unpublished materials) mention the Holy Spirit more frequently. His "Autograph Directory," dating from his last years, characterizes consolation as a gift of the Holy Spirit (cf. *DirAutog* 11; Palmer, *Giving*, p. 8).

Exaggerated suspicion of personal inspiration and Ignatius's own failure to identify the Spirit both reflect the historic neglect since the first centuries of the church in Western Christianity (more than in the East) of the work proper to the Holy Spirit. Today we need to remedy that error, specifying more clearly the role of the Spirit in our lives and in history. The Spirit is clearly operative, even pervasive, in Ignatius's vision and practice. Identifying that presence can help greatly to overcome a pernicious "Spiritphobia."

of it" (1 Cor. 12:27; cf. Rom. 12:5). "Body" in the Bible means the entire person, body and soul. Jesus' followers become the presence of God in history, God's body, the temple of the Spirit (1 Cor. 3:16–17). God, who became human in the incarnation, now leavens the mass of humanity with the divine life.[8]

This Spirit is the Spirit of Christ. Jesus lives in those who allow the Spirit to reproduce in them his way of thinking and acting. This is the decisive test of the presence of God's Spirit, rather than some other. The Spirit makes it possible to live as Christ did, in community. This is the beginning of "a new sky and a new earth" (2 Pet. 3:13; Rev. 21:1), a new world.

For Ignatius, contemplating Christ crucified and risen fosters this transformation of our hearts and minds and actions. Ignatius does not attribute this transformative process explicitly to the Holy Spirit, however. This is one example among many where the Spirit's presence is hidden in the *Exercises.*[9]

The New Testament says that we experience the risen Christ through the Holy Spirit. How and where does that take place? Ignatius points to an answer in the two additional points he proposes for contemplating the appearances of the risen Christ: the divinity, hidden in the passion, now reveals itself, and Christ consoles his discouraged followers [224]. What do these clues suggest about experiencing the risen Christ today?

RECOGNIZING THE RISEN ONE

The glory of God, hidden during the passion, bursts forth in the risen Christ. Christ takes the initiative in "allowing himself to be seen" (*ophthe,* 1 Cor. 15:5–8). But not by all. Who recognizes him? *Those who (still) believe in him,* after church and state have him executed as a reprobate; those who believe that he was right and his accusers wrong; those who, despite his "failure," recognize his greatness ("glory"), not only despite the way he died, but because of it. Only those who recognize the glory hidden can recognize the glory manifest.

Those who believe in him and follow him experience the consolation of the Spirit, who inflames their hearts and enables them to live like him.

My friend Linda, a long-time political activist, recently underwent a profound religious conversion. One day, after telling about how much stress she was under, she asked, "Can you explain why I am so happy these days? I'm sometimes just driving along, and I feel so joyful. Everything seems so beautiful. I don't understand it." Linda could find no sufficient cause for the consolation that sustains her as a mother and activist.

In Christ's resurrection, the glory of God shone forth precisely where it had been hidden. This suggests that we may find him hidden-yet-manifest among the victims today. And it seems we do. In poor communities, visitors are often surprised to find what they least expected: joy, and also hope, gracious acceptance, and generosity. This happens all the time in Central America. Where does the joy and hope come from? Not from good food, robust health, or power, none of which is much in evidence. No; the poor communicate joy *in spite of everything.*

This is the consolation without prior cause which Ignatius assures us comes only from God [330]. The apparent facts cannot account for it, which indicates that the resurrected one is here, consoling the afflicted [224], producing hope against hope and the energy needed to struggle against the odds. The poor people then pass on that consolation to visitors (cf. 2 Cor. 1:4) who return home renewed in hope.

Although this experience is not universal, I am struck by how widespread it is. If so, can it be the "consolation without prior cause," which Ignatius introduces in the context of the election and for which indifference is a precondition? Are we romanticizing the poor?

That question assumes that indifference and consolation without cause are rare, perhaps reserved for a spiritual elite. But why should we suppose that few poor and uneducated people have the interior freedom needed to receive that consolation?[10] They have less to lose, less to cling to.

My friend Teresa Pérez says that if they killed her serving the parish community, she would welcome it. That is indifference. Her joy is notorious and contagious. Many like her have given their lives for their friends and many more would do so, if necessary. Among them we find striking generosity (*"Mi casa es su casa"*), humor, and an undertow of stubborn joy — despite the conditions of their lives. Is this where the new world is beginning?

Like other poor regions, Central America is engulfed in permanent crisis with few prospects for change soon. And yet, when people gather they sing with enthusiasm:

Todavía cantamos, todavía pedimos,
Todavía soñamos, todavía esperamos.
We still keep singing, we still keep seeking,
We still keep dreaming, we still keep hoping.

If God raised up a victim of injustice to usher in a new world, we do well to look for Christ among the downtrodden today. That is where we should find hope against hope and the beginnings of a new world. That turns out to be the case in places like South Africa, Colombia, and Pine Ridge, South Dakota.

CONCLUSION

For Christian faith, Christ's resurrection signifies the beginning of a new creation, in which egoism and death are defeated. We share in this new creation in the measure that Christ's Spirit transforms us. Contemplating his victory-in-defeat nourishes that transformation, deepening hope and joy and pointing us to where we can find Christ, consoling the crucified of today.

In early writings like the *Exercises,* Ignatius failed to identify the transformative work of the Holy Spirit in explicit terms, even though the Spirit is pervasively present in his vision. The testimony of the scripture helps us better identify what he experienced. For example, in the scriptures the risen Christ sends his followers out on mission — a central theme for Ignatius, too. The consolation of the Spirit inspires their action, just as he says. In the Bible, however, consolation is a social and political, as well as a personal, reality. These New Testament ideas can help us connect the dots and fill in some blanks in Ignatius's writings on mission and consolation.

Consolation, Action, and Liberation  22

Then I saw a new heaven and a new earth; for the first heaven and the first earth had passed away, and the sea was no more. And I saw the holy city, the new Jerusalem, coming down out of heaven from God, prepared as a bride adorned for her husband. And I heard a loud voice from the throne saying,

> *"See, the home of God is among mortals. . . .*
> *He will wipe every tear from their eyes.*
> *Death will be no more;*
> *mourning and crying and pain will be no more,*
> *for the first things have passed away."* (Rev. 21:1–4)

My friend Ben recently wrote from Alabama, where he is spending several months in jail for trespassing at Fort Benning, Georgia, to protest United States military policy in Latin America. Ben is paying the price for "doing something serious for peace," as he puts it. Along with his poor fellow-inmates, he puts up with degrading conditions, which he says "would crack me on the outside," adding, "For some odd reason — the Holy Spirit, obviously — I'm doing surprisingly well."

In the New Testament, when the risen Christ communicates the Spirit, he sends his disciples forth with a mission — a theme dear to Ignatius. The Spirit consoles the disciples, Ignatius says, and he understands consolation as moving people to action. In Muscogee County Jail, Ben is strengthened, consoled, for his mission. Broadly understood, as we see in the scripture, consolation includes the justice and peace Ben is working for. The Spirit brings that about working through Ben's praxis, and through ours.

CONSOLATION, PERSONAL AND COLLECTIVE

Consolation is a central characteristic of Christian life in the New Testament. The disciples, crushed by Jesus' death, now rejoice to learn that he is alive. He calms their fears: "Peace be with you," "Do not be afraid."[1] Two disciples who walked with him on the road to Emmaus finally recognize him and exclaim, *"Were not our hearts burning within us* while he was talking to us on the road?" (Luke 24:32). All this is consolation, *paraklesis* in Greek.

The first Christian communities "live in the consolation [*paraklesis*] of the Holy Spirit" (Acts 9:31). The fruit of the Spirit is "generous love, joy, peace, patient endurance" (Gal. 5:22–23), that is, consolation.

God consoles especially in time of tribulation. Paul praises "the God of all consolation, who consoles us in all our affliction (*thlipsis*), so that we may be able to console those who are in any affliction," with that same consolation. "For just as the sufferings of Christ are abundant for us, so also our consolation is abundant through Christ" (2 Cor. 1:3–7).[2]

Ignatius clearly selected the correct biblical term for what he calls "consolation." For both New Testament writers and for Ignatius, consolation is more than comfort for the sorrowful. It is also clarity and zeal for mission, inspiration to act, joy and courage under fire. However, whereas Ignatius limits consolation to personal experience, consolation has social and political dimensions, which we can appreciate from several different angles.

Consolation is contagious

We have already seen that consolation and desolation are shared realities. Desolation spreads in groups, when cynics scandalize the "little ones." Brutal repression can crush the hope of entire populations and spread lasting, collective desolation.

When I asked a group of adults from poor communities if they thought consolation, too, is contagious, they agreed with enthusiasm. They recalled how, at the anniversaries of Archbishop Romero's martyrdom and similar events, people gather to march, sing, pray, and dance, and return home renewed in hope. They noted how they fight desolation with fiestas. Celebrating the corn harvest, birthdays, arrivals, departures, and religious feasts reawakens hope and solidarity.

Consolation spreads when we sing "We've Come This Far by Faith" and "We Shall Not Be Moved." More than "just an emotional experience," what erupts is often the consolation that renews hope.

Community worship, above all the Eucharist, is all about fighting desolation and inflaming hearts to keep going, in the joyful conviction that good will triumph over evil and death.

Consolation is sometimes contagious in the interaction between the preacher and the congregation. When the preacher cries, "I have a dream today!" the people shout back, "Yeah!" "That's right!" The prophet rouses the Spirit in them, and their Amen rouses the prophet in return.

Consolation and the prophetic Spirit

The Spirit that consoles is a prophetic spirit. The prophets of Israel were inspired (consoled) to denounce injustice and announce the coming of justice and peace. Jesus applied Isaiah's oracle to himself: "The Spirit of the Lord is upon me, because he has anointed me to bring good news to the poor" (Luke 4:18; cf. 3:22). This same Spirit now consoles Christ's disciples, inspiring them to speak and act for justice.

Isaiah and Zechariah had foretold that the prophetic Spirit would produce justice and peace,[3] and the Spirit that comes at Pentecost inspires a new form of community life.

> All who believed were together and had all things in common; they would sell their possessions and goods and distribute the proceeds to all, as any had need. Day by day, as they spent much time together in the temple, they broke bread at home and ate their food with glad and generous hearts. (Acts 2:44–46)

In this new community poverty has disappeared: "There was not a needy person among them" (Acts 4:34).

Today, too, the church should be the chief place where the community of equals happens. It should be salt of the earth and light of the world, a city set on a hilltop for all to see—though the Spirit blows outside the church, as well.

Consolation as liberation

This new community is itself God's consolation. In the biblical traditions, consolation is a collective reality, practically synonymous with liberation and *shalom*.

During the exile in Babylon (587–538 B.C.E.), the prophet we call Second Isaiah announced that God was about to liberate his people from exile. At the head of the prophet's collected oracles (Isaiah 40–55), we find this summary proclamation:

> Console, console my people, says your God.
> Speak tenderly to Jerusalem, and cry to her
> that her warfare is ended,
> that her iniquity is pardoned. (Isa. 40:1)

The consolation which the prophet announces is the liberation of the exiles and their restoration to Jerusalem in justice and prosperity (*shalom*): "Yahweh has consoled his people, and will have compassion on his suffering ones" (Isa. 49:13). "Yahweh has consoled his people, he has redeemed Jerusalem" (Isa. 52:9; cf. 51:3). Creation itself will spring to new life to participate in this divine consolation:

> For Yahweh will console Zion;
> he will console all her waste places,
> and will make her wilderness like Eden,
> her desert like the Garden of Yahweh.
> (Isa. 51:3)[4]

When the Hebrew scriptures were later translated into Greek (the Septuagint version, mostly from the second and third centuries B.C.E.), the words "Console, console [*nahamu, nahamu*]" were rendered by the verb *parakleo*. The *paraklesis*/consolation of the New Testament reflects this earlier tradition.

Since the full consolation announced by the prophet and his successor, Third Isaiah (Isa. 56–66), failed to materialize fully in their time, their oracles continued to nourish Jewish hope and resistance during the following centuries of oppressive foreign rule and up to the time of Jesus. The spirit of these oracles suffuses the message of Jesus, especially in the Gospel of Luke. The aged Simeon who receives the infant savior in the temple represents those who are "looking for the consolation of Israel," which is "the liberation of Jerusalem" (Luke 2:25, 38; cf. 1:68; 23:51). In programmatic texts, Luke presents Jesus' ministry as fulfilling the Oracles of Consolation (Luke 4:16–19; 6:20–26; 7:22) which proclaim liberation to the poor and oppressed.[5]

Whereas Ignatius dwells on how the risen Christ consoles his disciples, the wider biblical conception of consolation — as liberation, justice, the flowering of nature — connects his insight to the social, political, and ecological significance of Christ's resurrection, which is the beginning of God's kingdom of justice and peace.

How does this reality come about? According to the scripture, it is God's work. And God works through human beings entrusted with a mission.

MISSION AND PRAXIS

The Spirit consoles for mission. The risen Christ sends the women who first encounter him to tell the others that he is alive (Matt. 28:10; etc.). He commissions the disciples: "You are witnesses of these things" (Luke 24:48); "Go make disciples of all nations" (Matt. 28:19). He singles out Peter: "Feed my lambs . . . feed my sheep" (John 21:15–17).

He will accompany them. "I am with you till the end of the age" (Matt. 28:20). The Holy Spirit will empower their mission. "As the Father has sent me, so I send you. When he had said this, he breathed on them and said to them, 'Receive the Holy Spirit' " (John 20:21–22; cf. Acts 1:8). The "Spirit of Truth" will be their *Parakletos,* a "consoling" defense lawyer, who will enlighten and strengthen them in the face of opposition,[6] dispelling fear and inspiring bold speech and action.[7]

For Ignatius, too, the consolation of the Spirit moves to action. What we call Ignatian spirituality is oriented to a life of action, of "labor in the Lord's vineyard."[8] Ignatius wrote to Francisco Borja that we should seek consolation and similar gifts, because with them "our thoughts, words, and actions . . . become clear and warm and upright for God's greater service."[9] He wrote to Teresa Rejadell that "consolation points out and opens up the way we are to follow and points out the way we are to avoid." It conquers all obstacles, for "when this divine consolation is present all trials are pleasant and all weariness rest. Whoever goes forward with this fervor, warmth, and interior consolation finds every burden light and sweetness in every penance or trial, however great."[10]

A classmate of mine and professor of nursing reports (in our college reunion book) that several years ago she and her husband decided to add to their family of five children. They adopted two infants, then a third child, all from Honduras. Two years later, they took in a severely ill and undernourished infant from Haiti. The mother concluded, "I am overtired, overworked, overextended, but most importantly, overjoyed." That joy does not come from the amenities or a life of ease. It points to the Spirit of the risen one, consoling and enabling this hardworking parent.

Working within us, the Spirit makes us collaborators of God (1 Cor. 3:9). We sense that happening according to the pattern of Jesus' resurrection—which was continuous, discontinuous, and a reversal with respect to his earlier existence. Consolation is continuous with everyday life (it is not strange or bizarre) but also discontinuous, insofar as it is disproportionate to apparent causes; and it reverses desolation. The "fruits of the Spirit"—joy and generosity—outstrip our powers and the miserable surface facts. Consolation does not eliminate pain and loss, injustice and failure. (The "reversal" remains incomplete.) It is peace, joy, generosity, courage, and hope despite these, and under trial (*thlipsis*).

God is at work in our weakness when we find the strength to give more and the courage to forgive, when results surpass our efforts. That is how God works: bringing Israel out of Egypt against Pharaoh's mighty army, delivering Goliath into young David's hands. The psalmist sings: "Some trust in chariots and horses; but we trust in Yahweh our God" (Ps 20). God bestows blessings on his beloved even while they sleep (Ps 127). Aged and barren mothers give birth to children who, though they may seem unlikely candidates, save their people.[11] We can see God at work feeding thousands who share just a few loaves and fishes, and compensating tired fisherman by filling their boats with fish. The young church grows and spreads because, while Paul plants and Apollo waters, God gives the increase (1 Cor. 3:6). There is evident disproportion between the divine treasure and the earthen vessels who bear it (2 Cor. 4:7).

Dorothy Day recognized this disproportion in the beginnings of the Catholic Worker. In the epilogue to her autobiography she wrote,

"We were just sitting there talking.... It was as casual as all that, I often think. It just came about. It just happened."[12]

Oscar Romero's diary exudes serenity and lightness of spirit in the midst of intense activity and conflict, momentous issues engaged and decisions taken. The disproportion with Romero's frailty is striking. More than human energy is at work.

God's action endows our praxis with a distinctive character. Gathered at Puebla in 1979, the Latin American bishops wrote:

> In the face of the historical challenges confronting our peoples, we find two extreme reactions among Christians. The "passivists" believe that they cannot or should not intervene, hoping that God will act and bring liberation all by himself. The "activists" adopt a secularized perspective. They view God as remote, as if he had handed over complete responsibility for history to human beings; thus they anxiously and frantically try to move history forward.
>
> Jesus' posture was different.... [He] appears acting within history hand in hand with his Father. His attitude is simultaneously one of total trust on the one hand and of the utmost commitment and co-responsibility on the other. Jesus knows that everything is in the hands of the Father, who watches over the birds of the air and the lilies of the field (Luke 12:22–33); but he also knows that the work of the Father is meant to come to pass through his own work.
>
> Since the Father is the principal protagonist, Jesus tries to follow his pathways and rhythms. His constant concern is to stay in strict and loyal harmony with what the Father wants.[13]

A famous maxim in the same spirit — in the style of a Zen *koan* — is attributed to Ignatius: "So trust in God as if all the success of affairs depended on yourself, and nothing on God. Nevertheless, so work in them as if you were to accomplish nothing in them, and God everything."[14] Pedro Ribadeneyra, Ignatius's collaborator, associated him with an outlook that at first seems to affirm the opposite, but that some consider complementary in practice: "In matters which he took up pertaining to the service of our Lord, he made use of all the human means to succeed in them, with a care and efficiency as great as if the success depended on these means; and he confided in God and depended on his providence as greatly as if all the other human means which he was using were of no effect."[15] These two perspectives are often expressed in the formulas: "Pray as if everything depended on God, and work as if everything depended on you"; and "Pray as if everything depended on you, and work as if everything depended on God."[16]

Puebla and the Ignatian formulas express faith that God works in and through us. That inspires a sense of mission, hope, bold action, and perseverance, even in trial, disappointment, and apparent failure.

CONCLUSION

The Spirit of Christ consoles, producing joy, peace, and generous action. We frequently emphasize the sacrifices involved in a life of service and forget the consolations that sustain it. As a result, many fail to seek consolation, and when it comes they barely take note of it and profit little from it. Others dismiss consolation as nonessential or even distracting from their work. Isn't this the too-human, often masculine, temptation to overlook signs of love and fail to respond to them?

As the Holy Spirit is the "down payment" on the full salvation still awaited (2 Cor. 1:22; 5:5; Eph. 1:13), personal consolation is a taste of a new world in the making. The consolation of the Spirit spreads and produces community. It includes liberation for the poor, healing for our wounded earth, and resurrection from death.

How are we to understand this "imperishable hope" for abundant life, even beyond the grave? Wisdom counsels modesty in speaking about God's final victory. Like the prophets and visionaries of old, we can only reflect on past and present experience of God's liberating action and project forward into the future. On that basis, neither a Platonic immortality of disembodied souls nor a beatific vision modeled on a movie theater does justice to God's promise and our deepest longings. The inspired testimonies in scripture tell us that the new world will be continuous with our bodily, social existence but also very different and a reversal of present sorrow, injustice, and death. All creation longs to share in this new creation, which begins even now, as God works through human beings.[17]

The Spirit makes us God's collaborators and multiplies the fruits of our labors. However, what counts in the end is not so much measurable results as steadfast fidelity, frequently despite apparent results. The catch of fish often appears on the opposite side of the boat from where we have been fishing. On the other hand, had we not been fishing, it is unlikely that we would have harvested the catch.

Action is most human when it is a grateful response. The Contemplation for Arousing Love, to which we now turn, crowns the Ignatian retreat. It invites us to see God working in all creation to "make all things new" and to respond in loving service.

23 Learning to Love Like God

And the one who was seated on the throne said,
"See, I am making all things new." (Rev. 21:5)

The Contemplation for Attaining (or Arousing) Love of God [230–37] is "the conclusion and apt climax" of the Spiritual Exercises.[1] Like the Foundation and Two Standards on which it builds, this Contemplation inculcates a new vision and way of life. Its purpose is to help us sense God everywhere in all our activities, and to "love and serve in everything" [233] in response; or, according to three well-known Ignatian catchphrases, to *find God in all things* as *contemplatives in action* in close *familiarity with God.*

The Contemplation functions in the Exercises as a kind of Pentecost—not a contemplation of the event recounted in the Acts of the Apostles, but an invitation to experience something like it,[2] that is, to experience God's self-gift (as Holy Spirit) and to see the world with new eyes. The Contemplation invites us to experience how "God is love" and labors in the world for abundant life.

THE CONTEMPLATION FOR ATTAINING LOVE

God is love.
(1 John 4:8)

Before presenting the Contemplation, Ignatius reminds us of two truths about love. First, "love ought to be expressed in deeds more than in words" ([230]; see John 14:21; 1 John 3:18). Second, "love consists in a mutual sharing of goods; that is, the lover gives and shares with the beloved what he or she has, or out of what he or she has or can do, and vice versa, so that if one has knowledge one gives to the other who does not have it. The same with honors and with riches, and the other reciprocates in the same way" [231].

Commentary. If love is shown in deeds, then contemplating God's love means contemplating God's deeds, especially how God bestows gifts on us. God's love should stir up active love in us.

Love consists of mutual sharing. God shares "knowledge" of reality in this Contemplation. It is surprising to read that lovers share "riches" and "honors"—the two key temptations in the Two Standards [142]! The emphasis is obviously on sharing. We can understand sharing riches—but what about honors? Love "honors" others; it accords them *respect,* perhaps our deepest human need. A friend once recommended imagining all people wearing signs around their necks reading "Take me seriously!" Love *recognizes,* above all, the dignity of those the world despises. Love listens to their stories—which is often all they have.

The main body of the Contemplation is preceded by two brief introductory steps, the composition and the grace sought.

The "composition." After first asking God to direct everything to the ultimate goal of life, we next imagine a scene to keep our attention focused [232]. Ignatius suggests imagining ourselves before God and the saints in glory.

The grace sought. Next (as in every exercise), we ask for what we want. Ignatius suggests that we request "interior knowledge of so much good received, in order that, entirely conscious of that, I may love and serve God in everything" [233].

Commentary on the "grace" requested. The purpose of the Contemplation is to arouse love in us; to become so aware of God's love that we are moved to respond by loving in the same way.[3] We ask to love and serve "in everything" (*en todo*)—that is, not just in response to forgiveness (the First Week) or to love Christ in order to follow him more closely (Second, Third, and Fourth Weeks), but to love and serve God in everything, in everyone, and in every aspect of daily life.

The body of the Contemplation consists of four points, which are four perspectives from which to consider God's love.

- *The first point* is to recall the blessings we have received in our lifetime, the blessings "of creation, redemption, and personal gifts," reflecting that all this comes from God's hand and demonstrates how much more "the Lord desires to give himself" to us. We then reflect on how it is only reasonable to offer God in return everything we have, and ourselves with it, just as God has done. With as much feeling as possible, we then make the following offering:

> Take, Lord, and receive all my liberty,
> my memory, my understanding, and my whole will,
> all that I have and possess.
> You gave it to me;
> to you, Lord, I return it.
> It is all yours; use it as you please.
> Give me your love and your grace;
> this is enough for me. [231]

Commentary on the first point. In twelve-step programs like Alcoholics Anonymous, participants take inventory of their past. They try to come to terms with both the damage they have done and their happy debt of gratitude to those who stood by them despite everything (compare [60] in the *Exercises*). The first point of the Contemplation is an exercise in reappropriating the past. Our new situation helps us see God's hand where we never did before. God has always been there, guiding and helping us, when we were largely unaware of it.

Few things humanize like gratitude, which is rarely inappropriate and difficult to overdo. Growing up in an affluent society, we frequently take for granted what most people through history could not and cannot: good nutrition, decent health, a measure of economic security, and life itself. From taking these things for granted it is a short step to supposing life owes us that and more. Then, instead of giving thanks for the most basic things, we let any snafu ruin our day. We have received everything as a gift. Poor people – grateful to be alive, to eat, to enjoy family and the beauty of nature – are our professors in the school of gratitude.

In the first point, we recall the blessings of "creation, redemption, and personal gifts" (which may refer to gifts from Father-Creator, Son, and Spirit, respectively). The principal gift is God's Self. God's self-communication is the ultimate meaning of God's dealings with the universe. Each in a different way, the three Persons of the Trinity invade history and our personal lives, dwelling in us and making us dwell in

God — as the Eucharist and Pentecost illustrate. The remaining three points of the Contemplation develop this idea of God's self-gift.

Whereas the "indifference" of the Foundation [23] is a freedom *from,* the prayer "Take and receive" specifies that this freedom is *for* giving ourselves and our lives to God. This is not about renouncing memory, intellect, will, and freedom, however, but enlisting these, with all our creativity, in service. "Give me your love and your grace" seems to mean: "Give me love for you and grace to love you."[4]

• *The second point* (which might constitute the subject of a different exercise altogether) is:

> to observe how God dwells in creatures: in the elements giving being, in the plants vegetating, in the animals feeling, in humans giving understanding; and so in me giving me being, life, and feeling and making me to understand; and similarly making me a temple, having created me in the divine image and likeness. [235]

We reflect on these matters, seeking what we want, and closing (as we are able) with the prayer "Take and Receive."

Commentary on the second point. Here, too, the idea is to sense how God is present in everything and everyone, making each be what it is. God gives everything its being out of love, moment by moment (J. Tetlow), and dwells in each gift. God blows in the breeze and flows in the streams; God leaps in the frogs and flies in the birds; God thinks, loves, and communicates in human beings. As the Mayan Indians say, God is *Corazón de la montaña, Corazón del cielo* — "Heart of the Mountain" and "Heart of the Sky."

• *The third point* is to "consider how God works and labors for me in all created things on the face of the earth." Ignatius says God "behaves as a laborer does," working in minerals, plants, animals, according to the nature of each [236]. We then reflect and close with the usual prayer.

Commentary on the third point. God labors in everything to bring all creation to fruition. Jesus perceived his Father working to give life (John 5:17), making the sun shine and sending the rain to fall on good and bad alike (Matt. 5:45). This suggests God's solidarity with workers who continue the divine work of creation. It also invites us to reflect on our proper place and role in the world in relation to other creatures.

• *The fourth point* is "to observe how all good things and gifts descend from above, for example my limited powers from the divine and infinite power on high, and likewise justice, goodness, mercy, compassion, etc., just as rays descend from the sun and waters from the spring, and so on" [237]. Once again, we reflect and converse with God as seems fitting.

Commentary on the fourth point. All goodness participates in God's goodness and reveals God as its source, especially moral goodness: "justice, goodness, compassion, mercy" [237]. According to the apostle James, "Every generous act of giving, with every perfect gift, is from above, coming down from the Father of lights" (James 1:17). In this point, the motive for loving God is not the gifts or what God does, but who God is.

These four points, which are really four exercises, aim to foster a deep appreciation of God's gifts and of God as the principal gift in all gifts. According to the Foundation [23], creatures can divert us from our final goal; according to the Contemplation, all creatures are sacraments by which God comes to us. The Foundation bids us use all creatures to serve God; the Contemplation presents God laboring in all creatures to serve us.[5] Created reality — things, people, events — is not a screen that God hides behind to then peek out at us. God is present *in* all creatures and events and comes to us in and through them. "The world is charged with the grandeur of God," wrote the poet Gerard Manley Hopkins. The Contemplation invites us "to seek God our Lord in all things, . . . loving him in all creatures and all creatures in him."[6] *Created reality has in itself an inexhaustible depth and richness at the heart of which we find God.* The Contemplation fosters seeing (and feeling and hearing, etc.) this richness and growing more aware of God loving us in and through everything that exists and everything that happens (sometimes despite things that happen). This awareness awakens the response of grateful love and service to the world.

More specifically: in all things and daily events, God offers us the Kingdom, a new creation. Present and laboring in all things and events, God makes forgiveness, love, community, justice, and peace possible. When we accept the offer, by loving and serving in response [233], the Reign of God happens here and now. In this way God makes all things new (cf. Rev. 21:5).

THE CONTEMPLATION AND THE PASCHAL MYSTERY

God has made known to us the mystery of his will,...
to gather up all things in Christ. (Eph. 1:9–10)

The place of Christ in the Contemplation has been the subject of debate since soon after Ignatius's death. At first glance, there appears to be no mention of Christ.[7] Is he absent from the Contemplation? No. In fact, the cryptic references to Christ provide us with clues to developing the Contemplation's social implications. What are these references?

The first point includes the "blessings of redemption," which are summed up in Christ himself.[8] He is also the most complete example of God's presence in the world, which is the subject of the second point. According to the traditional (scholastic) schema implicit in point two, Christ is the key to understanding how God dwells in all creatures.

However, biblical thinking and good Christian theology seek God's presence not simply in persons and things but also in historical events and processes. God acts and saves in history. Therefore, the third point of the Contemplation speaks of "how God works and labors for me," how God "behaves as a laborer" [236]. This recalls the Third Week, when the retreatant "frequently call[s] to mind the labors, the fatigue, and suffering which Christ endured" [206].[9] According to John's Gospel, Jesus and his Father labor to bring life to the world: "My Father is still working, and I also am working" (John 5:17), and God's saving presence is most clearly revealed in the labor of Jesus' passion and death and in his resurrection (cf. John 17:1).

CONTEMPLATION IN THE POST-EINSTEINIAN UNIVERSE

> *The creation itself will be set free from its bondage to decay and will obtain the freedom of the glory of the children of God.* (Rom. 8:21)

Our wounded earth, with its endangered species and ecosystems, participates in the great drama of dying and rising. The whole creation groans in labor to give birth to a new world. The Contemplation for Attaining Love reflects the Pauline vision, in which all creation is taken up into ("recapitulated" by) the saving work of Christ (Eph. 1:10).

The scientific model of a mechanical universe which has dominated modern culture makes it difficult to accept such a vision, or to recognize a divine presence in the cosmos. That model has now collapsed in light of more recent discoveries. Today, scientists, naturalists, and philosophers are inviting us to a new sense of wonder.[10]

The prescientific universe which Ignatius found oozing with God is a far cry from the Newtonian-Einsteinian universe of modern times. The modern mechanical outlook is even more distant from the world as biblical writers understood it. As David Toolan puts it, the world of the prophets is "full of big chances . . . contingencies . . . breaks in symmetry." For all its stability, the universe of biblical writers has a place "for minorities of one or more that subvert a ruling order," a place for "the reign of God — against all the odds." That universe is "sacramental," full of "signs that give grace — both the grace of stability and the grace of instability" (445). There surprises are possible. God can work there, healing, setting free, enabling improbable catches of fish.

The Newtonian universe seems to exclude all this. While the modern scientific revolution has greatly enhanced our understanding of reality, "the ingenious Lawgiver who (at least for the theistic Newton) stands behind such laws [of physics] is not the Holy One that Jews and Christians worship as immanent in all creation and 'closer to us than we are to ourselves.' Rather, it is the Absentee Landlord of deism. For once Newton's God creates the cosmic machine, it will run by itself — and God can retire" (443). This reading of reality makes it difficult to contemplate the self-giving God laboring in all creation.

In recent decades, a richer understanding of the universe has come into view. The post-Einsteinian universe of quantum physics, quarks and strings has begun to restore the unity of the universe and our communion with it. The cosmos now "appears a lot more irregular, even chaotic, than we had supposed, and the realm of life and human being appear to belong here. The poetry is back in nature." Reality is characterized by "interconnection, process, fluctuation, and openness," with self-organizing organisms swimming upstream against the tide of entropy (446). In the "new" post-Einsteinian universe, some even claim to detect the beginnings of thought, freedom, and communication in nonhuman reality. In any event, today "the gap between nature and human culture has narrowed considerably" (452). All this is a far cry from the modern scientific paradigm of atomistic fragmentation and the rigid determinism of infinitesimal billiard balls interacting in gravitational fields.

God — and prophets — can more easily find a home in this universe of open systems communicating matter, energy, and even "information" to each other. This universe invites us to kneel and bow our heads in awe once again and to discover the Holy Mystery in quasars, in the sweep of evolution, in the beauty of falling snow, and in crucified and rising people.

The third point therefore gives the distinctly Christian clue to finding God "in all things." (The other three points, though also Christian, are compatible with non-Christian cosmologies.[11]) God's saving presence in history is disclosed above all in Jesus' cross and resurrection and in the crosses and resurrections — the ongoing paschal mystery — of suffering and struggling humanity. God's glory shines forth from the worn faces of those who labor, like God, to bring creation to fruition, often under unjust conditions. Divine glory shines in the victims of history, the poor and meek (*'anawim*) who refuse to adopt the methods of their assailants. And it shines, above all, in those who suffer and even die for what is right. In these ambassadors (Matt. 25) who complete what is lacking in Christ's sufferings (Col. 1:24) God draws near in mercy.

We cover retreat house walls with landscapes, tropical flowers, and koala bears, whose beauty surely points to their Creator. What about giving equal space to crucified-and-rising people and images like Fritz Eichenberg's print "The Christ of the Breadline," which portrays Christ's presence among our urban outcasts?

Every butterfly and blade of grass reveals the God of Jesus, but only if we can recognize God in broken human beings as well. We can avoid the God of Jesus in sunsets and flowers, if we try, but not in the poor who place us unavoidably before that God. If we cannot recognize God's face there, it is doubtful that any butterfly on earth will reveal the God of Jesus to us. When we can find God in our jails and AIDS hospices, we can find God coming to meet us everywhere else.

We all suspect that the world is a crueler place than we dare to admit. Since the poor confront us with this evil, it is tempting to avoid them. But if we let their stories break our hearts, they can open our eyes to marvels we scarcely dared imagine. They reveal the revolution of love that God is bringing about in the world.

There is a lot of dying going on, but a lot of rising as well. That is the deepest meaning of history and of our lives. But we perceive the daily resurrections only if we open our eyes to the crucifixions. To share the hope of the poor, we must let their suffering move us and place us before the Holy Mystery laboring among us.

CONCLUSION: A WORLD CHARGED WITH GOD

As we have seen, Ignatius calls the Spirit by other names, especially in early and published writings. Some detect veiled references in this Contemplation. Its title, the first preliminary note [230], and the first point (including the prayer "Take and Receive") speak of love, gifts (including self-gift), and sharing (*communio*), applying these expressions to God. These same words—Love, Gift, *Communio*— have been used to identify the Holy Spirit since the time of Augustine.[12] The second point of the Contemplation recalls that God makes of us a temple, a clear reference to the Holy Spirit.

Once we recognize the Contemplation for Attaining Love as a Pentecost exercise, the overarching trinitarian structure of the Ignatian Exercises becomes clear, as José María Lera says: "The Father, in the loving divine design, traces the plan of creation (Principle and Foundation [23]). The Son realizes that plan and invites human beings to follow him (the central and most important section of the Exercises)." Finally, the Spirit realizes God's plan in and through us, making us "daughters and sons in the Son,...'loving [God] in all things and all things in [God]...'" (Contemplation for Attaining Love).[13] The Foundation reveals the Creator's plan; the subsequent Weeks reveal Christ; the Contemplation reveals the Spirit.

The Contemplation rounds out the Foundation. Whereas the latter states that we are created "to praise, reverence, and serve God" [23], the former specifies that this means to "to love and serve in everything" [233]. Whereas, according to the Foundation, we should use creatures only to the extent that they aid our salvation, the vision of the Contemplation is richer: We are to "love and serve *in everything"* out of gratitude, that is, love all creatures in God and love God who is working in all of them (cf. *Const* 288).

However, if the Contemplation is primarily about the Spirit, it is also eminently trinitarian. It invites us to perceive reality with new eyes, which is the work of the *Spirit* who guides into all truth (cf. John 16:13). What our new eyes see, however, is the *Creator* giving us all good things through the *Son.* Above all, it is through the Son that the

Father communicates the Spirit (God's self-gift) to us. We respond to God's gift by "loving and serving in everything" [233], filled with the Spirit who remakes us in the image of Christ. Like the Contemplation, these trinitarian formulae express the way a self-giving God *invades* reality—especially ourselves—and labors to transform it.

God presses upon us, permanently, inviting us to respond by habitually seeking out and acting on God's purpose. Prayer and contemplation are obviously integral to this vision of life, and doing without them would be an evasion of reality. On the other hand, we do not withdraw from the world of action in order to pray, since it is precisely in the world that God is to be found.

We now turn to the subject of prayer itself.

PRAYER

Ignatius of Loyola takes a revolutionary approach to prayer. Part 6 introduces contemplation and prayer in the Ignatian spirit.

While the best way to grow in prayer is just to do it, some orientation can be helpful and even necessary for praying well. We begin with some introductory thoughts on contemplation and prayer, including the model prayer Jesus taught his disciples. We will then review what the *Spiritual Exercises* teaches about prayer. Finally, we will discuss prayer for active people.

24 Introducing Prayer

Then Jacob woke from his sleep and said, "Surely Yahweh is in this place – and I did not know it!" (Gen. 28:16)

It is true that love is the one thing necessary. However, love is like a beautiful flower that thrives only under the right conditions, including soil, water, air, light, and protection. Love needs the right conditions to thrive. Among these are contemplation and prayer.

CONTEMPLATION

I have had the good fortune to have lived in communities, and in several countries, with people of cultures, races, and histories different from my own. Each time I entered a new place, everything seemed strange, sometimes very strange. Then, with time, I could begin to understand. Or so I thought. Only much later would I realize that I didn't really understand much at all! Things were actually much more complex than I had thought.

Life is like that. Reality is too rich to take in on the fly. On any given day we grasp only a fraction of what goes on. Large chunks of reality escape our notice. To some extent we live on the surface of life, with reality only partly in focus. Small wonder dozing disciples, napping bridesmaids, and negligent stewards proliferate in the gospels, along with calls to watch, stay awake, and pray! Watch, stay awake, and pray. We can reflect on that by parts. First, watch and stay awake (contemplation). Then, pray.

How do we awaken more, and stay awake? How can we grow steadily in understanding reality, in order to respond to it better? Earlier I proposed ten "touchstones," which boil down to three requirements. First, we need to let reality "get to us," especially the reality of suffering. Second, we need to undergo personal transformation and to discern interior movements. Third, we need the challenge and support of a wisdom-bearing community. In all that, I suggested, our lives should become a permanent rhythm of action-contemplation-action.

Here I mean contemplation in the broad sense, not sitting on a pillow and concentrating for hours at a time, however helpful that might be for some people sometimes. By contemplation, I mean paying close attention to reality and allowing the truth to sink in, penetrate us, and stir our feelings and thoughts. We need contemplation in this sense the way we need food, water, and recreation, the way we need to brush our teeth and practice other daily disciplines. Without it, we fall into one of those unreflective lives that is hardly worth living.

Contemplation in this broad sense is not quite the opposite of action. Rather, action and contemplation are complementary, overlapping poles of our existence. If we consider our entire lives as praxis (free, conscious activity), then action and contemplation are two forms of praxis.[1] Contemplation is not simply passive and receptive; it also assumes active forms [cf. 45–54, 199, 206]. When it becomes a habit, it seeps into action. Action then becomes more contemplative.

PRAYER

In the perspective of faith, contemplation stops short unless it engages the Holy Mystery at the heart of reality, a personal Mystery that addresses us and invites a response. Simply contemplating the world around us is often insufficient for discovering, and always insufficient for really knowing, the personal Heart-of-Reality that gently closes in on us from without and from within. For this we need the help of treasuries of wisdom to connect the empirical dots and extend the reach of our cognitive powers. So, besides contemplating reality itself, we also contemplate words of wisdom, especially scripture, which purifies, orients, supplements, and extends our knowledge, without replacing our cognitive powers or constraining their proper functioning. The Word of scripture takes us via the express lane into the heart of reality to encounter the Holy Mystery and the world around us in light of that Mystery.[2]

If we accept that God is present in and among us, how seriously do we take that presence? Even believers can prefer to do what they believe God wants without going to the considerable trouble of engaging God in prayer.

So maybe the first thing we need to ask in this prayer business is whether we take God seriously. For starters, I suggest considering that God is more real than the desk, the tree, the rain – more real than we are.

If God is real, then God is close, present – more present than the desk, more present than we are. It is not that the desk, tree, and rain are real and concrete and God is a kind of ghost lurking in or behind them. God is more concrete and more present than everything else.

And God is present as one who addresses us personally and invites us to intimate friendship and collaboration. If we take this seriously, then praying is realism. To ignore God, present and addressing us, would be evasion of reality.

Some people stall in prayer because it seems like talking on the phone to someone whom we cannot know, someone who never reveals his or her thoughts or feelings. It is pretty difficult to communicate under these conditions, to say nothing of developing a relationship! But this problem seems to arise from a misunderstanding.

An axiom as old as Moses teaches us that no image or concept can capture the reality of God. God is unlike any creature, and our cognitive powers are puny, and prejudiced to boot. While I believe this is true, we don't want to overdo it. According to the Contemplation for Arousing Love,[3] God communicates to us through the world. Every leaf and sunset speaks to us of God. God addresses us even more clearly through human beings, made in the divine image.

In the Christian view of things, we have a carpenter from Nazareth turned preacher and healer who discloses God more fully than anything or anyone else. Jesus is the wholly adequate Image of God. And we have a Spirit who struggles to disclose this God to us, and who, when we don't know how to pray, prays within us with sighs too deep for words (cf. Rom. 8:26). In that case, we need not worry about who is at the other end of the line. On this testimony, we can rest assured that our dialog partner is like Jesus, Someone of "steadfast lovingkindness," above all, who will not give a stone to children who ask for bread but will respond with compassion to sincerity and human weakness. That is what "covenant" is about—steady, reliable commitment.

Equally radical, perhaps, is the idea that in covenant and in prayer we do not take the initiative. God seeks us out from the beginning. Eventually, we may wake up to God knocking on our door. We then face the challenge of learning to cooperate with God's efforts to communicate.

Not that God is distant. The God of Christian faith is in immediate contact with us at all times, available twenty-four hours a day, on call. To say God is "Trinity" means that God is busy in the world. God is active self-giving love, "coming at us" as Creator in everything, as Christ who is one of us and as Spirit humanizing and divinizing us. If we want to accept the insistent offer of friendship of this "extroverted," immediately present God, we will, normally, communicate to our Friend what we are thinking and feeling and inquire what is on our Friend's mind.

At least now and then! Since life goes on, and since God calls to collaborative action, there is plenty to do besides pray. There are dishes to wash and repairs to be made. However, as in any intimate relationship, at some point in the day, we will want to sit down together and ask, "How are things going?" We will want to sort out the day together. There will be personal incidents to share and other issues to discuss, like how the Reign of God is faring at work or in the Middle East. As in other intimate relationships, some days we will spend more time together, some less, depending on our need and pressing demands.

Prayer, then, is a normal part of a life of discerning and doing the most loving thing. If we persevere at that kind of life, in time not only will prayer likely be about action, but contemplation will seep into action, making all of life a "dancing with God." We become "contemplatives in action." And, since God calls many friends and collaborators, we will want community prayer to nourish our vision and commitment.

In short, contemplation and prayer are necessary for a full life. It is true that love is the one thing necessary and that we love God by loving our neighbor. But that does not make prayer dispensable any more than eating, breathing, and bathing are dispensable. All of these are necessary acts of love. If we go without them even for a short time, love of neighbor can suffer considerably! In the same way, serious commitment to our neighbor cannot survive for long without prayer. Although the effects might not appear right away, we can say about prayer what the great Pablo Casals is reported to have said about practicing cello: "If I fail to practice one day, God notices. If I fail to practice two days, I notice. If I fail to practice three days, the audience notices."

What does prayer look like in practice? When his disciples asked about that, Jesus taught them a prayer.

"THE PRAYER THAT JESUS TAUGHT US"

> *He was praying in a certain place, and after he had finished, one of his disciples said to him, "Lord, teach us to pray, as John taught his disciples."* (Luke 11:1)

Jesus taught his disciples the "Our Father." More than a formula, it contains the key elements of good prayer. The theme of this prayer and all prayer is twofold: (1) that God's will (the "Kingdom") be done and (2) that our basic needs be met—nourishment, forgiveness, and protection against falling away.

Luke's version of the prayer is more primitive. Matthew's additions appear below in brackets:

> [Our] Father [in heaven],
> hallowed be your name.
> Your kingdom come,
> your will be done [on earth as it is in heaven].
> Give us this (or each) day our daily bread;
> and forgive us our sins [Matthew: "debts"]
> as we ourselves [have] forgive[n] everyone indebted to us.
> And do not bring us into temptation,
> [but deliver us from evil (or, the Evil One)].
> (Luke 11:1–4; Matt. 6:9–13)

Our Father. This prayer is communal ("our," "us," "we") even when prayed "in secret," as Jesus prayed and recommended that others pray (Matt. 6:6).

While it is legitimate to address God as Mother and in other ways, Jesus' invitation to call God Father is revolutionary good news. He means that his disciples form a family of sisters and brothers (and mothers). The new family is to have no patriarchal earthly fathers.[4] Jesus' Father is different — caring and life-giving, practically maternal. We are to address God as *Abbá* the way Jews addressed their fathers in trust and freedom.[5] Paul says that we are no longer slaves but sons and daughters of the Head of the household and therefore heirs to the farm, that is, to the world (cf. Gal. 4:6–7; Rom. 4:13). This is as if, today, we had passed from being stock clerks in the basement to being the children of the CEO and heirs to the firm. We now go to the top floor of company headquarters without an appointment. We breeze in to see our father whenever we please. "We have access to God in boldness and confidence" (Eph. 3:12; cf. Heb. 4:16; 10:19).

In heaven expresses God's transcendence. Not that God is outside the universe, but that God is not another entity. God is at the heart of reality as the source of all that is and all goodness.

Hallowed be your name means "may all people recognize your goodness and holiness." This expresses reverence and praise. According to the Ignatian Foundation, we are created to "praise, reverence, and serve God" [23]. These words indicate different ways of loving God. Praise and reverence, which are not widely valued in modern society, humanize us, as Etty Hillesum discovered while a graduate student in her twenties. She wrote in her journal:

> *Good Friday morning, 8:30 [1942].*... Something I have been wanting to write down for days, perhaps for weeks, but which a sort of shyness — or perhaps false shame? — has prevented me from putting into words. A desire to kneel down sometimes pulses through my body, or rather it is as if my body had been meant and made for the act of kneeling. Sometimes, in moments of deep gratitude, kneeling down becomes an overwhelming urge, head deeply bowed, hands before my face.[6]

Etty was surprised by the urge to kneel before the Mystery that was taking hold of her life. Falling to her knees, she experienced the consolation that comes when we discover part of our true self.

Praise and reverence are salutary acts of gratitude in a society that takes life's blessings for granted. (On prayer of thanks, see 2 Cor. 1:11; Col. 2:7; 3:17; 4:2; and 1 Thess. 5:8.) While it is infantile to multiply words when asking for something (cf. Matt. 6:7), the same rule does not apply to multiplying expressions of love and praise, as every lover and poet knows — provided the words come from the heart. This is what we do in song, litanies, rosaries, mantras, and similar repetitive prayers. (At least it should be.)

The remainder of the Lord's prayer is a series of petitions. *Your kingdom come, your will be done on earth....* This is the principal and all-encompassing petition. We don't ask for just anything — to win beauty contests or to beat out the business competition — but that God's Reign come, with its justice, peace, and abundant life. All petitions should fit under that umbrella.

It is striking how much prayer of petition we find in the Bible, especially in the New Testament. "So I say to you, Ask, and it will be given to you; search and you will find; knock, and the door will be opened for you" (Luke 11:9). "Very truly, I tell you, if you ask anything of the Father in my name, he will give it to you.... Ask and you will receive" (John 16:23–24).[7] In the *Spiritual Exercises* prayer of petition (the "grace" and the colloquies) gives direction to every prayer exercise. In the *Constitutions,* where Ignatius outlines the life of active apostles, prayer is almost exclusively petition for individuals, decisions and missions.[8]

Prayer of petition presents difficulties today. To some, it can seem a bit vulgar, even selfish, perhaps a beginner's way of praying that we should outgrow in favor of something more sublime. Also, it is difficult to see how it "works." For one thing, we find it uncomfortable to think of God listening to our prayers and then intervening in the world in a magical or miraculous way. For another, prayer of petition frequently seems to fail. Good people pray for good things, and then nothing seems to happen.

As for the first objection, if God is the source of all we are and have, we never outgrow our absolute need for God. Rightly understood, dependence on God is unlike any other. Because it is of God's nature to create freedom, the more dependent on God we become, the more free and mature we become.

Nor does divine action supplant or compete with ours. As Basque philosopher Xavier Zubiri says, "God's movement is not a second movement added to my own." Rather God works in and through me. Therefore, to ask God's help "is not to ask assistance from someone who is outside and whom one requests to draw near to help . . . [but] to ask that God intensify God's own activity within us."[9] Here Zubiri gives us a happy paraphrase of the Lord's Prayer: May God's Kingdom come ("intensify") in us and among us!

This is not to pray for a magical or strictly miraculous action that violates nature's laws, even if God might well work that way. We have more – really abundant – evidence of what I prefer to call surprises that are disproportionate to apparent causes: accelerated healing processes, telepathic communication, extraordinary coincidences, and even sudden social changes that, like the draft of fish in the gospels, point to an intensification of God's work that we need not explain as exceptions to nature's ways – especially in a post-Einsteinian universe.

I recently asked a group of forty people in Chalatenango, El Salvador, how many had personally experienced such disproportionate surprises, which they could only attribute to God, or had heard testimonies about such phenomena which they could not reasonably doubt. Then I asked how many were present among us that day "by pure miracle of God" who had rescued them during the civil war in the eighties. Practically everyone in the group fell into one of these categories!

God's surprises exhibit the continuity, discontinuity, and reversal of Jesus' own resurrection.[10] Faith perceives creation bursting its bonds and entering into the liberty of God's children (cf. Rom. 8:21).

But why does prayer sometimes go unanswered? According to the letter of James (4:3), one reason is that people seek self-gratification rather than God's Reign. But why does persistent prayer for healing and for peace also seem to go unanswered? Faith can only respond that, while the visible results of prayer may disappoint us, God's faithful love invites us to trust that, whenever genuine faith is present, God works real change in and among us, even if we cannot perceive this clearly.

Give us each day our daily bread. The second half of Jesus' prayer asks for help in facing three challenges of daily life: material needs, social offenses, and moral temptation. What could be more basic?

The petition for daily bread asks God to supply our material needs, one day at a time. This is not only a prayer for poor people who lack refrigeration (and must find bread every day). It is also for moderns who exchange dependence on one another and on God for a spurious self-sufficiency, only to find ourselves dependent on capital and technology to ensure bread (and Scotch!) far into the future. Like his multiplication of loaves, Jesus' prayer suggests that if we would concentrate more on sharing ("seek first God's Reign and its justice") than on producing and hoarding, we would all have daily bread, and fewer worries as well (cf. Matt. 6:33–34).

Forgive us our sins just as we forgive those who are indebted to us. We ask God's forgiveness, aware that we must forgive others in the same way (Matt. 5:14–15). In Jesus' native Aramaic, "debt" and "sin" are the same word, and so are "debtor" and "sinner." Sin makes us debtors of God and neighbor. Luke's version, especially, may refer to material debts as well as sin: "Forgive us our sins as we forgive everyone indebted to us."

And lead us not into temptation, but deliver us from evil. The first half of this couplet means, "Do not let us succumb to trial and so abandon you." It may refer to extreme trials, like that of Job or the great testing which must precede final victory (Mark 13:14–20, 24; 1 Pet. 4:12; etc.). Others read simply, "Help us through our trials!"

While Jesus' prayer contains the basic elements of all prayer, it is not the only prayer. Since prayer is highly personal and we pray in all kinds of circumstances, prayer assumes an endless variety of forms.

VARIETY

Prayer can be silent or vocal, sung or spoken, whispered or shouted. We can pray with formulas (like the psalms) or without them. We can pray alone or with others. If with others, prayer can be formal and "high," as in the church's liturgy, or informal and "low," as in popular piety. We can kneel, stand, or sit; we can dance or express ourselves through other gestures.

In prayer we use our senses (eyes, ears, touch): we feel, imagine, desire, remember, understand, ponder, evaluate, decide.

We can experience and express the gamut of emotions: pleasure and joy, sorrow, trust, gratitude, regret, hope and longing, love, indignation, frustration, weariness, boredom, resignation, awe, amazement. We can express ourselves in praise, thanksgiving, petition, lament, complaint, contrition, declaration, and promise.

Just as when we communicate with other people, with God we do well to listen as much, or more, than we talk. And, as lovers find with each other, we sometimes find it enough with God just to be together, doing nothing special.

The subject of prayer can vary greatly. We can pray over the world with its joys and sufferings (my day, the family, our neighborhood, the Middle East). Or, we can pray over the *word* about reality, especially the Word of God. Third, we can also attend to our internal word. Finally, we can focus directly on God.

When it comes to prayer, one size does not fit all. What "works" for Fran may not do much for Terry, at least not now. What worked well last year might not this year. What was good in my twenties will give way to something else in my thirties. The kind of prayer depends on our personality, our mood, our health, and the situation.

The important thing is to try something, notice what helps, be constant at daily prayer, and seek wise counsel. Learning to pray is a little like learning a language or a sport. How do we know what works? In general, we stay with *what brings consolation and produces effective love.*

Ignatius of Loyola was one of the great masters of prayer. The next chapter gathers what he says about prayer in the *Spiritual Exercises.* However, that doctrine serves only as a point of departure for prayer in the Ignatian spirit. What is most novel and characteristic in Ignatius's approach is the way he relates prayer to daily life.

School of Prayer 25

In the morning, while it was still very dark, he got up and went out to a deserted place, and there he prayed. (Mark 1:35)

When it comes to prayer, Ignatius presents a paradox. Though he was a great mystic and teacher of prayer, he was suspicious of people who spent long hours praying. Apart from the *Spiritual Exercises,* he left few writings on prayer. In fact, few of the "methods" of prayer in the *Exercises* originated with him. Still, he was a revolutionary, breaking with the monastic ideal of prayer and insisting on integrating prayer and action. His style is especially suited to people leading busy lives.

Prayer in the Ignatian spirit meshes with daily life. Above all, it focuses on discernment with God: evaluating past events, present situations, and future possibilities. It is also prayer of petition concerned with the mission.

Here I will present some fundamental principles of prayer in the Ignatian spirit and summarize the methods proposed by the *Exercises* for prayer. Since prayer in a retreat differs from prayer in everyday life, "The Exercises are essentially a point of departure."[1] Still, much of what Ignatius says about prayer in the *Exercises* can be adapted for prayer in daily life.

SOME BASICS

Ends and Means. The purpose of prayer is to grow in effective love of God. So in prayer we seek devotion — that is, the consolation that draws us to deeper union with God — the better to love and serve in everything we do.

All the means of prayer, including the amount of time, the hour of day or night, the place, posture, subject matter, and order, should serve this end. The means vary, depending on individuals and circumstances. Ignatius roundly criticized those "masters" who imposed their own way of praying on others.[2] For God guides each one of us along a path suited to our individual needs. To discover that path, it often helps to try different kinds of prayer [89]. Ignatius wrote to Francisco Borja,

> That level [of prayer] is best for each individual, in which God our Lord communicates himself more . . . , because God sees and knows what is most suitable for the person and . . . shows him [or her] the way. For our part, in order to find that way with God's aid, it helps a great deal to seek and try out many different ways [of prayer], in order to walk by the way most clearly indicated and the happiest and most blessed way for the person.[3]

Follow the consolation. How can we recognize our way? Basically, we *follow the consolation* (discreetly, as the Rules for Discernment explain).[4] The main thing is to notice what helps us find God, what brings devotion and consolation. Ignatius suggests entering prayer

> at times kneeling, at times sitting, at times lying on my back, at times standing, always pursuing what I want. We need to notice two things: The first is that if I find what I want while kneeling, I won't change my position; and if lying down, the same thing; and so on. Second, on the subject matter where I find what I want, I will rest there without anxiousness to move on until I am satisfied. [76]

Through consolation, the Spirit nudges us forward. We want the subject of prayer to stir our feelings and move our will — and eventually our hands and feet. In prayer, we collaborate with God, who frees us by enlisting our "loves" in generous service.[5]

As Teresa of Avila said, we do not go to prayer to know much but to love much. Nevertheless, understanding is also an objective of prayer, and thinking is part of prayer — more for some than for others. However, we need not be anxious about "covering ground" in prayer, since "it is not much knowledge that fills and satisfies the soul, but sensing and savoring things internally" [2].

PRAYER IN THE SPIRITUAL EXERCISES

According to an old Jesuit joke, you can't smoke while you pray; but it's okay to pray while you smoke! Of course, we can pray anywhere at any time—on the corner, on a bus, in an elevator. However, we also need to set aside time just for prayer, that is, for formal prayer. Many people find it helpful to have a special time, or times, for this each day, and even a special place.

The subject matter of the prayer could be (1) a personal issue or something in the news ("reality") or (2) a text, especially from scripture. For longer periods of prayer, Ignatius divides the subject matter into three or more "points" to ponder.

When entering into prayer, he recommends that, after asking God's help to pray well, we focus our imagination on a scene related to the subject matter and then ask God for what we want (see the boxed text "Helps to Prayer"). For example, in the prayer we might want to know and love Christ better in order to follow him more closely [48, 104]; or we might want guidance in facing some challenge during the day that is beginning, or peace in time of war or health for sick friends.

Conversation is the heart of prayer. Although in the *Exercises* Ignatius suggests conversing with God toward the end, conversing is appropriate any time it brings the fruit we are seeking. We converse "as one friend speaks to another, or as a servant to one's master" [54; cf. 199], that is, with the freedom and confidence of God's children, on the one hand, and with reverence, on the other. We express our feelings and desires and we listen to God. Conversation can also be just looking, just "being there," as lovers are accustomed to enjoy each other's presence.

Meditation and contemplation. In the *Exercises,* Ignatius distinguishes between discursive meditation and imaginative contemplation. In the former we think more; we remember, ponder, strive to understand. The meditations of the First Week [50–64] and the Two Standards [136–47] are examples of this kind of prayer. We would meditate over a passage in Paul's letter to the Romans in this way.

HELPS TO PRAYER

God is the first actor in prayer. Though our response should be wholehearted, we should avoid strain and excessive concern for technique. As a wise guide once told me, the soul has no muscles. Still, there are many things we can do to enter better into prayer. Ignatius recommends pausing briefly before prayer to consider with whom we are about to converse and how God loves us [75]. We then ask God to direct our prayer to the single goal of love and service [46, 49; cf. 23].

Next, we recall what we intend to pray about. It might be a crisis at work or a passage from scripture. Then we picture an image that can help focus our imagination on the subject of the prayer: Christ, a person we want to pray for, the gospel scene we want to contemplate, etc. [47]. Next we ask God for what we want in the prayer. Finally, Ignatius recommends ending formal prayer time with a vocal prayer like the Our Father.

In our busy, noisy times, many people feel the need to spend a few moments just calming down, centering themselves, as they begin prayer. Relaxation techniques can help. These frequently involve concentration — which, paradoxically, relaxes and recollects us.[6]

Ignatius suggests a few remote preparations for prayer, especially in a retreat. If we pray in the morning, it helps to review the subject matter the night before, for example, reading the passage we plan to pray about, and to recall the subject matter again just before falling asleep. On waking in the morning, it helps to recall the subject matter before other worries crowd in on us [73–74]. Many people prefer to pray when they get up in the morning, because it is a quiet time for focusing.

For Ignatius, "contemplation" means imaginatively re-creating a scene from the gospels or some other story, reliving it in our imagination and reflecting on it. (I have been using "contemplation" in a wider sense here; Ignatius himself broadens its scope in the Contemplation for Attaining Love [230–37].) In the contemplations of the Second, Third, and Fourth Weeks, we allow the story to unfold in our imagination like a film, even giving ourselves a bit part. We enter into a story like that of Christ's birth, considering above all the people involved: we (1) observe them, (2) listen to what they say, and (3) note what they do (not necessarily in that order), reflecting on what promises to bear fruit [110–17].[7] Ignatius recommends three additional points, or perspectives, when contemplating Christ's passion: notice what Christ suffers, how his glory is hidden in that suffering and how he suffers for our sins [195–97]. When contemplating an appearance of Christ risen, besides the first three points, he suggests two more: consider how Christ's glory is now revealed and how he consoles his despondent followers [223, 224].

Repetitions. In the course of a retreat day, with its four or five hour-long exercises, Ignatius recommends for the afternoon "repetitions" of the morning exercises. The repetitions require less effort on our part. In them, we repeat the earlier exercises, "pausing [only] on those points where [we] felt greater consolation or desolation or greater spiritual feeling" [62], that is, passing over the dry spots of the earlier exercises.

For example, you may have meditated in the morning on the Beatitudes of Matthew (Matt. 5:1–12). Two or three beatitudes moved you or enlightened you. Or maybe you felt challenged or irritated by "Blessed are the sorrowful." In the afternoon repetition, you pause to consider those two or three beatitudes. That is most likely where the "action" is for you, either the action of the enemy or of the Spirit, or both. Those beatitudes surface areas of resistance or areas of growth for you to consider. In a repetition we take note of earlier desolation and seek to understand it, but we avoid getting pulled into its vortex [cf. 318].

The principle behind the repetitions applies outside the retreat. The idea is to take note of interior movements, especially in prayer, and

HOLISTIC SPIRITUALITY

Although "bringing the senses to bear" can take a simple elementary form, it is not necessarily an inferior form of prayer. By allowing God's Word to shape our senses, feelings, and imagination, this exercise helps reintegrate our scattered self.

Prayer moves our feelings, that is, the appetites of bodily sensibility, so that they will incline the will and the intellect toward what is good. Imagination plays a key role in this. By fashioning symbols that are at once sensible and universal, our imagination can make concrete reality present to our understanding, bridging senses and feelings, on the one hand, and intellect and will, on the other. In this capacity, imagination cooperates with God's Spirit, reintegrating senses, emotions, will, and reason — which otherwise operate on their own, in an uncoordinated way — so that even now we are becoming that spiritual body (body transfigured by the Spirit) which we shall one day fully be (cf. 1 Cor. 15:44).

The imagination can produce narcissistic fantasy, however. In "bringing the senses to bear" on the subject of prayer, the interior senses savor liberating symbols, especially the

later return to what occasioned them, in order to learn what they have to teach us.

Application of the Senses. The last hour-long exercise of the retreat day is the "Application of the Senses," literally, "bringing the senses to bear" on the subject of an earlier prayer [66–71, 121–26, 133, 227]. This involves using the imagination to "see," "hear," "feel," "taste," "touch" and "smell" the material prayed over earlier and, as always, to reflect and seek devotion. This is praying with the interior senses, which include not only interior sight but all the senses.

biblical symbols of the Reign of God and the anti-reign.[8] The Spiritual Exercises bring the senses to bear on Jesus above all. He in turn invites us to imagine and sense life-giving water, bread, the wedding-feast, a sower, his seed, a dragnet, a prodigal son. Through these symbols, the Spirit works to integrate us and unite us to God.

"Bringing the senses to bear" illustrates the holistic character of Ignatian spirituality, which engages the senses, feelings, body, imagination, intellect and will and unites contemplation with action.

Commenting on the application of the senses, Hugo Rahner writes: "As Ignatius and his earliest disciples never tired of emphasizing, there is no such thing as a technique of meditation for its own sake, since genuine meditation is only possible when a person is also prepared to put what he has contemplated into action. *Intelligo ut faciam*—I understand in order that I may act. But the ideas formed in the mind alone must be made to touch the heart before action is possible: and this synthesis of mind and heart takes place precisely in the Application of the Senses, which, because it affects body and soul together, is the most delicate and sensitive form of prayer."[9]

Like the repetition, applying the senses is a less taxing prayer for later in the retreat day. With both types, prayer becomes simpler, involving less thought.

This kind of prayer can be appropriate when we are tired. Prayer using the imagination or the senses is generally more restful and regenerative than discursive meditation. Writing to Teresa Rejadell, Ignatius recommended restful forms of prayer and even "pious recreation, letting the understanding roam where it will, over good or [morally] indifferent things, avoiding only bad things."[10]

DIFFICULT PRAYER

At times prayer can be a difficult desert-like experience. It can resemble conversing with a person who strikes us as dull. When conversing with poor, sick, or mentally and emotionally handicapped people, it sometimes takes patience to discover the riches hidden under layers of poverty, including our own, and the scars left by life's hard knocks.[11] "Inside each person there is a giant scratching to get out," someone once said. Dealing with God can be like that. This shouldn't surprise us, since God hides precisely in such places. Just as we sometimes need faith, imagination, and patience to uncover the riches of people who might not attract us at first, we need these virtues to find God, who labors to overcome our resistance and insensitivity in both cases.

Prayer is no less valuable when God seems absent. Though we might feel little warmth while visiting a sick friend or someone in prison, that doesn't make our care less genuine or our visit less valuable. Since delight and consolation are not essential to good prayer, their absence should not discourage us. Difficult prayer may be more genuine than easy prayer.

It is normal to pass through crises of growth in prayer, like the "dark nights" that John of the Cross describes. Some believe periods of dry prayer can signal the beginning of deeper union with God.[12] Most experienced teachers tell us that prayer tends to simplify over the years. However, Ignatius showed little interest in specifying stages of growth in prayer. Such schemas may have less relevance for assessing the prayer of active people. As Joan Scott says, development in prayer "will happen without our keeping looking at the map."[13]

CONCLUSION

The Spiritual Exercises are a wonderful school of prayer. But, like any good school, they prepare for life. They ready us to find God in the world in the midst of activity. With their many responsibilities, parents, laborers, and community workers rarely find time for retreats or lengthy formal prayer. My friend George prays while contemplating passengers on the New York subway. My co-worker Mayra rises at 5:00 a.m. and spends three to four hours commuting each day, returning home at night to cook supper for her family. She has no alternative but to find God on a crowded bus bumping through traffic. Our final chapter discusses the prayer of busy people like them.

26 Worldly Prayer

Pray without ceasing.
(1 Thess. 5:17)

BEYOND THE MONASTIC IDEAL

Ignatius urged others to seek and find God in all things, as "contemplatives in action."[1] He prized familiarity and ease in conversing with God.[2] What he had in mind was revolutionary in his time and it remains so today.

For most of the last two thousand years, Christians have measured their prayer against the monastic ideal, and a false monastic ideal at that. The early Fathers of the Church and the medieval theologians consistently presented the contemplative life (Mary) as superior to the active life (Martha). Although the contemplative vocation was not for everyone, it was held up as the standard by which all could measure their lives and their prayer: I may not be called to be a nun or monk, but I can strive to approach that ideal by withdrawing from secular concerns at times and particularly in prayer. I cannot devote myself to long hours of prayer in solitude, but the more time I can dedicate to this kind of prayer the better. Here monasticism itself is distorted: the ideal proposed is not simply to seek God in community, prayer and silence, but by withdrawing from all worldly concerns.

In Ignatius's day, too, masters of the spiritual life proposed prayer as the privileged, even exclusive means of union with God, and monastic prayer as the ideal form of prayer. Ignatius broke with this weighty tradition.[3] For him, solitude and lengthy prayer is not the chief standard by which to evaluate our prayer, nor is prayer always the preferred means to union with God.

Some people are called to more prayer than others, and even to lengthy prayer. At times we all need to get away and pray for longer periods. For most people, however, that is neither possible nor desirable as a frequent practice. For parents, laborers, and community workers, lengthy daily prayer would require neglecting important responsibilities. If God calls us to such tasks, then God must want us to pray in ways that will help us fulfill them, not undermine them. While busy people can learn much from others who pray for long stretches, they need not imitate them in order to pray as they ought and be just as united to God.

Few are tempted to excess in prayer these days. Instead, we need to recall how much we need it. But proposing the monastic ideal to people who do not have that vocation is a sure-fire way to quash interest in prayer. And for those who need an excuse not to pray, nothing serves like an impossible ideal.

UNITED WITH GOD IN THE PRAXIS OF LOVE

> *"Those who love me will keep my word, and my Father will love them, and we will come to them and make our home with them."* (John 14:23)

Contemplativus in actione, yes. But a more exact formulation of what Ignatius had in mind would be *united to God in seeking and doing God's will.*[4] We are united to God not by prayer as such but by seeking and doing what God wants. Sometimes this means praying. More often it means some other kind of activity. "A Jesuit told Ignatius that he found God primarily in solitude and by meditating or praying privately. Ignatius responded, 'What do you mean? Do you draw no profit from helping your neighbor? For this is our practice.' "[5]

An administrator of the Jesuit College of Coimbra in Portugal, Manuel Godinho, was deeply troubled. Providing for the material needs of the school community engrossed him in details and conflicts that he considered distractions impeding his spiritual growth. Ignatius wrote to him with affection, assuring him that accepting such distractions in order to serve God actually united him to God. "For the distractions which you accept for his greater service, in conformity with his divine will interpreted to you by obedience, can be not only the equivalent of the union and recollection of uninterrupted contemplation, but even more acceptable to him, proceeding as they do from a more active and vigorous charity."[6]

For Ignatius, if we are seeking to do God's will, we are no less united to God in busy confusion than in formal prayer. We need be no less united to God washing the dishes than when at the Eucharist. If possible, we should find no less devotion in driving the school bus than in prayer.[7] "Whatever you do, in word or deed, do everything in the name of the Lord Jesus Christ giving thanks to God the Father through him" (Col. 3:17). When we habitually seek to do the most loving thing, our whole life is a pleasing offering to God (cf. Rom. 12:1–2).

How many millions of laborers and domestic workers, how many poor and unlettered people untrained in formal prayer, experience union with God like this? God is present to them, "mortified" as they are by poverty and the struggle to fulfill their daily responsibilities.

When we serve God habitually, everything we do becomes a kind of prayer. Thomas Aquinas applied the term "prayer" in this broad sense: "As long as one is acting in one's heart, speech, or work in such a way as to tend towards God, one is praying. One who is directing one's whole life towards God is praying always."[8]

As contemplation suffuses action, we are "praying always" (cf. Luke 18:1; 1 Thess. 5:17). Ignatius wrote: "In the midst of actions and studies, the mind can be lifted to God, and by means of this directing everything to the divine service, everything is prayer."[9] This is a gift which nonetheless requires our collaboration. For one thing, praying informally, or "always," presupposes praying formally, that is, setting aside some time for prayer in the strict sense. "I recognize the truth in the old axiom 'To work is to pray,' " writes theologian Walter Burghardt, "but to make work your only prayer is to risk spiritual shipwreck."[10]

Praying (formally) is not an escape from everyday responsibilities, however. It should flow out of action and lead to action, each nourishing the other. "Meditation and contemplation would seem to be wasted," wrote Jerónimo Nadal, "if they do not issue in petition and some devout desire—and ultimately in some action."[11]

More fundamentally, finding God in all things depends on seeking God in all things, above all seeking and doing God's will. It is not possible to be a Christian contemplative in just any kind of action. In our spreading materialist wasteland, more and more people thirst for contemplation, including political wheeler-dealers, tycoons, and military top brass, stressed out by the rigors of their professions. Are we to suppose that everyone doing deep-breathing on a meditation pillow is communing with the God of Christians? Not necessarily. What unites us to God is the practice of love. If prayer, or any other religious act, is not grounded in that, it is an offense to God.[12] God becomes present in the self-giving love [cf. 230–31] of which Jesus is the best example. When we act as he did, God is united to us and acts in us. As Ignacio Ellacuría said, following him today means being a contemplative in action for justice, united to God in the struggle for a more just world.[13]

DISTRACTIONS AND RECOLLECTION

Jesus looked up to heaven and said, "... I am not asking you to take them out of the world, but to protect them from the evil one." (John 17:15)

Since distractions can undermine prayer, it is important to put worries and obsessive concerns aside as much as possible. That can even permit us to deal with those same concerns later with better perspective. It also keeps desolation at bay [cf. 319]. Nevertheless, sometimes "distractions" are really invitations to make our prayer more real. By giving them a trial welcome, we can discover whether they lead to consolation and fruitful action or not. Praying about real problems can make prayer more turbulent or even painful. But that does not make it shallower. It makes prayer more real. Christians (including those in monasteries) bring the world, with all its joy and anguish, into their prayer. What is more fitting than bringing our daily cares and activity before God and asking for guidance?[14]

Perhaps we need to rethink recollection. Traditional teaching has rightly stressed its importance for prayer. Recollection means being able to focus our minds and hearts on the subject matter of prayer to the exclusion of other things. Calming down and centering certainly helps enter into prayer better. This is short-term recollection. It is even more important, however, to cultivate a deeper, habitual recollection. This means having our minds and hearts habitually focused on things that really matter, like the well-being of those around us and the life-and-death issues of war and peace, unemployment and environmental crisis.

While short-term recollection is helpful for prayer, it is no substitute for this more basic habitual recollection. A retreat, a monastic setting, or a summer in the country can provide conditions for avoiding distractions and interruptions in prayer. It is helpful to pray in a peaceful climate, especially when facing major challenges. But prayer need be no less genuine or profound outside such settings!

The praxis of discipleship – truth-telling, defending the weak, and challenging injustice – generates conflict and inner turmoil, but also peace at a deeper level. I can be as calm as you please meditating at pool-side and be out of touch with reality and with God. On the other hand, my head might be throbbing and my nerves jangling from a tense morning of crisis intervention in the rehab center. In the midst of it all, I may offer a silent prayer or step back for a few minutes of discernment, stressed out though I may be. For all my inner turbulence, my prayer need be no less genuine, no less profound, than that of a monk engrossed at Mass. If I am recollected at the deeper level of the Foundation, my stuttering prayer will arise from there, where I am habitually in touch with reality and with God. The peace of the hot tub has little to do with the peace that the world cannot give.

By all means, let us get centered for prayer and seek out quiet conditions when we can. Let us recognize our periodic need to get away for longer periods of solitude. But let us not confuse this with the ideal form of prayer. When all is said and done, a brief prayer in which we struggle to discover the more loving thing to do is far preferable to a serene and lengthy prayer that shields us from the harsh demands of love. The best preparation for prayer is to let the world's crosses break our hearts, and then respond. That can lead us into the noisiest neighborhoods and the most upsetting situations – but also into the deepest prayer.[15]

This is good news for busy people and for poor people in noisy apartments, with long bus rides and tedious jobs. How many of them actually lead lives of deep prayer, perhaps unconsciously? Probably many more than we usually suppose.

QUALITY AND QUANTITY

> *When you are praying, do not heap up empty phrases as the Gentiles do; for they think that they will be heard because of their many words.* (Matt. 6:7)

How long should busy people pray? Each one must decide for himself or herself. More prayer is not automatically better. Writing to Borja, who spent long hours in prayer, Ignatius recommended that he cut his prayer and penance in half, observing tactfully that "there is greater virtue for the soul and greater grace to be able to delight in its Lord in a variety of tasks and in a variety of places than in only one." On another occasion he wrote:

> It would be good to realize that not only when they pray do human beings serve God, for if that were so, our prayers would fall short if they were less than twenty-four hours a day, if that were possible for us, since everyone should be given over to God as completely as possible. But in fact at times God is served more by other things than by prayer, and so much so that God is pleased that prayer be omitted entirely for these things, and much more that it be shortened.[16]

Since students need to expend most of their mental energy on studies, Ignatius strictly limited the time Jesuit students devoted to formal prayer. Outside that time, he advised them to "practice seeking the presence of our Lord in all things, in conversations with someone, walking, seeing, tasting, hearing, understanding and in everything they might do." This practice of "finding God in all things" is less taxing than "lifting ourselves up to more abstract divine matters." It can also occasion "great visitations from the Lord, even in a brief prayer."[17] This kind of prayer is familiar from the Contemplation for Attaining Love.[18] Ignatius urged students to offer God their studies and other labors.

Ignatius's personal secretary wrote of him, "I notice that he rather approves the effort to find God in all things than that one should spend a long time in prayer."[19] He was wary of people who engaged in long hours of prayer. A close observer, Luis Gonçalves da Câmara, says that Ignatius used to comment that of one hundred persons given over to much prayer, ninety are deceived.[20] He knew from experience that long hours of prayer frequently camouflaged willfulness. However appropriate lengthy prayer might be at times, what is essential is readiness to do God's will. A person of inner freedom was a "mortified person" in the language of the day. Gonçalves observed, "When the Father [Ignatius] speaks of prayer, it seems he always presupposes the passions to be very much tamed and mortified, and he esteems that above all."[21]

In 1553, Jesuits in Spain complained to Ignatius's envoy, Nadal, that they were dedicating too little time to prayer, no more than an hour, and that they were embarrassed to tell others. On returning to Rome, Nadal proposed that Ignatius permit the Jesuits, or at least Jesuit students, to pray longer. Ignatius vehemently objected, adding that "for a truly mortified person, fifteen minutes is sufficient to be united with God in prayer" and that such a person will actually pray more in fifteen minutes than an unfree person in two hours.[22]

Ignatius praised prayer very highly, says Gonçalves, "above all that prayer in which one places God always before one's eyes." Though he spent hours in prayer himself, he was convinced that his own practice was no valid criterion for leading others in so personal a matter.[23]

The prayer of active people will often consist of brief periods of formal prayer during the day and of "finding God in all things."

THE INDISPENSABLE PRAYER

Friends, colleagues, and lovers communicate in many ways. So do believers and God. When people share an important project, like raising a family or a scientific enterprise, their communication will most often be about "How is it going?," "How are you/we doing?" That will be the heart of their communication and will serve as the minimum when time is scarce. The prayer called "examen" is like that.

For a long time the examen was the prayer that people schooled in Ignatian spirituality learned to hate because they were taught that it meant cataloguing their sins for a quarter of an hour. If couples and colleagues were to end each day like *that,* we would have to fear for their relationships and their projects. Today we can view the examen through a wider lens and appreciate better what Ignatius was driving at when he insisted that this was, for Jesuits at least, the indispensable prayer.[24] He himself reviewed his experience week by week, day by day, even hour by hour.[25]

Examen is that pause (or two or three) each day when we take stock of things. Examen means reviewing the day, or part of it, with God, assessing what has happened in order to do better in the future. God and I ask, How are we doing? How is it going? How can tomorrow be better?[26] When it comes to formal prayer, something like the examen would seem to be a necessary minimum.

Examen flows out of practice and back into it. If we are struggling with a moral problem, we will focus on that: Where did I slip up? Where was I in danger? What worked and what did not? [cf. 24–30]. If we are not struggling with a moral problem, then, in the examen we review our activities with special attention to consolation and desolation. Examen will be a privileged moment of that "dancing with God" in which we seek to discover where God is leading. In the examen, we step back to learn the "dance steps" of the day. Patterns of consolation and desolation (and other principles of discernment we have examined[27]) will suggest where God was present in events, where God was nudging and where we cooperated or resisted. Examen thus follows the logic of the Repetitions in the Exercises: we return to those places during the day where there were interior movements [cf. 62].

Besides reviewing our activity, the examen includes other elements as a matter of common sense and politeness. As we always greet a friend, the prayer begins with praise and thanksgiving. We ask for enlightenment in examining our activities; and, after that review, we express contrition and ask help for the future [cf. 43].

Examen in common can be especially fruitful for couples, friends, and co-workers.

Beyond that, we all need help in discerning what is going on in our lives. Call it spiritual accompaniment, guidance, or spiritual direction; we need someone with experience who will listen to us and give good feedback, helping us to avoid pitfalls and to sense where the Spirit is leading us.

CONCLUSION

It is good news for busy parents and workers that when we try to do what God wants we are united to God. Formal prayer should flow out of our daily responsibilities and help us to fulfill them better. Each of us must find the kind of formal prayer that draws us closer to God, including the restful types of prayer appropriate for busy people.

When we strive to love and serve as God desires, all of life becomes a prayer and an offering, and we learn, in the midst of our daily activity, to find God in all things.

The Penguin Is Real

Years ago, I took part in a study trip to Peru. It was my first encounter with mass poverty, the institutions that generate and manage it, and the serious efforts in progress to resist those evils, especially by people of faith. One morning that summer, while bumping through a coastal desert city in a crowded bus, I spotted a penguin waddling down the street! I could hardly believe my eyes. As we hurtled on, the penguin vanished from sight.

When I reported this vision to our group that evening, they laughed up a storm. A penguin *here*? No way! I began to think they must be right. After all, how could I be sure the black and white creature I had seen for only a few seconds was a penguin, especially here, in one of the world's driest deserts and not far from the equator?

The next day, having buried the memory of the penguin, I talked to Michael, who had been away the previous night. Michael informed me that he, too, had seen the penguin during the day. Was he kidding? No, he was not. Two of us had seen it. The penguin was real.

Ever since then, Michael and I have continued to remind each other, sometimes across vast continents and oceans, of the penguin of Chimbote, which became a symbol for us of that eye-opening, life-changing summer. In Peru we discovered fundamental truths about the world, about its suffering, and about hope that we will never forget. The penguin bonds us. It also reminds us that we need others in order to stick by our vision in a sometimes cynical world that smothers dreams and expects few surprises. Yes, a penguin in the desert. Yes, love is possible. A different world is possible.

If we were to trust the nightly news and the sitcoms, we might conclude that we are just lonely, violent creatures destined to spend our lives getting, spending, and bed-hopping. In this book, we have considered an alternative: On the one hand, things are far worse than they seem. On the other, they are far better. Sin abounds — but grace abounds even more. Whatever terrible things we have done, however cruel the world may be, healing and new beginnings are possible. We are not condemned to live behind cinder block and razor wire. If deep in our hearts we believe that justice will triumph some day, that is because it will. We are not alone in the universe. Something — Some One — is at work, transforming reality.

However, the world will change only if there are new human beings to change it, people who are free to love, to resist the lure of wealth, and to stand with the poor. That is the way of Jesus of Nazareth, whose Spirit guides us forward via consolation, teaches us to pray, fortifies us for trial, and discloses the divine goodness that shines forth in every thing and everyone. A new world is not only possible, it has already begun. The penguin is real.

Unfortunately, commitments once made with enthusiasm often stall out and even reverse direction over time. To "hang in there" requires discipline, and plenty of support. As I have said, love is like a delicate flower. It requires proper conditions to thrive. Over the years I have tried to cull from wise veterans what they think is necessary in order to persevere and produce lasting fruit over the long haul. The following checklist summarizes what I have learned:

- First, we need community. As Michael and I learned from the penguin, we need companions who share our vision. We need a community that can support and challenge us to stay faithful, that can nourish and deepen our alternative vision and praxis. That is what church should be.
- We need regular contact with poor and suffering people.
- We need daily prayer and contemplation.
- We need regular community worship.
- We need spiritual accompaniment, that is, regular recourse to someone to whom we can unburden ourselves and who can help us to avoid traps and make wise choices.
- We need a simple lifestyle.
- We need physical exercise and a moderate concern for our health.
- We need regular rest and recreation.

- We need study, especially of social reality.
- We need a sense of humor.

Honoring these needs can keep us responding to the Spirit, strong in the conviction that... the penguin is real! Despite setbacks and failings, a different world — of freedom, community, abundant life — is in the making.

Appendices

Appendix I (to Chapters 7 and 8)
The Kingdom Meditation?

According to William Peters, the Ignatian exercise traditionally called The Kingdom "is one of the most difficult for any [retreat] director to give, and it is probably the most difficult to understand."[1] In addition, the history of interpretation "shows no uniformity of opinion as regards the importance, place, and function of the exercise *Del Rey*. Neither is there uniformity of opinion as regards the interpretation of the exercise itself."[2] Peters may exaggerate, but the problem is real.

It is not even clear what the exercise should be called. St. Ignatius's "Autograph Directory" reads at the beginning (in Spanish): "The call of the temporal king helps to contemplate the life of the eternal King" [91]. This kind of descriptive title stands at the head of several exercises (cf. [45, 190, 218]). While Peters abbreviates the title to *"Del Rey,"* Santiago Arzubialde abbreviates it to "The Call."[3] Neither abbreviation follows automatically from the descriptive title but depends on what each writer considers the focal point of the exercise. The traditional title, "The Kingdom," is based on the 1548 Latin Vulgate version of the *Exercises,* which served as the standard Latin text until a new translation was published in 1835. The Vulgate inserts the title "The Contemplation of the Kingdom of Jesus Christ" at the beginning of the exercise. George Ganss defends this title, along with the abbreviation "The Kingdom," as reflecting Ignatius's mind, reminding us that he personally used this papally approved version from 1548 to 1556.[4]

So, what should the title be? More important, what is the exercise chiefly about: the cause (the Kingdom), the caller (the king), or the call itself?

The aim of the exercise is related to its place in the *Spiritual Exercises* as a whole. At least for the last 150 years, it has commonly been treated as one of two central meditations of the retreat, forming a binary together with the meditation on Two Standards [136–48]. The principal authority for this opinion is Ignatius's companion and official expositor, Jerónimo Nadal, who saw in this exercise and in the Two Standards meditation the nucleus of the Spiritual Exercises.[5] Peters holds, on the contrary, that "the exercise *Del Rey* is extremely low-keyed, and has a rather unobtrusive, perhaps even unimportant, place in the Spiritual Exercises." On occasion it might even be omitted.[6] Peters points out that the early directories (manuals written to guide the director of the Spiritual Exercises) specify that the exercise is to be given on a transitional rest day between the First and Second Weeks. It is to be repeated only once, with no other exercises prescribed for that day. In the autograph version, it is not designated as either a meditation or a contemplation. The retreatant is simply to "consider" the call, first of the temporal king, then of the eternal king—both presented in rather vague terms—

somewhat aseptically, as if from a distance.[7] "Consider" means just that, to ruminate over the themes presented.

Peters also objects to the way he believes the exercise has been used to pressure retreatants into making a premature commitment. This happens, he says, when one makes the Kingdom the focal point of the meditation, makes the meditation central to the Exercises as a whole, and overemphasizes the final self-offering of this exercise [98]. That leads directors to present the meditation in a semipelagian tone, that is, emphasizing the will-power and effort of the retreatant, and even in an aggressive, martial spirit. Peters considers this entirely foreign to Ignatius's intention. He further argues that militarist metaphors for the Christian life and mission were rare in Ignatius's writings and those of the Jesuits, in general, until the restoration of the Society of Jesus in the early nineteenth century.[8]

I believe the call, rather than the cause (the Reign of God) or the king (Christ), is the central focus of the exercise. Hence the title of this book's chapter 7, "The Call." I agree with Peters that the exercise presents the call, not as something to be experienced during the exercise itself, but as something to be anticipated in the future. Chapter 8 briefly explains the cause to which Christ calls: the "Reign of God." Ignatius presents this in the exercise on the Incarnation [101–9], which immediately follows "The Call." There Christ receives his mission, which he will then invite others to share. Christ himself, the one who calls, is the central focus of all the gospel contemplations of the second and subsequent weeks. It is in contemplating Christ (cf. chapter 9), especially in the Second Week, that one can expect to hear his call. I will now explain my reasons for interpreting "The Call" in this way and offer some comments on presenting the exercise today.

Arzubialde is surely correct to infer from Ignatius's long title that the *call* is the "meaning and finality" of the exercise.[9] The whole text points in that direction. The "grace" requested in the exercise should dispel any doubts: According to the Second Prelude, the exercise is guided by the petition not to be deaf to Christ's call but prompt and diligent in responding to it [91]. However, while the call is the main focus, the one who calls and the enterprise to which he calls are clearly essential elements as well.

The call is central to Ignatian spirituality as a whole. In the Exercises the theme recurs in the Two Standards meditation and throughout the Second Week. It underlies the whole idea of Ignatius's apostolic spirituality of laboring in the vineyard as Christ's companion.[10]

Today it is necessary to remove unnecessary obstacles to acceptance of this notion. First, contemporary individualism and the global crisis of authority militate against the very idea of discipleship. However attractive Christ may be, it is important to stress that his call is a personal invitation rather than a command from a distance: My own know my voice. I know them and they know me. I call each one by name (cf. John 10:3–4). Nor does Christ call slaves or drones but companions and friends (John 15:15). He comes not to be served, but to serve (Matt. 20:28).

Second, Christ does not summon people to an alien task but to the vocation which fulfills them as human beings (through the cross, to be sure). The idea of a vocation itself requires explanation today (cf. chapter 7), since most people do not think of their lives in such terms. They tend to view their future in terms of career, or lifestyle options. Forging a vocational identity can be especially problematic, due to the contradictory role models that confront people in today's rapidly changing, pluralistic, society. So vocation deserves emphasis.

Third, the call of Christ comes not as a harsh demand, but in the form of consolation attracting to generous service. This cannot be programmed or forced. In The Call, one only "considers" Christ's call in anticipation of actually experiencing it later. (The First Prelude invites the retreatant to "see with the eyes of the imagination" the places Christ visited [91]—only the places. Christ has not yet appeared on the scene.) Today, too, it is fitting to have people consider the call from a distance, in parable ("Consider something like this..."), without pressure for an immediate response, which people are rarely prepared to give. While contemplating Christ's life during the Second Week, most retreatants experience the call in the form of consolation attracting them toward him. Hence Ignatius's descriptive title: Considering "the call of the temporal king helps [us] contemplate the life of the eternal King" in the exercises of the Second Week [91].

What about the *cause* to which Christ calls? In the present exercise, Ignatius describes it only in general terms: Christ wants to conquer the entire world and so enter into his Father's glory. However, in the very next exercise on the Incarnation [101–9], the Trinity observes humanity on the way to perdition and decides to send the Son to save all humanity from damnation and for eternal life. *This* is the cause for which Christ labors and to which he invites others to collaborate. "The person is invited, not only to share in salvation (this is the object of the First Week), but also to share in the mission of salvation: to associate himself or herself with Christ in leading the whole world... back to the Father."[11] Since Ignatius could count on a common understanding of God's saving work and the mission of the church, he saw no need to spell this out further. We can presume no such common understanding. We must spell out the nature of God's Project more clearly today. Chapter 8 does this, identifying Christ's mission with the Reign (or Kingdom) of God.

Ignatius does not explicitly identify Christ's cause as the Kingdom. He does not entitle this enterprise The Kingdom; in fact, the word is absent from the autograph text of the exercise. Subsequent exercises of the Second Week omit the gospel stories and passages which refer directly to the Kingdom. All this certainly reflects the fact that Ignatius understood the Kingdom not as scripture scholars explain it today, namely, as God's saving work in the world, but as church tradition had understood it ever since patristic times, namely, as referring principally to the community of the blessed in heaven (and also to the church on earth).

Although I do not believe the traditional title of this exercise ("The Kingdom") points to its central theme, it has the merit of correctly specifying the mission which Christ calls people to share. Today everyone agrees that the "Reign of God" constitutes the sum and substance of Jesus' proclamation in the synoptic gospels. He calls all to open themselves to God's coming Reign. This symbol admits of a variety of interpretations, since God's saving activity takes different forms in different contexts, and different cultural settings require different expressions. The history of Christianity bears witness to this variety. But it also bears witness to poisonous misrepresentations of the Reign of God, such as its reduction to a Platonic immortality of the soul or, less frequently, a purely earthly kingdom.

For all its richness and variety, "Reign of God" cannot mean whatever we please. It always refers to the action of the same God who loves, gives life, combats evil and injustice, forgives, and remains faithful to the divine promises. It means regenerated human beings living in communion with God, with one another, and with all creation. The church should be the clearest manifestation of this reality.

Though Peters criticizes militaristic interpretations of "the Kingdom," in fact Ignatius did see God's saving enterprise as resembling a military campaign.[12] The crucial meditation on the Two Standards further develops this imagery. This agrees with the New Testament, according to which God's Reign faces an organized counterproject. The New Testament excludes a privatized, purely psychologized, or nonconflictive presentation of the Reign of God which would disguise God's challenge to dehumanizing social relations and institutions. "Reign of God" remains a political symbol which signifies, among other things, the subversion of politics (and militarism) as usual.

As for the person of *Christ* who calls, he is the focus of everything that follows "The Call." In the Second Week, he will appear, preaching [91].[13] For, although he came to serve, he does teach and lead. ("You call me teacher and lord—and you are right" [John 13:13].) He does this not in a domineering way, but as role model and mentor [cf. 93]. Christ himself shows us his cause and our place in it. This does not obviate the need to present the cause in general terms (as the gospels, the *Exercises,* and chapter 8 of this book do). But it is Christ who communicates interior knowledge of this to those who contemplate his life. As they come to know him, love him, and follow him in practice [104], Christ himself, dealing directly with the individual [cf. 15], will draw each one to collaborate in the "Kingdom," according to his or her particular calling. More precisely, Christ's Spirit will draw them, via consolation, into their vocation.

Appendix II (to Chapter 10)
The Meaning of the Two Standards

The Two Standards meditation shows us the demonic logic that undermines commitment and Christ's counterstrategy through which commitment deepens. On some points my presentation of the meditation (in chapter 10) clashes with the way it is frequently interpreted. Many hold, for example, that the first step in the enemy's strategy—coveting riches—refers not merely to the desire for material wealth, but more broadly to the desire for any created good whatever: for wealth, yes, but also for health, a long life, intelligence, a career, honor, and so forth. On this reading, the "highest spiritual poverty" [146] of Christ's standard, which stands in direct opposition to covetousness, is equivalent to the "indifference" of the Foundation [23]. That is, the "spiritual poverty" of Christ's standard is not interior detachment from material wealth alone, but from *"all* created things," including health, riches, honor, and a long life.[1] In addition, most interpret "humility" and "pride," the crucial last element of each "standard," as interior attitudes with no particular social significance.

I consider these interpretations to be misleading. And since the Two Standards meditation stands at the heart of the *Spiritual Exercises* and Ignatian spirituality, it is important to substantiate my interpretation more thoroughly.

The first point to establish is that covetousness in the Two Standards is nothing other than the desire for material wealth. The exercise on the Three Types of Persons [149–56], immediately following the Two Standards meditation, confirms this decisively. The Two Standards concludes with a triple colloquy in which the retreatant begs to be received under the standard of Christ "in the highest spiritual poverty" and, should God be pleased, "no less in actual poverty," as well as "humiliations and insults" [147]. Then, in the meditation on Three Types of Persons, three sets of entrepreneurs have come to see that their attachment to huge sums of money (ten thousand ducats) threatens their salvation. The solution for them is indifference with regard to their wealth [155]. The meditation closes with the same triple colloquy as the Two Standards [156, 147]. In the text of the *Exercises,* a note then follows, spelling out the point of the Three Types in unmistakable terms: "...when we feel an inclination or repugnance against actual poverty, when we are not indifferent to poverty or riches, it is a great help, in order to extinguish such a disordered inclination, to ask...that the Lord choose one for actual poverty" [157]. The goal of this meditation, therefore, is not simply indifference, as most commentators recognize, but indifference *with respect to one's possessions.* However symbolic the ducats may be, there can be no doubt that "poverty" and "riches" have a concrete meaning in the parable of the Three Types of Persons. Together with the note [157], the parable confirms that in the preceding meditation on Two Standards, "riches" means material wealth and "spiritual poverty" is the freedom to part with one's possessions.

Additional evidence confirms this and throws still more light on the Two Standards.

In 1927 the Spanish Jesuit Luis Teixidor pointed out an apparent dependency, whether direct or indirect, of Ignatius on St. Thomas Aquinas with regard to "covetousness" in the Two Standards.[2] When Ignatius says that the enemy "tempt[s] people to covet riches," he adds "as he [the enemy] is ordinarily accustomed to do" [142]. This last expression, added to the Spanish autograph of the *Exercises* in Ignatius's own hand, includes the Latin words *ut in pluribus* for "ordinarily." In the *Summa Theologica* where Aquinas treats of "one sin as the cause of another" (1a 2ae, q. 84) under the article "whether or not covetousness is the root of all sins" (art. 1), he argues that, yes covetousness is the root of all sins, though not in every specific case, since "judgement in the moral order considers what is usually [*ut in pluribus*] the case, not what is always the case."[3] Both the context and the expression concur with the text of the *Exercises.*

Finding traces of Thomist influence in the *Exercises* is understandable.[4] The main lines of the Two Standards meditation date from Ignatius's Manresa days (1522–23) and even earlier, from his convalescence at Loyola. However, in reaction to attacks on his orthodoxy and investigations by the Inquisition, Ignatius continued to refine his early jottings up until 1535, with the help of his studies in the scholastic tradition at the University of Paris.[5]

Teixidor's discovery would amount to little more than a curiosity were it not for other parallels that he failed to pursue. These confirm the link he discovered and shed additional light on the Two Standards. As I said, in the first article of question 84 St. Thomas considers "whether or not covetousness is the root of all sins." However, the very next article asks "whether *pride* is the beginning of all sin." Recall that in paragraph [142] of the *Exercises* Ignatius says that, after first tempting us to covetousness, the enemy "leads to all other vices" from the three-step progression riches-honors-*pride*.

In art. 1 Aquinas follows his predecessors[6] in referring to the basic scriptural text on covetousness (*cupiditas* = *avaritia*) as the "root" of all evil: "Those who desire to be rich fall into temptation and the snare of the devil, into many senseless and hurtful desires that plunge people into ruin and destruction. *For the desire for riches is the root of all evils*" (1 Tim. 6:9–10). Aquinas argues that covetousness is the root of all sins—covetousness in the narrow, concrete sense, that is, as greed for material wealth. "For we observe that because of riches a person acquires the power to commit any kind of sin" or "to obtain all manner of temporal goods, as the text of Ecclesiastes says, 'all things obey money' (Eccles. 10:19, Vulgate)."

In arriving at this conclusion Aquinas considered, and discarded, two extended senses of the word "covetousness," first, "the immoderate craving for any sort of temporal good" (including, e.g., "health, a wife, . . . knowledge, and high places"[7]) and, second, "the propensity of corrupt nature to crave transient goods inordinately." The first sense is more concrete but general; the second sense is more abstract. He recalled that certain authors held that covetousness is the root of all sins in the second sense, since "all sin grows out of love for the goods of this earth." However, he rejected the abstract and general meanings of covetousness in favor of the narrow concrete meaning:

> All this, while true, does not seem to be in accord with St. Paul's meaning [in 1 Tim. 6]. . . . For he is clearly speaking in the text against those who, "because they seek to become rich, fall into temptation and the snare of the devil. . . ." Hence it is manifest that he is speaking of covetousness as the immoderate desire for riches.

In the next article (art. 2), about pride as "the beginning of all sin," Aquinas comments on the traditional basis for this thesis, Sirach 10:14 (Vulgate), which reads "Pride is the beginning of all sin." This has been the consistent teaching of the Christian tradition.[8] Once again, Thomas considers three possible meanings. Pride "stands, first, for the disordered will for personal excellence." Second, it means "a particular sort of explicit contempt for God, the refusal to be subject to his command." In this sense, all sins have an element of pride. Third, pride "stands for the proclivity arising from fallen nature towards this contempt."[9]

These three senses parallel the three meanings of covetousness in the previous article of the *Summa*. Once again Aquinas notes that certain authors hold that pride as a general proclivity (*inclinatio,* the third, most general sense of pride) is the beginning of all sin. They argue that, just as covetousness (as a general proclivity) "concerns sin as a turning to a passing good," pride as a general proclivity concerns "sin as a turning away from God," something that is part of all sin. However:

> While this may be true, it is not according to the mind of the Wise Man [the author of Sirach], who said, *The beginning of all sin is pride.* He obviously is speaking of pride as it is the inordinate desire to excel. This is clear from what he adds, *God has overturned the thrones of proud princes* [Sirach 10:17], and from the import of the whole chapter.

Thus Aquinas understands the beginning of all sin to be pride in the sense of the "inordinate desire to excel," by which he means arrogance, personal ambition, will to power—in accord with Sirach 10.

Finally, St. Thomas explains the relationship between covetousness as the root of all evil and pride as the beginning of sin. He says that while pride is what is first intended (order of intention, final cause), covetousness is the first to go into action (order of execution): "The end in acquiring earthly goods is that through them a person may attain distinction and eminence," that is, honor. Thomas continues: "Hence, from this point of view, pride, or the will to excel, is put as the beginning of sin."

This is another striking agreement with the *Spiritual Exercises,* which describes the enemy as first tempting people to covet riches "that they may the more easily attain the empty honor of the world, and come to swollen pride" [142]. (Unlike Ignatius, Thomas specifies that riches are sought with the conscious intention of acquiring honors.) Aquinas adds: "The vices, such as avarice, called the 'root' of sin, and pride, called the 'beginning' of sin... are first absolutely speaking in the genesis of sins."[10] From pride, Aquinas says, spring the "capital vices" and from these all other vices.[11] Again, the similarity to the Two Standards is striking.

Teixidor discovered a link between what Aquinas and Ignatius say about covetousness as the root of all evil. However, Aquinas goes on (1) to argue that pride leads to all other vices and (2) to explain the genesis of sin as a progression from covetousness to pride by way of *honors.* Ignatius affirms both points in [142]. For both Thomas and Ignatius, riches lead to honors, honors to pride, and pride to all other vices.

This link between the *Summa* and the *Exercises* further confirms that "riches" in the Two Standards refers to material possessions, not to any created good (health, honor, a long life, etc.). To paraphrase St. Thomas: while "indifference" to *all* created goods is clearly central in the Spiritual Exercises, this is not what Ignatius has in mind when he says that the enemy first tempts people to desire *riches.* Ignatius is not thinking about a generic element in all sin, namely, "the immoderate craving for any sort of temporal good," nor what is metaphysically first in sin, namely, "the propensity of corrupt nature to crave transient goods inordinately." (Thomas rejected these two abstract meanings of avarice for 1 Timothy 6.) As usual, Ignatius is thinking concretely and practically, in this case about the usual first step in the process of moral decline, the desire for material possessions.

This is why, in the *Constitutions* of the Jesuits, Ignatius calls evangelical poverty a "firm rampart" of religious life, the outside wall which resists the first assaults of the enemy.[12]

The Thomistic link suggests, second, that Ignatius understands pride to be the beginning of sin in the same way as Aquinas does, seeing the beginning of sin as pride in the concrete sense of chapter 10 of Sirach: selfish ambition, arrogance, will to power—the kind of pride that springs from worldly honors. The earliest Latin translations of the *Spiritual Exercises* render Ignatius's *crescida soberbia* as *arrogantem superbiam.*

This is further confirmed by Ignatius's opposition to honors for Jesuits, his abhorrence of and strictures against ecclesiastical and social ambition in the Society of Jesus,[13] and his insistence on humble tasks and obedience. These measures and the strictures regarding poverty are so many practical means of implementing the standard of Christ.

Christ calls all to "the highest spiritual poverty" and some to "actual poverty" [146]. "Actual poverty" means material want. What about "spiritual poverty"? In Ignatius's time "spiritual poverty" could mean detachment from material riches or, in a wider sense, detachment from all created things (as in the Foundation).[14] However, if "riches" means material riches and "actual poverty" means material poverty, then "spiritual poverty" in the Two Standards clearly means detachment from material riches, not from health, honors,[15] a long life, and so forth. As I said earlier, the parable of the Three Types with its accompanying note [157] makes this crystal clear. "Spiritual poverty" is not identical to "indifference" but a crucial instance of it, the freedom to give up possessions. It is not a question of the most fundamental virtue from a psychological or ontological point of view, but of a practical tactic against the first attack of the enemy.

Finally, the "humility" of Christ's standard is not a generic element of all virtue or a general subordination of the creature to the Creator, which would ground all virtue. At least it is not limited to that. Humility is practical lowliness, the opposite of arrogant pride. Ignatius's "three kinds of humility" [165–67] indicate a progression. All include obedience to God. The "humility" of Christ's standard, however, appears to be the third kind of humility [167]—the desire to share poverty and rejection with Christ and his friends. It is the capacity to identify with those the world considers to be unimportant.[16]

The "humiliations" of Christ's standard are the opposite of the honors the world bestows on "important" people. They are a share in the contempt it visits on "unimportant" people, the persecution of those who stand with them, as Christ did.

From all this it follows that being received under the standard of Christ—arguably the central theme of Ignatian spirituality—means rejecting the pursuit of wealth and preferring to share the material poverty and contempt experienced by the poor. Joining Christ means joining the poor. Serving God's Reign means assuming their cause, just as God does (Luke 6:20–21). "Praise, reverence, and service of God" [23] is thus correctly translated as "the service of faith and the promotion of justice," as recent General Congregations of the Jesuits have stated, and as their superior general Pedro Arrupe (1965–83) saw so clearly.

Abbreviations

[32]	Numbers in brackets without further indication refer to paragraphs of St. Ignatius's *Spiritual Exercises,* according to the standard numbering. See the note at the foot of p. 8. For versions of the *Spiritual Exercises,* see the bibliography below.
Autobiog	Autobiography of St. Ignatius. See bibliography.
CIS	Centrum Ignatianum Spiritualitatis, Rome.
Cusson, *BibTheol*	Gilles Cusson, S.J., *Biblical Theology and the Spiritual Exercises* (St. Louis: IJS, 1988).
DirAutog	The so-called "Autograph Directory," brief instructions of Ignatius Loyola for administering the Spiritual Exercises. In *Obras,* pp. 312–15; Eng. trans. in Palmer, *Giving,* pp. 7–10.
IJS	The Institute for Jesuit Sources, St. Louis, Missouri.
Ivens, *Understanding*	Michael Ivens, S.J., *Understanding the Spiritual Exercises: Text and Commentary. A Handbook for Retreat Directors* (Herefordshire/Surrey: Gracewing/Iñigo Enterprises, 1998).
LettIgn	*Letters of St. Ignatius of Loyola,* selected and translated by William J. Young, S.J. (Chicago: Loyola University Press, 1959).
Manr	*Manresa,* a journal of Ignatian spirituality, Madrid.
MHSI	Monumenta Historica Societatis Iesu (Historical records of the Society of Jesus)
Obras	San Ignacio de Loyola, *Obras,* transcription, introductions, and notes by Ignacio Iparraguirre, S.J., Cándido de Dalmases, S.J., and Manuel Ruiz Jurado, S.J., 5th revised and corrected edition (Madrid: B.A.C., 1991).
Palmer, *Giving*	Martin E. Palmer, S.J., *On Giving the Spiritual Exercises: The Early Jesuit Manuscript Directories and the Official Directory of 1599* (St. Louis: IJS, 1996).
Peters, *SpEx*	William A. M. Peters, *The Spiritual Exercises of St. Ignatius: Exposition and Interpretation* (Jersey City, N.J.: Program to Promote the Spiritual Exercises, 1967).

Pousset, *LFF*	Édouard Pousset, S.J., *Life in Faith and Freedom: An Essay Presenting Gaston Fessard's Analysis of the Dialectic of the Spiritual Exercises of St. Ignatius,* trans. and ed. Eugene L. Donohue, S.J. (St. Louis: IJS, 1980).
SSJ	*Studies in the Spirituality of Jesuits,* published five times a year (four as of 2004) by IJS.
Toner, *CommRules*	Jules J. A. Toner, *A Commentary on Saint Ignatius' Rules for the Discernment of Spirits: A Guide to the Principles and Practice* (St. Louis: IJS, 1982).
Toner, *DecisMakg*	Jules J. A. Toner, *Discerning God's Will: Ignatius of Loyola's Teaching on Christian Decision Making* (St. Louis: IJS, 1991).

Notes

In the notes to the text I use abbreviations to refer to works that I cite frequently. For other works cited, the initial reference will be a complete one. References to the same work in subsequent chapters will refer readers back to the initial reference by indicating in parenthesis the chapter and the note in which the initial reference occurred. For example, "(ch. 2 n. 3)" indicates that the complete reference can be found in note 3 of chapter 2 of this book.

Chapter 1. Spirituality for Solidarity

1. Karl Rahner, "Ignatian Spirituality and Devotion to the Sacred Heart," *Christian in the Market Place* (New York, 1966), p. 126.

2. See the pioneering work of Katherine Dyckman, Mary Garvin, and Elizabeth Liebert, *The Spiritual Exercises Reclaimed: Uncovering Liberating Possibilities for Women* (New York: Paulist Press, 2001).

Chapter 2. Free to Love

1. Dorothy Day, *Selected Writings: By Little and by Little,* ed. Robert Ellsberg (Maryknoll, N.Y.: Orbis, 1991), p. 264. She was quoting Dostoyevsky's Father Zossima in *The Brothers Karamazov.*

2. George E. Ganss, S.J., *The Spiritual Exercises of St. Ignatius* (St. Louis: IJS, 1992). Here I follow Ganss's translation of Ignatius's original Spanish. Numbers in brackets refer to the standard paragraph numbering for the *Spiritual Exercises.*

3. Ibid., p. 151. The comments are Ganss's own.

4. Indifference "is a potential, to be activated when appropriate" (Ivens, *Understanding,* p. 31).

5. Indifference presupposes desire and is perfectly compatible with strong desires or repugnance. See Cusson, *BibTheol,* pp. 118–31; Edward Kinerk, "Eliciting Great Desires: Their Place in the Spirituality of the Society of Jesus," *SSJ* 16, no. 5 (November 1984): 1–29; Dolores Aleixandre, "El deseo y el miedo: Reflexiones desde la Biblia y desde la espiritualidad ignaciana," *Manr* 66 (1994): 121–30.

6. I translate Ignatius's *afección* as "inclination." *Afecciones* "are propensities and not mere emotions" (Ganss, *Spiritual Exercises,* p. 148). In the scholastic terminology of Ignatius's time, "affect" referred to "every capacity of the human person (from the 'lowest' faculties to the 'highest') to be drawn to or to enjoy an object in any way perceived as 'good,' together with the correlative capacity to hate and recoil from objects in any way perceived as 'bad.' In its highest form this capacity is a quality of the will." Michael Ivens, "The First Week: Some Notes on the Text," *The Way Supplement* 48 (Autumn 1983): 5. Affectivity is not only central to interior bondage; as we shall see, Ignatius was one of those rare geniuses who recognized that affectivity (in the form of "consolation") is also decisive for interior liberation.

7. In the Great Commandment, "love" includes trust-filled allegiance to Yahweh. See William L. Moran, "The Ancient Near Eastern Background of the Love of God

in Deuteronomy," *Catholic Biblical Quarterly* 25 (1963): 77–87. This is the "praise, reverence, and service" of God of the Ignatian Foundation.

8. See Anthony de Mello, *Awareness: A de Mello Spirituality Conference in His Own Words,* ed. J. Francis Stroud, S.J. (New York: Doubleday, 1990). We have many real needs but only one absolute need.

9. Ignatius does not specify this in the Foundation. Scholars also debate whether the text refers directly to Christ. There are other ambiguities, as well. Does the Foundation present life as a mere test track for heaven or hell? Does it suppose that giraffes and oceans exist just for us humans and our salvation? Whatever the terse Foundation might seem to suggest, Ignatius's wider vision and other writings lead us beyond this kind of narrow thinking.

Chapter 3. The Reality of Evil

1. The Weeks of the Exercises reflect a progression in life as well as in the retreat. They are not stages of growth that people definitively transcend but successive moments that will recur later on, as well, enriched by what preceded. Having experienced later moments, we reexperience earlier ones in a new light.

2. In this book, "liberal" does not refer to welfare-state policies or permissiveness but, more broadly, to the middle-class or bourgeois ethos shared by liberals (in the narrow sense) and conservatives alike. The chief virtue of liberalism is personal freedom; its chief vice is individualism.

3. See J. I. González Faus, *Proyecto hermano: Visión creyente del hombre* (Santander: Sal Terrae, 1987), p. 274 n. 36.

4. United Nations Development Programme (UNDP), *Human Development Report 2001* (New York: Oxford University Press, 2001), p. 9.

5. See World Health Organization, Fact Sheet No. 251, June 2000.

6. UNDP, *Human Development Report 1997,* p. 24; idem, *Informe sobre desarrollo humano, 1998* (Naciones Unidas, N.Y.: Mundi-Prensa, 1998), p. 2; *Vida Nueva* (Spain), September 19, 1998, pp. 24–29.

7. UNDP, *Human Development Report 1999,* p. 3.

8. Sandra Postel, "Carrying Capacity: Earth's Bottom Line," in Lester R. Brown et al., *State of the World 1994: A Worldwatch Institute Report on Progress toward a Sustainable Society* (New York and London: W. W. Norton, 1994), p. 5.

9. UNPD, *Human Development Report 2003,* pp. 11–12; "Pots of Promise," *The Economist,* May 24–30, 2003, pp. 69–71. For an outstanding summary account of global despoilment, see Enrico Chiavacci, "A Carefully Hidden Reality," *Concilium* 283 (1999/5): 30–38.

10. Although Ignatius has an acute sense of sin as a vast enterprise, or anti-reign (as we shall see), it should not surprise us that he shows little awareness of what today we call structural or institutional sin.

11. Cf. Jon Sobrino, *Jesus the Liberator: A Historical-Theological Reading of Jesus of Nazareth* (Maryknoll, N.Y.: Orbis, 1993), pp. 186–89.

Chapter 4. Forgiveness

1. Ignatius does not develop the themes of guilt and forgiveness in much detail. This chapter seeks to supply that need in response to contemporary sensibilities.

2. "He who passively accepts evil is as much involved in it as he who helps to perpetrate it. He who accepts evil without protesting against it is really cooperating with it" (Martin Luther King, *Stride Toward Freedom,* 1958; in *A Testament of Hope: The Essential Writings of Martin Luther King, Jr.,* ed. James Melvin Washington [San Francisco: Harper & Row, 1986], p. 429).

3. See Sobrino, *Jesus the Liberator* (ch. 3 n. 11 above), pp. 95–99.

4. *Selected Writings* (ch. 2 n. 1), p. 80.

5. Heb. 7:23–29; 9:12, 25–28; 10:1–18.

6. "While we were living in the flesh [that is, following the impulses of human nature], our sinful passions, aroused by the law, were at work in our members to bear fruit for death.... Apart from the law, [the power of] sin lies dead" (Rom. 7:5–8).

7. Ignatius recalled experiencing "great sorrow and confusion" for his sins but no "fear of his sins or of being condemned" for them, since he was certain of God's love and forgiveness (cf. *Autobiog* 33).

8. Some consider it unfashionable to speak of victims. Discouraging a victim-syndrome of passive self-pity is one thing; denying the objective reality of victims is something else. Victims are those who are harmed by objectively unjust actions, policies, relationships, and institutions. Being a victim does not preclude being a self-directed agent.

9. Cf. Isa. 6:5. On the fascination and awe evoked by the Holy, see Rudolf Otto's classic, *The Idea of the Holy* (New York: Oxford University Press, 1958).

Chapter 5. Reform of Life

1. Alcoholics Anonymous and other twelve-step programs follow closely the dynamic of the First Week of the Spiritual Exercises and what traditional ascetical theology has called the "purgative way." See Jim Harbaugh, *A 12-Step Approach to the Spiritual Exercises of St. Ignatius* (Kansas City, Mo.: Sheed & Ward, 1997). Like several other recent works on Ignatius, this inviting book has come to my attention too late to benefit from it here.

2. See [32–43] for Ignatius's sixteenth-century formulations.

3. Ignacio Ellacuría, "Las iglesias latinoamericanas interpelan a la Iglesia de España," *Sal Terrae* 3 (1982): 230.

4. Dyckman et al., *The Spiritual Exercises Reclaimed* (ch. 1 n. 2), pp. 74–75. The authors draw on suggestions of Margaret Miles.

5. Besides Augustine's *Confessions* and Ignatius's *Autobiog,* see C. S. Lewis, *Surprised by Joy: The Shape of My Early Life* (London: Geoffrey Bles, 1955); Dorothy Day, *The Long Loneliness* (New York: Harper, 1952); Thomas Merton, *The Seven Storey Mountain* (New York: Harcourt, Brace, 1948); Etty Hillesum, *An Interrupted Life: The Diaries, 1941–1943 and Letters from Westerbork,* foreword by Eva Hoffman, introduction and notes by Jan G. Gaarlandt (New York: Henry Holt and Co., 1996).

6. Bernard Lonergan, *Method in Theology* (Toronto: University of Toronto Press, 1990), p. 240. Regarding conversion, see pp. 104–7, 237–43. Lonergan distinguishes intellectual, moral, and religious conversion. Moral conversion "sublates" intellectual conversion, and religious conversion "sublates" the other two. That which sublates does not annul what is sublated, but rather places it on a firmer footing, enriches it, and brings it toward perfection. Ibid., pp. 241–42.

7. Ibid., pp. 105, 107.

8. Cf. John R. Sachs, "Current Eschathology: Universal Salvation and the Problem of Hell," *Theological Studies* 52, no. 2 (June 1991): 227–54.

Chapter 6. Rules for Discernment

1. Literally, "Rules to aid us toward perceiving and then understanding, at least to some extent, the various motions which are caused in the soul: the good motions that they may be received and the bad that they may be rejected" [313, Ganss trans.].

2. See chapter 15.

3. The situation of this group is not obvious. Some believe Rule 1 refers only to hardened egoists (e.g., Daniel Gil, *Discernimiento según San Ignacio,* 2d ed. [Rome: CIS, 1983], p. 99). Others believe it also includes converted people who are backsliding (e.g., Jules Toner, *CommRules,* pp. 52–54), pointing out that the expression "mortal sin" which Ignatius uses here could mean simply "capital vice" not "mortal sin" in the modern sense. In parallel fashion, commentators debate over Rule 2. Cf. Daniel Gil and Miguel A. Fiorito, "La primera regla de discernimiento de S. Ignacio. ¿A quién se refiere . . . ?" *Stromata* 33 (1977): 341–60. Since Ignatius habitually thinks in practical, pastoral terms, I believe his first rule refers to people who, though they may not be hardened egoists (who sometimes seem incapable of feeling bitter remorse), are nonetheless ensnared in serious moral problems (martial infidelity, theft, cover-up, gambling problems, and the like). Rule 2 refers to those who are committed to serious reform.

4. Day, *Selected Writings* (ch. 2 n. 1 above), p. 12. The "special emotions . . . came only at hearing the word of God." However, consolation is not always occasioned by the explicit word of God or overt religious symbolism.

5. Letter of Ignatius to Teresa Rejadell, June 18, 1536, *LettIgn,* pp. 21–22; *Obras,* p. 732.

6. *Selected Writings,* p. 75.

7. "Desolation . . . points out the unredeemed areas of our lives. It indicates the next growth-point." William Broderick, "First Week: Rules for Discernment," in *Presenting the First Week, The Way Supplement* 48 (Autumn 1983): 35. In desolation, we experience the pull of concupiscence, that is, weakness.

8. Letter to Teresa Rejadell, June 18, 1536, *Obras,* p. 730; cf. *LettIgn,* p. 19.

9. Ignatius uses a sexist example of a woman upbraiding a man.

10. Cf. Daniel Gil, *Discernimiento,* pp. 238–39. Permanent struggle with the enemy is an *existential,* that is, a constitutive structure of the human condition.

11. Ibid., p. 304.

12. "Whoever puts a stumbling block before [or: scandalizes] one of these little ones . . ." (Matt. 18:7).

13. Cf. [32]. "Transcendent origins" does not mean "from some other world." It means origins other than ordinary objects of experience, activity at the "deepest level" of reality. See Dean Brackley, *Divine Revolution: Salvation and Liberation in Catholic Thought* (Maryknoll, N.Y.: Orbis Books, 1996), Chapter 3 on Rahner and pp. 100–102 on transcendence in the thought of Xavier Zubiri and Ignacio Ellacuría.

14. Therefore, natural feelings of depression or joy "can [also] fall within the scope of [Ignatius's] rules, insofar as the good or evil spirits can take these emotions and work on them for their respective ends." Ganss, *Spiritual Exercises* (ch. 2 n. 2 above), p. 191.

15. Brigitte-Violaine Aufauvre, "Depression and Spiritual Desolation," *The Way* 42, no. 3 (July 2003): 47–56, provides helpful indications of the difference between ordinary depression and spiritual desolation.

Chapter 7. The Call

1. The paradox is that Max Weber found the notion of vocation crucial to the birth of capitalism. See his classic, *The Protestant Ethic and the Spirit of Capitalism* (New York: Scribner, 1958).

2. Dag Hammarskjöld, *Markings* (New York: Alfred A. Knopf, 1964), p. 205.

3. I am grateful to Ita's brother, Bill Ford, for the full text. Judith M. Noone, M.M. (*The Same Fate as the Poor* [Maryknoll, N.Y.: Orbis, 1984], p. 117) and Phyllis Zagano (*Ita Ford: Missionary Martyr* [New York and Mahwah, N.J.: Paulist Press, 1996], p. 1) quote parts of the letter.

4. "Those who lose their life for my sake will find it" (Matt. 10:39; 16:25; Mark 8:35; Luke 9:24; 17:33; John 12:25; cf. Acts 20:35). "Find" here means "win, obtain." "Life" is *nephesh* (Hebr.) = *psyche* (Gk.), meaning life, soul, self, that is, the person as a whole.

5. Ignatius administered the First Week of the Spiritual Exercises to many, but he insisted that the rest of the Exercises should be presented only to those who were open in principle ("indifferent") to whatever God might ask of them. Without that magnanimous attitude [5, 23], they would profit little from Jesus' call for total commitment (if they could hear it at all) or from subsequent exercises.

6. Actually, the word "king" appears only here [95, 97] in Ignatius's autograph text of the *Spiritual Exercises.* The title "The Kingdom" does not come from Ignatius; nor does the word appear in the autograph. See "Appendix I: The Kingdom Meditation?" below.

7. Translation of Ignatius's text following David L. Fleming, S.J., in *Draw Me into Your Friendship: A Literal Translation and a Contemporary Reading of the Spiritual Exercises* (St. Louis: IJS, 1996), p. 85. Joseph Tetlow also creatively rewrites the exercise in his *Choosing Christ in the World: Directing the Spiritual Exercises of St. Ignatius Loyola according to Annotations Eighteen and Nineteen. A Handbook* (St. Louis: IJS, 1989), pp. 148–49.

8. Ignatius expects that people making the Exercises will experience this call as they contemplate Christ's life during the Second Week which is about to begin. Christ is absent from the imaginative composition at the beginning of The Call. Ignatius has us imagine the "synagogues, villages and towns" where he preached [91]. But Jesus has not yet arrived on the stage. In this exercise, one only "considers" his call [94–96], somewhat abstractly and at a distance, as it were, in order better to hear it and respond generously later, when it actually comes. See Appendix I, below.

9. For this translation of [97], see Peters, *SpEx,* pp. 76–77.

10. I follow the text of Fleming, *Draw Me,* p. 87. According to Gilles Cusson (following J. Clémence), the first-mentioned response, that of any decent person (based on "judgment and reason" [96]), commits respondents to Christ's *cause* (*trabajo*). The additional measures, of those with more desire [97], link them closer to Christ's *person.* See *BibTheol,* pp. 197–204. In taking account of resistance to the call, Ignatius follows the logic of Jesus' Parable of the Sower (Mark 4:1–9). The "seed" of God's Word is exposed to a variety of threats. It can fall on rocky soil and fail to take root (without a solid base, the hearer succumbs to trials). Seed that germinates can still be

choked by thorns (the desire for riches and other mundane cares [cf. 97]). This is why good intentions of "total commitment" [96] often fail to "bear fruit thirty, sixty and a hundredfold" (cf. Mark 4:13–20).

11. Robert Coles, *The Call of Service: A Witness to Idealism* (Boston: Houghton and Mifflin, 1993), pp. 3–7.

12. These reflections are inspired by Édouard Pousset, *LFF,* chapter 1, "Freedom."

Chapter 8. The Reign of God

1. See www.wsfindia.org, www.portoalegre2003.org, etc.

2. Here I follow the widely accepted interpretation of the beatitudes by Belgian scholar Jacques Dupont. See Jacques Dupont, *Les Béatitudes: La bonne nouvelle* (Paris: Gabalda, 1969).

3. The dispositions (and behavior) of the disciple are at issue, however, in the beatitudes in Matthew (Matt. 5:1–12).

4. "Reign of God" does not refer primarily to a place. The expression refers to God's activity as king, specifically as a king who rescues the weak and the oppressed of all kinds. "Entering" God's Reign (Matt. 5:19; etc.) means living under the regime that God's Reign brings about. God's Reign is therefore a "political" project; but it is "not from this world," for God's are not the politics of violence and self-interest, but the "politics" of truth and humble service (John 18:36; Matt. 20:25–28). For a more detailed presentation of Jesus' proclamation of the Reign of God, see chapter 6 of my *Divine Revolution* (ch. 6 n. 13 above), "Jesus and the Reign of God."

Chapter 9. Contemplation of Christ

1. This is what happens with all masterpieces, or "classics." See David Tracy, *The Analogical Imagination* (New York: Crossroad, 1981), especially chapter 3.

2. In the *Spiritual Exercises,* see [110–17].

3. See the prayer of St. Richard of Chichester, paraphrased in the musical *Godspell:* "Day by day, three things I pray: to know Thee more dearly, to love Thee more clearly, to follow Thee more nearly" [*sic*]. Cited in Ivens, *Understanding,* p. 91.

4. "A contemplation is a film that I create with my imagination. I move the characters, I direct them, I make them come and go, I write the script, I frame the dialogues, etc. It is, besides, a film in which I place myself, like those films in which the director or script writer also participates." José Ramón Busto, S.J., "Exégesis y contemplación," *Manr* 64 (1992): 15–23 at 21.

5. One considers what the persons "say *or might say*" [123]. "Ignatius was concerned to bring the gospel reality into intimate and personal encounter with the contemporary reality of the exercitant's own experience and history. How otherwise was Christ to become incarnate in the world, in greatly different times and cultures, in the faith and life of the believing community?" (Joseph Veale, "Manifold Gifts," *The Way Supplement* 82 [Spring 1995]: 46). See also Ernest C. Ferlita, "The Road to Bethlehem—Is it Level or Winding? The Use of the Imagination in the Spiritual Exercises," *SSJ* 29, no. 5 (November 1997): 11–13. For examples of what "happens" in Ignatian contemplation, see Michael Kennedy, S.J., *Eyes on Jesus: A Guide for Contemplation* (New York: Crossroad, 1999), and idem, *Eyes on the Cross: A Guide for Contemplation* (New York: Crossroad, 2001).

6. Dietrich Bonhoeffer, *The Mystery of Holy Night,* ed. Manfred Weber, trans. Peter Heinegg (New York: Crossroad, 1997), pp. 14–15.

7. Cf. Sandra M. Schneiders, *Women and the Word: The Gender of God in the New Testament and the Spirituality of Women* (New York: Paulist Press, 1986), pp. 52–53.

8. Ibid., p. 51.

9. Cf. ibid., pp. 58–61.

10. Cf. Dyckman et al., *The Spiritual Exercises Reclaimed* (ch. 1 n. 2 above), p. 187. The authors provide a rich synthesis of a range of feminist writers on this subject.

11. Cf. Jon Sobrino, *Jesus in Latin America* (Maryknoll, N.Y.: Orbis, 1987), pp. 135–37.

12. William C. Spohn, *Go and Do Likewise: Jesus and Ethics* (New York: Continuum, 1999), describes very well how the story of Jesus shapes the dispositions and moral perception of followers today. They use their imagination to creatively reinterpret his message and reincarnate his attitudes and praxis for today.

Chapter 10. The Two Standards

1. Matt. 16:18–17:8.

2. Literally, "Meditation on Two Standards, the one of Christ, our supreme captain and lord; the other of Lucifer, mortal enemy of our human nature" [136].

3. We need not actually seek honors; they normally follow on riches as a matter of course. See Peters, *SpEx,* p. 95.

4. See Sirach (Ecclesiasticus) 10:15 (Latin Vulgate), "Pride is the beginning of sin," the classic text for this thesis up to Ignatius's day. The context of the verse clarifies that "pride" is the arrogance of the powerful. However, Sir. 10:15 seems to conflict with 1 Tim. 6:10, "The love of money is the root of all evil," just quoted. Thomas Aquinas reconciles the two verses in a way that agrees with the Two Standards. He also insists that covetousness in 1 Tim. 6:10 refers to material wealth and that pride in Sir. 10:15 refers to arrogance. See Appendix II, "The Meaning of the Two Standards," at the end of this book.

5. While personal transformation is God's work, we cooperate by actively resisting (Latin: *agere contra*) our unfreedoms. As the Official Directory of 1599 put it, "if you want to straighten a crooked stick you must bend it to the opposite side so that it will end up midway between the two and thus straight" (Official Directory of 1599, no. 217; text in Palmer, *Giving,* p. 336). The image comes from Aristotle, *Nicomachean Ethics,* ii, 9. The early Directories were sixteenth-century manuals for directors of the Spiritual Exercises. For the *agere contra* principle in the *Spiritual Exercises,* see especially [16, 157] and also [13, 97, 146–47, 167, 319, 324–25, 350–51].

6. In the Pauline letters, see 2 Cor. 4:7–12; 6:3–10; 11:21–33; 1 Cor. 4:9–13; Phil. 3:10–11.

7. Ivens, *Understanding,* pp. 109, 111. Michael Ivens's masterful commentary, to which I am indebted, is arguably the best in English. Here, I believe he makes a wrong turn.

8. Cf. Ignatius's account of the celebrated vision at La Storta, near Rome, where he was "placed with the Son" (*Autobiog* 96).

9. Concerning the danger of riches and the importance of renouncing them, see, in the Gospel of Luke alone: Luke 3:10–14; 6:24; 12:15, 33; 14:33; 16:9–13, 19–30; 18:22–30; 19:8–9; etc. For interpreting Ignatius on this point, see Appendix II.

10. See the reflections in Dyckman et al., *The Spiritual Exercises Reclaimed* (ch. 1 n. 2 above), especially pp. 196–99.

11. Joaquín Losada, "El contenido teológico de la meditación de dos banderas, combate espiritual y combate escatalógico," *Manr* 58 (1986): 50; my emphasis. "The symbol of the two cities... avoids the risk of proposing the meditation and the process of election in a privatized and individualistic way.... We need to maintain this communitarian, ecclesial horizon... throughout the meditation" (ibid.).

Chapter 11. Downward Mobility

1. According to British sociologist Anthony Giddens, the globalization of risk has given the world a "menacing appearance." "The possibility of nuclear war, ecological calamity, uncontainable population explosion, the collapse of global economic exchange, and other potential global catastrophes provide an unnerving horizon of dangers for everyone" (*The Consequences of Modernity* [Stanford, Calif.: Stanford University Press, 1990], p. 125).

2. "Individualism lies at the very core of American culture," wrote Bellah et al. (*Habits of the Heart: Individualism and Commitment in American Life* [New York: Harper & Row, 1985], p. 142). Like upward mobility, individualism is ambivalent. In a positive sense, it is a "belief in the inherent dignity of the human person." However, in a negative sense, individualism is the belief "that the individual has a primary reality whereas society is a second-order, derived or artificial construct" (ibid., p. 334). Bellah et al. feared that individualism, in the aberrant sense, has grown "cancerous" in the United States (ibid., p. vii). See, more recently, Robert D. Putnam, *Bowling Alone: The Collapse and Revival of American Community* (New York: Simon & Schuster, 2000).

3. See Manuel Castells, *The Information Age: Economy, Society, and Culture,* vol. 2: *The Power of Identity* (Oxford: Blackwell Publishers, 1997).

4. In the last fifty years, whole majorities in some countries have escaped from poverty. See Eric J. Hobsbawm, *The Age of Extremes: A History of the Short Twentieth Century, 1914–1991* (New York and London: Pantheon, 1994), especially chapter 9, "The Golden Years." Millions continue to escape poverty in East Asia, especially China.

5. I describe the way of the world and then the way of Christ as ideal types, that is, internally coherent models which throw light on reality without themselves occurring in pure form in real life. See *From Max Weber: Essays in Sociology,* trans., ed., and with an introduction by H. H. Gerth and C. Wright Mills (New York: Oxford University Press, 1958), pp. 59–60, 294, 323–24.

6. Cf. René Girard, *The Girard Reader,* ed. James G. Williams (New York: Crossroad, 1996), "Part I: Overview of the Mimetic Theory" and passim. See also the Girardian study by Gil Bailie, *Violence Unveiled: Humanity at the Crossroads* (New York: Crossroad, 1995). On covetousness, consumption, and capitalism, see John Kavanaugh's now classic *Following Christ in a Consumer Society: The Spirituality of Cultural Resistance* (Maryknoll, N.Y.: Orbis, 1981).

7. Kenneth L. Becker, "Beyond Survival: The Two Standards and the Way of Love," *The Way* 42, no. 3 (July 2003): 125–36, relates the two standards to psychologist Abraham Maslow's hierarchy of needs. Maslow's first two needs are what I call "security" (they are related to riches/poverty); the next two, acceptance and recognition, are related to honors/contempt. Becker links Maslow's fifth and final need, self-actualization, to love, drawing on Jung's psychology.

8. See, for example, Peter L. Berger and Thomas Luckmann, *The Social Construction of Reality: A Treatise in the Sociology of Knowledge* (Garden City, N.Y.: Anchor Books, 1967).

9. For a beautiful exposition of the nature and implications of the ladder model of society, see Trina Paulus, *Hope for the Flowers* (Ramsey, N.J.: Paulist, 1972). Like Kavanaugh's *Following Christ,* this book is still in print.

10. Chuck Collins, Betsy Leondar-Wright and Holly Sklar, *Shifting Fortunes: The Perils of the Growing American Wealth Gap* (Boston: United for a Fair Economy, 1999), p. 5. Figures are for 1997 and are based on economist Edward Wolff's analysis of Unites States Federal Reserve data.

11. Immanuel Wallerstein, *After Liberalism* (New York: The New Press, 1995), p. 198.

12. See Lester C. Thurow, *The Future of Capitalism: How Today's Economic Forces Shape Tomorrow's World* (New York: William Morrow and Co., 1996), pp. 1–2. The U.S. in the 1990s was a notable exception.

13. Manuel Castells, *The Information Age,* vol. 3: *The End of Millennium,* 2nd ed. (Oxford: Blackwell Publishers, 2000), chapters 2 and 3.

14. See Ignacio Ellacuría, "Utopia and Prophecy in Latin America," in *Mysterium Liberationis: Fundamental Concepts of Liberation Theology,* ed. I. Ellacuría and J. Sobrino (Maryknoll, N.Y.: Orbis, 1993), pp. 299–300.

15. *Milwaukee Journal-Sentinel,* February 15, 1998.

16. There are many books available to help discern lifestyle questions. In the past, many have benefited from Richard J. Foster's *Freedom of Simplicity* (San Francisco: Harper & Row, 1981). José Hobday's more recent *Simple Living: The Path to Joy and Freedom* (New York: Continuum, 1998) is clear and engaging.

17. For an excellent account of how people grow and mature in the vocation to solidarity, see Margaret Swedish and Marie Dennis, *Like Grains of Wheat: A Spirituality of Solidarity* (Maryknoll, N.Y.: Orbis Books, 2004).

Chapter 12. Humility and Solidarity

1. "The name" here means the person of Christ.

2. Homily, January 14, 1979, in Mons. Oscar A. Romero, *Mons. Oscar A. Romero, Su pensamiento,* vol. 6 (San Salvador: Arzobispado de San Salvador, 2000), p. 120.

3. The Spanish diplomat Pedro Ortíz (to whom Ignatius administered the Exercises) and his brother Francisco, a Franciscan friar, wrote a treatise in which they refer to the "kinds of humility" as three kinds of love. See Cusson, *BibTheol,* pp. 264–67.

4. Ganss translation. My phrasing in describing the first two kinds follows Tetlow, *Choosing Christ: in the World* (ch. 7 n. 7 above), p. 163.

5. Cited in José M. Guerrero, "Tres maneras de humildad [=amistad]," *Manr* 38 (1996): 267.

6. See Carlos Domínguez, "Las tres maneras de humildad: Una relectura desde la teología y el psicoanálisis," *Manr* 68 (1996): 293.

7. Brian E. Daley, "'To Be More like Christ': The Background and Implications of 'Three Kinds of Humility,'" *SSJ* 27, no. 1 (January 1995): p. 30. See Ignatius's revealing comments in *DirAutog* 9. The third kind of humility is an affective disposition rather than a practical norm. Cf. José María Castillo, "La 'tercera manera de humildad' en los Ejercicios Espirituales de S. Ignacio," *Proyección* [Universidad de Granada, Spain] 46 (April–June 1999): 123–36.

Chapter 13. Expanding the Soul

1. An earlier version of this chapter appeared in *SSJ* 34, no. 4 (September 2002): 1–22.

2. Valerie Saiving, "The Human Situation: A Feminine View," in *Womanspirit Rising: A Feminist Reading in Religion,* ed. Judith P. Christ and Judith Plaskow (San Francisco: Harper & Row, 1979), pp. 25–42. The essay was first published in 1960. For further development of Saiving's thesis and its relevance for spirituality, see Dyckman et al., *The Spiritual Exercises Reclaimed* (ch. 1 n. 2 above), pp. 163–66.

3. Saiving argues that boys need to struggle to distinguish themselves from their mothers, who are their primary caregivers in infancy, in ways that girls do not; and that boys and men experience the need to perform and to affirm their psychosexual identity in ways that girls and women do not.

4. See T. S. Eliot, "The Love Song of J. Alfred Prufrock" in his *The Complete Poems and Plays, 1909–1950* (New York: Harcourt, Brace and World, 1962).

5. Letter of June 18, 1536, in *Obras,* pp. 729–34; cf. *LettIgn,* pp. 18–24.

6. *Obras,* p. 731; emphasis added. Ignatius takes for granted "that we must attribute all the good that we see in creatures" to God working in them (*LettIgn,* p. 18).

7. *LettIgn,* p. 22.

8. Cf. Ignatius's reflections on "loving humility" vs. fearful humility in his *Spiritual Diary* (*Diario Espiritual*), nos. 178–87 (*Obras,* pp. 408–11). Selections of Ignatius's *Spiritual Diary* are available in English in *Ignatius of Loyola: The* Spiritual Exercises *and Selected Works,* ed. George E. Ganss, S.J. (New York: Paulist, 1991), pp. 229–70.

9. "Hence we must examine the matter closely; and if the enemy uplifts us, we must abase ourselves by recounting our sins and miseries. If he keeps us down and depresses us, we must raise ourselves up in true faith and hope in our Lord" (*LettIgn,* p. 20).

10. See my "A Radical Ethos," *Horizons* 24, no. 1 (Spring 1997): 7–36, and Dietmar Mieth and Jacques Pohier, eds., *Changing Values and Virtues, Concilium* 191 (1986).

11. The so-called "Rules for Scruples" [345–51].

12. Santiago Arzubialde, "Raíces de la teología espiritual en Dos Banderas," *Manr* 56 [1984]: 297.

13. Cited in Rogelio García Mateo, S.J., "El 'Rey eternal': Ética política y espiritualidad," *Manr* 60 [1988]: 143–44.

14. See *Obras,* p. 733; Young, *Letters,* pp. 22–23.

15. See the first essay in Nietzsche's "A Genealogy of Morals" (1887), especially secs. 10 and 11, in *The Complete Works of Friedrich Nietzsche,* ed. Oscar Levy (New York: Russell & Russell, 1964); see also Max Scheler, *On Ressentiment and Moral Value-judgments* (1912), on which I comment below.

16. Max Scheler, *El resentimiento en la moral* (Buenos Aires: Espasa-Calpe Argentina, 1938), p. 80. Though not as much as Nietzsche, Scheler, too, exaggerated the reach of ressentiment, for example, attributing modern humanitarian liberalism almost entirely to ressentiment (cf. *Ressentiment,* chapter 4). He later retreated from that sweeping diagnosis.

17. René Girard, *The Girard Reader* (ch. 11 n. 6 above), p. 252. Girard believes that mimetic (imitative) rivalry, especially with one's role models, is at the root of ressentiment. "The impassioned admiration and desire to emulate stumble over the

unfair obstacle with which the model seems to block the way of his disciple, and then these passions recoil on the disciple in the form of impotent hatred" (ibid., p. 40).

18. See chapter 11 and my "A Radical Ethos," pp. 24–52.

19. See Daley, "To Be More like Christ," (ch. 12 n. 7 above), pp. 6–7, 36–39. I am modifying, even Christianizing, Aristotle's rather elitist portrait of the magnanimous individual. See *Nicomachean Ethics,* 1099a32–b5, 1122a18–1125a15.

20. Scheler, *Resentimiento,* pp. 90–93; emphases in original.

21. *Const* 622. Many more examples could be cited. Among them, cf. [5] and the prayer, "Take, Lord, and receive . . ." [234].

Chapter 14. Life in the Spirit

1. See the discussion of making, keeping, and changing commitments in Dyckman et al., *The Spiritual Exercises Reclaimed* (ch. 1 n. 2), pp. 293–97.

2. See Aristotle, *Nicomachean Ethics,* Book vi, Chap. 7, and Thomas Aquinas, *Summa Theologica,* 1a 2ae, q. 94, a. 4; 2a 2ae, q. 47, a .2.

3. Cf. John Paul II, *Veritatis splendor* (The Splendor of the Truth, 1993), no. 52.

4. This is the *Magis* (= More) Principle; see also [152, 155, 179, 183, 185].

5. Anne E. Patrick, *Liberating Conscience: Feminist Explorations in Catholic Moral Theology* (New York: Continuum, 1996), p. 198.

6. See Ignatius's remarkable letters to Jerónimo Vignes of November 17 and 24, 1555; January 18 and May 17, 1556, in *Obras,* pp. 1072–76. Selections from the first two letters in *LettIgn,* pp. 404–6.

7. Nor does Christian discernment proceed primarily by utilitarian criteria, that is, by calculating the greatest overall good for the greatest number. The mystery of iniquity is too profound, the work of God too sublime, and our perception too limited for us to calculate the relevant consequences of our actions. While they are important, Christian discernment based on the New Testament principles of discipleship relies more heavily on the belief that the praxis of discipleship shapes us to better assess and respond to reality. Cf. Spohn, *Go and Do Likewise* (ch. 9 n. 12 above), p. 120.

8. In the same way, it was not crucial whether one ate, or not, meat sold in the market which may have been offered in pagan rituals (Rom. 14; cf. 1 Cor. 8; 10:25–33). What mattered was that each one act out of faith and with charity toward the neighbor, especially toward one's "weaker" neighbor. The subjective state of my neighbor places a limit on my freedom.

Chapter 15. More Rules for Discernment

1. *DirAutog* 11.

2. Letter to Teresa Rejadell, June 18, 1536, *LettIgn,* p. 22.

3. "The one of them [consolation] He gives, the other [desolation] He permits" (ibid., p. 21).

4. Toner, *CommRules,* p. 218.

5. Although "the good angel as well as the bad can console the soul" [331], God is the ultimate cause of all consolation. In fact, consolation is best understood as nothing less than the touch of God (the effect of God's self-communication), the indwelling Spirit, overflowing into consciousness. Following this understanding, I interpret the "good angel" [331; cf. 329] as the Holy Spirit. All kinds of things can serve as a

contributing cause, "triggering" — that is, occasioning and even inducing — consolation. However, only God *gives* consolation in the strict sense.

6. Gil, *Discernimiento* (ch. 6 n. 3 above), pp. 309–10.

7. As a student, Ignatius used to feel great consolation and attraction to prayer, but he soon realized that this was a temptation, because it tired him and undermined the studies he had undertaken to serve God better. *Autobiog* 54–55.

8. "The bad spirit tends to piggyback on still-open psychological wounds or on weaknesses of human temperament that one has not appropriated" (Carlos Rafael Cabarrús, S.J., "Discernimiento: La osadía de 'dejarse llevar,'" *Diakonía* [Managua] [May 1986], p. 21). The movements of the good Spirit can also "'ride' on our wounds,... to close and cure them" (ibid., p. 15). Divine grace heals, liberates, and humanizes; evil aggravates weaknesses and dehumanizes.

9. Francisco Suárez, *De Religione Societatis Iesu,* L. IX, cap. V, nn. 38–41 (ed. Vives, 1860, *Opera omnia,* t. XVI, 2). See Daniel Gil, "Algunas reflexiones sobre la consolación sin causa," *Manr* 41 (1969): 39–64, and 121–40 at pp. 47–54. Gil disputes Karl Rahner's interpretation of Suárez on this point (ibid., p. 49 n. 25). Cf. K. Rahner, "The Logic of Concrete Individual Knowledge in Ignatius Loyola," in idem, *The Dynamic Element in the Church* (New York: Herder and Herder, 1964), pp. 84–170.

10. Suárez, *De Religione,* n. 40.

11. See Gordon Zahn, *In Solitary Witness: The Life and Death of Franz Jaegerstaetter* (Collegeville, Minn.: Liturgical Press, 1964; reissued 1977).

12. Suárez, *De Religione,* nn. 40–41. The quotation is from n. 40. Cf. Gil, "Algunas reflexiones," p. 126 and passim.

13. *Autobiog* 14; cf. ibid. 8–9.

14. Cabarrús, "Discernimiento," p. 22.

15. Here, as in the first two rules of the first series [314–15], it is not clear precisely what distinguishes the two kinds of persons. See chapter 6 note 3 above.

Chapter 16. Three Ways to Make Decisions

1. Cabarrús, "Discernimiento" (ch. 15 n. 8 above). The early directories for the Spiritual Exercises — sixteenth-century manuals compiled by pioneer Jesuit retreat directors — characterize indifference as "resignation of the will" and "abandonment" into God's hands. Palmer, in *Giving,* collects these works in English translation. Cf. Ignatius's own hand-written directory, *DirAutog* 17; in Palmer, *Giving,* p. 9. The original versions of the directories are found in *Monumenta Ignatiana,* Series 2, *Exercitia Spiritualia de Sancti Ignatii de Loyola et eorum Directoria,* vol. 2, *Directoria Exercitiorum Spiritualium (1540–1599),* ed. Ignatius Iparraguirre, S.I. (Rome: MHSI, 1955).

2. That means one is "more inclined, should it be for the equal service of God, toward that which is most in accord with the counsels and example of Christ our Lord" (*DirAutog* 17; trans. in Palmer, *Giving,* p. 9). Several early directories repeat this criterion. "Counsels" here refers to the evangelical counsels of poverty, chastity, and obedience. In Ignatius's day, the subject matter of the "election" in the month-long retreat was ordinarily the retreatant's "state of life." The retreatant decided whether to remain a layperson and eventually marry (observing the "commandments") or adopt one or more of the evangelical counsels, enter a religious order, etc. The Ignatian procedures need not be limited to decisions of this kind, however.

3. The last opinion is Karl Rahner's in "The Logic of Concrete Individual Knowledge" (ch. 15 n. 9 above), p. 128 n. 25.

4. Although some identify the experience of the "first time" with consolation without prior cause [cf. 330, 336], Ignatius nowhere expressly indicates that consolation is essential to this experience (cf. Toner, *DecisMakg,* p. 116).

5. Alfredo Campaio Costa, "The 'Times' of Ignatian Election: The Wisdom of the Directories," *The Way* 42, no. 4 (October 2003): 80. "Malia's" experience is certainly exceptional, however. See below.

6. *Autobiog* 27.

7. Toner, *DecisMakg,* pp. 112–13. The extended quotation is from a written account by "Malia."

8. *DirAutog* 18.

9. Gil, *Discernimiento* (ch. 6 n. 3 above), p. 171. The "action" in question might be specific, or vague and general.

10. *DirAutog* 18. Later he adds, "The person may proceed by presenting one side to God on one day and the other on the next, . . . and noting in which direction God our Lord gives the greater indication of his divine will—like someone presenting various foods to a prince and noting which of them is to his liking" (*DirAutog* 21; trans. in Palmer, *Giving,* p. 9). This text does not specify that the expected "indication" is consolation, and the context suggests that this exercise can be used in any of the "times." Some early directories propose it for the second "time," however. Moreover, while writing the Constitutions of the Society of Jesus, Ignatius followed this procedure, receiving indications of God's will through consolation and visions (see his *Spiritual Diary* in Ganss, ed., *Ignatius of Loyola* [ch. 13 n. 8 above], pp. 238–70) and *Autobiog* 100 (ibid., p. 111; *Obras,* p. 177).

11. In the second time, one makes a "judgment by affective connaturality that the object of the volitional impulse is what is to be chosen" (Toner, *DecisMakg,* p. 137). Some early directories stress that in the second time one proceeds without discursive reasoning (see the Directories of Polanco 82, Miró 86, Cordéses 130 and the Official Directory of 1599, 190, 220, 221; Eng. trans. in Palmer, *Giving*). Weighing reasons is proper to the third time.

12. Referring to the retreat context, Michael Ivens writes: "Nor is the 'inwardness' of the election process – attention to the quality of motivation, to movements of spirits, and to responses to the Gospel—a substitute for looking outward, seeking to discern the word of God in events and situations and in prophetic voices that help interpret the claims these make on us" (*Understanding,* p. 128 n. 75).

13. We should exercise extra caution in drawing practical conclusions from desolation. Cf. Toner, *DecisMakg,* pp. 154–56.

14. Ibid., pp. 158–59.

15. See ibid., pp. 166–68.

16. On communal discernment, see John Carroll Futrell, *Making an Apostolic Community of Love: The Role of the Superior according to St. Ignatius of Loyola* (St. Louis: IJS, 1970), chapter 6; idem, "Communal Discernment: Reflections on Experience," *SSJ* 4, no. 5 (November 1972); Jules Toner, "A Method for Communal Discernment of God's Will," *SSJ* 3, no. 4 (September 1971); idem, "The Deliberation That Started the Jesuits: A Commentary on the *Deliberatio primorum Patrum,*" *SSJ* 6, no. 4 (June 1974); Ladislas Örsy, "Towards a Theological Evaluation of Communal Discernment," *SSJ* 5, no. 5 (October 1973); Piet Penning de Vries et al., *Communal Discernment: New Trends,* Subsidia ad Discernendum 14 (Rome: CIS, 1981); William A. Barry, "Toward Communal Discernment: Some Practical Suggestions," *The Way Supplement* 58

(Spring 1987): 104–12; Andrew Hamilton, "Correct Weight for Communal Discernment," *The Way Supplement* 85 (Spring 1996): 17–27; Virginia Varley, "Fostering the Process of Discerning Together," ibid., pp. 84–97.

17. Cf. *Const* 622–23. See also *Const,* Part VII, chapter 2.

18. *DirAutog* 20.

19. The love from God and for God does not exclude other motivations but rather aligns them with this deepest motivation. See Official Directory of 1599, 174.

20. "In what touches ourselves and our standard of living we will always do better and be more secure the more we cut down and reduce expenses and the closer we come to our High Priest, our model and rule, Christ our Lord" ([344], trans. in Ivens, *Understanding,* p. 240). Cf. 2 Cor. 9:7.

21. Toner, *DecisMakg,* p. 210. The same "clincher" that applies to the prior process of coming to a (tentative) judgment also applies to terminating the search for confirmation. Ibid.

22. Cf. Toner, *CommRules,* pp. 50–51, 66, 228.

23. However, see the qualifications of Toner, *DecisMakg,* pp. 121–27 and Ivens, *Understanding,* p. 136.

24. See José Nevado, S.I., "El segundo tiempo de elección en los Ejercicios," *Manr* 39 (1967): 41–54; Sampaio Costa, "The 'Times' of Ignatian Election," pp. 73–88. Besides according preference to the second method over the method of the third time in *Spiritual Exercises* [178] and *DirAutog* 19, Ignatius preferred the second method in practice at critical moments in his life: at the time of his conversion, in his decision to go to Jerusalem, in the deliberation over poverty in his *Spiritual Diary,* in opposing the cardinalate for Francisco Borja (cf. *Obras,* pp. 909–10; *LettIgn,* pp. 257–58), and in writing the Constitutions of the Society (cf. *Autobiog* 101). However, by the time Gil González Dávila wrote his directory about thirty years after Ignatius's death, he felt the need to warn "that for a person to be guided on his or her own solely by interior movements and feelings is highly dangerous and the source of all the illusions and illuminations [*alumbramientos*] by which the devil has been waging a mighty war against the Church of God." After developing this thesis, he concluded: "For this reason it is said that the third method of the election is surer" (González Dávila 135 and 140, in Palmer, *Giving,* pp. 258–59; translation slightly altered). The Official Directory later incorporated this judgment: "the third way by means of reflection and reasoning is safer and more secure" than the second (no. 190; cf. no. 204; in Palmer, *Giving,* pp. 330, 333).

25. Tad Dunne, "The Cultural Milieus of the Spiritual Exercises," in *A New Introduction to the Spiritual Exercises of St. Ignatius* (Collegeville, Minn.: Michael Glazier, 1993), p. 20.

26. See Karl Rahner, "The Logic of Concrete Individual Knowledge" (ch. 15 n. 9 above), especially pp. 103–9, 128 n. 25, and Harvey D. Egan, *The Spiritual Exercises and the Ignatian Mystical Horizon* (St. Louis: IJS, 1976). Avery Dulles, "Finding God's Will," *Woodstock Letters* 114 (Spring 1965): 139–52, provides a clear summary of Rahner's difficult essay. Thomas Green, *Weeds among the Wheat* (Notre Dame, Ind.: Ave Maria Press, 1984), pp. 87–88 presents the three methods as distinct but considers the third incomplete and untrustworthy without the second. According to Green, in the third we guess at what God is saying to us; in the second we actually "hear" it.

27. Cf. *Spiritual Exercises* [20]; Toner *DecisMakg,* pp. 169–70. The early directories clearly affirm the sufficiency of the third method. See Toner, *DecisMakg,* pp. 249–50.

Ignatius at least implicitly affirms the sufficiency of the second method in [178]. In a letter to Ramírez de Vergara (March 30, 1556), he validates the sufficiency of the third method when the second fails to indicate a clear path. Ignatius wrote to him: "it is true that, in order to pursue better and more perfect things, the inclination of reason is sufficient." Although the will and affections provided no clear indications to Ramírez, Ignatius assured him that, should he follow the clear lead of reason, God would then incline the will as well and make the execution easy (*Obras,* p. 1086; *LettIgn,* pp. 416–17). In the 1539 "Deliberation," Ignatius and his companions relied essentially on the third method of pros and cons in deciding to found the Society of Jesus (English text in Futrell, *Making an Apostolic Community,* pp. 187–94 and Toner, "The Deliberation That Started the Jesuits" [both references in n. 16 above]).

28. Ignatius recorded his parallel use of both in his *Spiritual Diary.* See paragraph no. 15 in Ganss, ed., *Ignatius of Loyola* (ch. 13 n. 8), p. 241.

29. Toner, *DecisMakg,* p. 286.

30. See ibid., p. 312.

31. See ibid., chapter 5.

32. Cf. Luis Gonçalves da Câmara, *Recuerdos ignacianos: Memorial de Luis Gonçalves da Câmara,* Benigno Hernández Montes, S.I., ed., with commentary (Bilbao and Santander: Mensajero and Sal Terrae, 1991), p. 143 (§182). Hereafter, I refer to this work as the *Memorial,* as it is frequently known, and to paragraphs according to the standard numbering. Detachment from the results of our actions is also a cardinal principle of the Hindu scriptures, the *Bhagavad Gita.*

33. Cf., among others, Ivens, *Understanding,* p. 37. For a different interpretation of the subject of this note, cf. Michael J. Buckley, S.J., "The Structure for the Rules for the Discernment of Spirits," *The Way Supplement* 20 (1973): 19–37.

Chapter 17. The Way of Truth and Life

1. Michael Ivens distinguishes between the necessary "here-and-now dispositions, especially in relation to the impending election" of the retreat, and those "habitual dispositions" that are the labor of a lifetime. Ivens, *Understanding,* p. 123.

2. The *Spiritual Exercises* specifies criteria 1a (Reason), 2, 3, 4, 5, 8, 9, and 10 in its own way. I have added 1b (Science), what 3 says about the victims, 6 and 7 to address the concerns mentioned above.

3. Rationality takes many forms. See, for example, Stephen Toulmin, *The Uses of Argument* (Cambridge: Cambridge University Press, 1958); David Tracy, *Plurality and Ambiguity: Hermeneutics, Religion, Hope* (Chicago: University of Chicago Press, 1987); Ivone Gebara, *Longing for Running Water: Ecofeminism and Liberation* (Minneapolis: Fortress, 1999), chapter 1, "Knowing Our Knowing: The Issue of Epistemology."

4. Understanding life requires entering into its drama and letting that drama enter us. This is the way we come to know other people and new places. We must adjust to them practically and emotionally, as well as conceptually. In the Bible, knowledge is a matter of experience by the whole person, unlike Western thought which distinguishes sharply between sense and feeling on the one hand and conceptual knowledge on the other. Basque philosopher Xavier Zubiri takes exception to this dualism. (See his *Inteligencia sentiente: Inteligencia y realidad* [Madrid: Alianza, 1980].) For him human beings are animals of "sensing intelligence," *inteligencia sentiente.* There is no such thing as pure reason or intelligence separated from the senses and feelings.

5. Cf. John 9; 3:19–20; 2 John 4; 3 John 3–4; 2 Thess. 2:12; Eph. 4:17–19; 5:8–14; etc.

6. See also Phil. 1:9; 1 Cor. 2:16. "Perception is a function of character; it is not a morally neutral faculty but one that sees only that which the person already values. Transformation of the person down to her most important values, therefore, is necessary to correct the vision of the heart" (Spohn, *Go and Do Likewise* [ch. 9, n. 12 above], p. 86).

7. See E. Gilson, *The Christian Philosophy of St. Augustine* (New York: Random House, 1960), Part I, chapter 1.

8. Cf. Spohn, *Go and Do Likewise,* especially chapters 2 and 5. These are part of the support system of a committed life.

9. According to Jacques Maritain, Thomas Aquinas taught that "the very mode or manner in which human reason knows natural law is not rational knowledge, but knowledge *through inclination.* That kind of knowledge is not clear knowledge through concepts and conceptual judgments; it is obscure, unsystematic, vital knowledge by connaturality or congeniality, in which the intellect, in order to bear judgment, consults and listens to the inner melody that the vibrating strings of abiding tendencies make present in the subject" (J. Maritain, *Man and the State* [Chicago: University of Chicago Press, 1951], pp. 91–92; emphasis in original). While these natural inclinations may not be identical with those arising from consolation, the two at least overlap.

10. Paul Ricoeur, *The Symbolism of Evil* (Boston: Beacon, 1967), pp. 347–57.

11. See the classic work of Paulo Freire, *Pedagogy of the Oppressed* (New York: Herder and Herder, 1970).

12. On the Spiritual Exercises and social awareness, see the seminal article of Elinor Shea, "Spiritual Direction and Social Consciousness," in *The Way of Ignatius Loyola,* ed. Philip Sheldrake (S.P.C.K: London, 1991), pp. 203–15; originally published in *The Way Supplement* 54 (Autumn 1985).

13. See the inset on pp. 86–87 above.

14. The literature is vast. See the two classics: Karl Mannheim, "The Utopian Mentality" in idem, *Ideology and Utopia: An Introduction to the Sociology of Knowledge,* trans. Louis Wirth and Edward Shils (New York: Harcourt, Brace & World/Harvest, n.d.; original German ed., 1929) and Ernst Bloch, *The Principle of Hope* (Cambridge, Mass.: MIT Press, 1995).

15. Cf. Gustavo Gutiérrez, *A Theology of Liberation: History, Politics, and Salvation,* trans. and ed. Sister Caridad Inda and John Eagleson, rev. ed. with a new introduction (Maryknoll, N.Y.: Orbis, 1988), pp. 135–40. For a good example of realistic-utopian thinking, see Ignacio Ellacuría, "Utopia and Prophesy in Latin America" (ch. 11 n. 14 above), pp. 44–88.

16. Toner, *DecisMakg,* p. 313.

17. Cf. Tracy, *Analogical Imagination* [ch. 9 n. 1 above], pp. 236–37, 324–27, 420.

18. Lonergan, *Method in Theology* (ch. 5 n. 6 above). For the transcendental precepts see pp. 53, 55.

19. Gil Bailie, *Violence Unveiled* (ch. 11 n. 6 above), chapter 13.

20. I suspect that, like Anne Patrick, I learned to think in these terms under the influence of James Gustafson, who taught both of us at the University of Chicago. See Patrick, *Liberating Conscience* (ch. 14 n. 5 above), p. 188.

21. Classical orthodox theologies, including Catholic moral theology prior to the Second Vatican Council (1962–65), so stressed moral norms that discernment

was often reduced to weighing and applying norms. This legalistic approach often neglected actual conditions and the complex reality of the person acting. Liberal theologies, including post–Vatican II *aggiornamento* theology, rehabilitated discernment, devoting greater attention to the subject who discerns. Finally, political and liberation theologies stress the importance of understanding objective reality, especially the reality of the victims, and discernment as a response to that reality.

22. Since poles overlap, there is more than one legitimate way to match criteria and poles.

Chapter 18. The Grace of Compassion

1. Hillesum records these last words in her diary: "We should be willing to act as a balm for all wounds." Hillesum, *An Interrupted Life* (ch. 5 n. 5), p. 231. Page references in the text refer to this volume.

Chapter 19. The Solidarity of God

1. See chapter 9.

2. Ignatius adds "in his humanity," avoiding the idea of a suffering divinity.

3. Two examples can illustrate what I mean. Hurricane Mitch devastated Central America in 1998. As in most "natural" disasters, it was the poor who suffered. In El Salvador, the government had resettled destitute war refugees on flatlands subject to perennial flooding. Long before, agribusiness had deforested the area and depleted the soil. The consequences of Hurricane Mitch were disastrous for the poor settlers. The same pattern was repeated with the earthquakes of 2001, which destroyed mainly the precarious adobe homes of the poor, especially those constructed on hillsides. We could do a similar analysis of illness. Natural disasters occur, but much of our suffering, and most of its bitterness, come from *un*natural, moral causes.

4. E.g., Rom. 3:25; 1 John 2:2; 4:10; 1 Pet. 1:18–19; Eph. 5:2; Heb. passim.

5. Jon Sobrino, *Jesus the Liberator* (ch. 3, n. 11, above), p. 246. "In history there is no such thing as love without solidarity and there is no solidarity without incarnation. Solidarity that was not prepared to share the lot of those with whom it wanted to show solidarity" would not be solidarity, or love, at all. Ibid., pp. 244–45.

6. Cf. ibid., pp. 245–49. See also Pousset, *LFF,* p. 157. Compared to our creeds, official liturgies and unofficial religious discourse, the Bible shows little interest in stressing God's omnipotence. Every reference to God as "Almighty" in the Revised Standard Version (and NRSV) of the Old Testament is a translation of the Hebrew *El Shadday.* Although we do not know exactly what *El Shadday* means, we do know it does not mean "Almighty God." In the New Testament, every example of "Almighty" is a translation of the Greek word *Pantocrator,* which there means "All-sovereign" rather than "Almighty," a subtle but important difference, since God's sovereignty is not "of this world."

7. Elie Wiesel, *Night* (New York: Bantam Books, 1986), p. 62.

8. On the debated identity of the least brothers and sisters in Matthew 25, see the careful analysis of John R. Donohue, S.J., "The 'Parable' of the Sheep and the Goats: A Challenge to Christian Ethics," *Theological Studies* 47 (1986): 3–31.

Chapter 20. Blessed Are the Persecuted

1. Solidarity is the essence of religion, which all other religious practices (prayer, ritual, etc.) must serve. See James 1:27; Matt. 7:12; 25:31–46; Rom. 13:8–10; Hos. 6:6; Mic. 6:8; etc.

2. When protesting abortion, I hope Maria will locate this problem in its social and cultural context and not reduce it to a question of personal sin. The society that offers women the option of abortion simultaneously denies many of them the social, educational, and health options and resources they need to provide for themselves and their families, which helps account for the alarming incidence of abortion. According to the Alan Guttmacher Institute (www.guttmacher.org/sections/abortion.html) 39 million abortions were performed in the United States in the thirty years following the Supreme Court's 1973 *Roe v. Wade* decision. This disregard for the life of the unborn is part of the more general disregard for life reflected in the lack of housing and medical coverage for millions, the frequent application of the death penalty, domestic and social violence, and growing militarism.

3. For some of what follows, I draw on Jon Sobrino, *Spirituality of Liberation: Toward Political Holiness* (Maryknoll, N.Y.: Orbis, 1988), chapter 5, "The Spirituality of Persecution and Martyrdom."

4. See also Luke 1:30, 38; 8:50; 24:36–41; Matt. 14:26–31; 28:5, 10; Luke 12:22–33; Rom. 8:31–39; 1 John 5:5. See the Old Testament roots of this radical trust in the face of threats in Deut. 7:17–24; 20:1–4; Josh. 1:1–9; Judg. 7:1–25; 2 Macc. 8:18; Ps 20:8; 44:2–8; Isa. 7:9; etc.

5. On rejoicing in persecution and consolation in trials, see James 1:2; Acts 5:41; 2 Cor. 1:4–5; 7:4; 1:4–10; 1 Thess. 3:7; John 16:33; Heb. 10:32–35; 1 Pet. 4:13, 19.

6. Homilies of July 15 and May 20, of 1979, in *Mons. Oscar A. Romero, Su pensamiento* (ch. 12 n. 2 above), 7, p. 75; 6, p. 362; translation from Jon Sobrino, *Spirituality of Liberation,* pp. 100–101. Preaching at a Mass for murdered priest Rafael Palacios, Romero said: "We can present, together with the blood of teachers, of workers, of peasants, the blood of our priests. This is fellowship in love. It would be sad, in a country where so many horrible murders are being committed, if priests were not also to be found among the victims" (Homily, June 30, 1979, in *Romero, Su pensamiento,* 7, p. 30).

7. Cf. Matt. 5:39; Luke 6:27–32, 35; Rom. 12:17–21; 1 Cor. 4:12; 2 Cor. 7:4; 1 Thess. 5:15; 1 Pet. 3:9.

8. The Greek word translated "guileless" here means "without duplicity" or "uncontaminated." It has nothing to do with naiveté.

9. Rom. 6:4; 8:17; Gal. 2:19; 2 Tim 2:11–12; Eph. 2:5–6; 3:6; Col. 2:12–13. See David M. Stanley, S.J., *A Modern Scriptural Approach to the Spiritual Exercises* (Chicago: IJS, 1967), pp. 210–11; Juan Manuel Martín-Moreno, S.J., "El don del Espíritu Santo en los Ejercicios Espirituales," *Manr* 59 (1987): 364.

Chapter 21. Resurrection and the Spirit

1. In this section I draw on Jon Sobrino, *Christ the Liberator: A View from the Victims,* trans. Paul Burns (Maryknoll, N.Y.: Orbis, 2001), especially chapters 1–3.

2. Cf. Col. 1:18; 1 Cor. 15:20.

3. "Jesus' resurrection is hope, first of all, for those crucified in history.... There is, then, a correlation between resurrection and the crucified analogous to the correlation between the Kingdom of God and the poor." Sobrino, *Christ the Liberator,* p. 84.

4. Cf. Rom. 6:3–8; Gal. 2:19–20; Col. 2:20; 3:1–3; 1 Thess. 5:10.

5. John 3:3–8; 2 Cor. 5:17; Gal. 6:15.

6. Cf. 1 Cor. 5:7; Col. 3:1–15; Eph. 4:13.

7. Cf. Rom. 5:5; 8:11. Although the Spirit filled Jesus during his ministry, the disciples only received the Spirit after his death. See John 7:37–39. On the cross Jesus gives over the Spirit, and blood and water flow from his side (John 19:30, 34). On the day of resurrection he breathes on the disciples and says, "Receive the Holy Spirit" (John 20:22).

8. The messianic age inaugurates a new temple, Christ's body (John 2:21; 4:20–24; Rev. 21:22). On the church as the body of Christ, see Eph. 1:22–23; 2:16; 5:30; Col. 1:18, 24; 3:15. According to these texts, the church is, quite literally, the body of Christ on earth. When I say that Christ rises in the disciples, I do not mean to reduce the resurrection to their subjective experience. Christ himself passed through death and was transformed.

9. See the boxed text "Spirit in Disguise" on p. 198–99. For the material there, among other sources, I draw on the trilogy of José María Lera, "Apuntes para una pneumatología de los ejercicios. En el XVI° centenario del Concilio I de Constantinopla," *Manr* 53 (1981): 327–58; idem, "Apuntes para una pneumatología de los ejercicios (II)," *Manr* 58 (1986): 99–128; idem, "La contemplación para alcanzar amor, el pentecostés ignaciano: Apuntes para una pneumatología de los Ejercicios (III)," *Manr* 63 (1991): 163–90. Lera's thesis is admirably summarized in Juan Chechon Chong, S.I., "La Contemplación para Alcanzar Amor [230–237], el Pentecostés ignaciano," *Manr* 72 (2000): 293–303. See also the rich study of Juan Manuel Martín-Moreno, S.J., "El don del Espíritu Santo en los Ejercicios Espirituales," *Manr* 59 (1987): 357–72.

10. "Some consider this experience [of consolation without prior cause] as something pertaining to the pinnacle of the spiritual life, or to properly mystical gifts. We do not believe Ignatius so understood it.... Experience also invites us to think that this occurs frequently" (Cabarrús, "Discernimiento: La osadía de dejarse llevar," [ch. 15 n. 8 above], p. 30).

Chapter 22. Consolation, Action, and Liberation

1. Matt. 28:8, 10; Luke 24:36–38, 41, 52; John 20:19, 21, 26; cf. 14:27–28.

2. For consolation in this sense, see also 1 Thess. 3:7; 2 Thess. 2:16–17; Rom. 15:4–5; 1 Cor. 14:3; 2 Cor. 7:4–7, 13; Phil. 2:1; Phm. 7; Col. 2:2; Heb. 6:18.

3. Isa. 2:15–20; 42:1–4; 59:15–21; Zech. 4:6.

4. On the "consolation" of the nonhuman environment, see also Isaiah 41:18–20; 43:19–21; 44:23; 48:21; 49:13, 19.

5. See also Luke 6:24; 16:25. On justice and the poor in Luke, see Richard J. Cassidy, *Jesus, Politics, and Society: A Study of Luke's Gospel* (Maryknoll, N.Y.: Orbis, 1978). See also Sharon H. Ringe, *Jesus, Liberation, and Biblical Jubilee: Images for Ethics and Christology* (Philadelphia: Fortress Press, 1985); Jerome H. Neyrey, ed., *The Social World of Luke-Acts: Models for Interpretation* (Peabody, Mass.: Hendrickson Publishers, 1991).

6. See John 14:15–17, 26; 15:26; 16:7–15.

7. References to this boldness (*parrhesia* and *parrhesiazomai* in Greek) abound. See especially 2 Cor. 3:12, 17 and Acts 4:13, 29, 31; 9:27–29; 13:46; 14:3; 18:25–26; 19:8; 26:26; 28:31. See also 1 Thess. 2:2, Eph. 6:19; Phil. 1:20; 1 Tim. 3:15; Heb. 3:6; 10:35; etc.

8. This image predominates in the *Constitutions,* not in the earlier *Exercises.* See Peter J. Schineller, S.J. "The Pilgrim Journey of Ignatius: From Soldier to Laborer in the Lord's Vineyard and Its Implications for Apostolic Lay Spirituality," *SSJ* 31, no. 4 (September 1999): 1–41.

9. *LettIgn,* p. 181 (September 20, 1548); in *Obras,* 832.

10. *LettIgn,* pp. 21–22 (June 18, 1536); in *Obras,* 732.

11. Luke 1:36–37; Judg. 6:15; cf. Gen. 18:14; 37:3–11; Exod. 4:10–13; 1 Sam ch. 1; ch. 16; Jer. 1:6–7; etc.

12. Day, *The Long Loneliness* (ch. 5 n. 5 above), p. 285.

13. Paragraph nos. 275–78, in *Puebla and Beyond: Documentation and Commentary,* ed. John Eagleson and Philip Scharper (Maryknoll, N.Y.: Orbis, 1979), p. 160.

14. The attribution dates at least to the Hungarian Jesuit Gabriel Hevenesi, *Scintillae Ignatianae* (Vienna, 1705). Trans. in Cusson, *BibTheol,* p. 71 n. 75.

15. P. Ribadeneyra, *De ratione quam in gubernando tenebat Ignatius,* cited in Joseph de Guibert, *The Jesuits, Their Spiritual Doctrine and Practice: A Historical Study* (Chicago: IJS, 1964), p. 148 n. 55.

16. See Hugo Rahner, S.J., *Ignatius the Theologian,* trans. Michael Barry (New York: Herder and Herder, 1968), pp. 25–31; and John W. Padberg, S.J., "Personal Experience and the *Spiritual Exercises:* The Example of Saint Ignatius," *SSJ* (1978): 320.

17. For a profound reflection on these themes, see James Alison, *Raising Abel: The Recovery of the Eschatological Imagination* (New York: Crossroad, 1996).

Chapter 23. Learning to Love Like God

1. George Ganss, "Notes for the Spiritual Exercises," in Ganss, ed. *Ignatius of Loyola* (ch. 13 n. 8 above). Although the text of the *Exercises* does not specify when this exercise should take place, today most agree that it is part of the Fourth Week, to be done after or possibly along with contemplations of the risen Christ. The Contemplation grows organically out of the four weeks and seems to presuppose them. See Cusson, *BibTheol,* pp. 312–17; Michael J. Buckley, "The Contemplation to Attain Love," *The Way Supplement* 24 (Spring 1975): 92–104 at pp. 92–93; and Peters, *SpEx,* pp. 11, 153–54.

2. See José María Lera, "La contemplación para alcanzar amor, el pentecostés ignaciano: Apuntes para una pneumatología de los Ejercicios (III)," *Manr* 63 (1991): 163–90; and Juan Chechon Chong, S.I., "La Contemplación para Alcanzar Amor [230–37], el Pentecostés ignaciano," *Manr* 72 (2000): 293–303. Ignatius fails to name the Spirit explicitly in this context. On this point, see "The Relationship of the Three Methods of Decision Making" in chapter 16 of this book and the boxed text "Spirit in Disguise?" on pp. 198–99 above.

3. We seek to "attain" love for God, that is, "arrive at" loving God, not "obtain" God's love for us (cf. Ivens, *Understanding,* p. 172). For the title of this chapter I borrow from Joseph Tetlow who calls the exercise "The Contemplation for Learning to Love like God" (Tetlow, *Choosing Christ in the World* [ch. 7 n. 7 above], p. 172). The title in

the Latin Vulgate version of the *Exercises* is *"Contemplatio ad amorem spiritualem in nobis excitandum,"* "The Contemplation for Arousing Spiritual Love within Us." Several early directories adopt this language.

4. For different interpretations of the prayer "Take and Receive," see Gabriel María Verd, S.J., " 'Tomad, Señor, y recibid', una oración polivalente," *Manr* 58 (1986): 77–88.

5. Cf. Pousset, *LFF,* pp. 198–99.

6. *Const* 288.

7. In early writings like the *Spiritual Exercises,* Ignatius sometimes attributes to Christ functions that are proper to the Father, for example, referring to Christ as "Creator and Lord" [53] and "Creator and Redeemer" [229]. Similar references in the Foundation [23], the election [169–89] and this Contemplation may also refer to Christ. See Jesús Solano, "Jesucristo en las denominaciones divinas de S. Ignacio," *Estudios Eclesiásticos* 30 [1956]: 325–42; José María Díez-Alegría, "La Contemplación para alcanzar Amor en la dinámica espiritual de los Ejercicios de San Ignacio," *Manr* 23 [1951]: 171–93; Miguel Angel Fiorito, "Cristocentrismo del Principio y Fundamento de S. Ignacio," *Ciencia y Fe,* separata, January–February 1961; Teresa Días Gonçalves, "Sentido cristológico del 'Principio y Fundamento,' " *Manr* 44 [1972]: 53–68; idem, "¿Es cristológica la contemplación 'ad amorem'?" *Manr* 45 [1973]: 289–308; Cusson, *BibTheol,* p. 57 n. 32. In the *Spiritual Diary,* in passages recorded two years before his death, Ignatius seems to express new awareness of the "individuality" of each of the three divine Persons. See Ganss, ed., *Ignatius of Loyola* (ch. 13 n. 8 above), pp. 245–50, paragraph nos. 52, 54, 63, 67, 72, and 73.

8. Among the "blessings" of the first point, the Vulgate version of the *Exercises* includes: "how much the most generous Lord has *borne and suffered* for my sake" (*Monumenta Ignatiana,* Series 2, *Exercitia Spiritualia,* nova editio, I. Calveras, S.I. et Candidus de Dalmases, S.I. eds., MHSI, vol. 100 [Rome: Institutum Historicum Societatis Jesu, 1969], p. 308; my translation and emphasis). This can only refer to Christ. Ignatius's faithful interpreter, Juan Polanco, repeats the idea in his Summary of the *Exercises;* text in I. Iparraguirre, ed., *Directoria Exercitiorum Spiritualium* (ch. 16 n. 1 above), p. 344.

9. Cf. Buckley, "The Contemplation," p. 102. Nadal pointed this out long ago (H. Nadal, *Apologia Exercitiorum,* in *Epistolae et Monumenta P. Nadal,* vol. 4 [Madrid: MHSI, 1905], pp. 863, 867–68). In the *Exercises* and in Ignatius's writings generally, *trabajo* (labor) frequently refers to hardship and persecution endured in the service to God. Cf. [93, 95–97, 116]; also [51]. Like Gaston Fessard (*La dialectique des Exercices Spirituels de saint Ignace de Loyola* [Paris: Aubier, 1956], pp. 147–64), Buckley believes that the four points of the Contemplation recapitulate the four weeks of the Exercises.

10. Theological reflection on the "new physics" and evolutionary biology is rich, vast and growing. Helpful recent accounts include David Toolan, *At Home in the Cosmos* (Maryknoll, N.Y.: Orbis, 2001); John F. Haught, *God after Darwin: A Theology of Ecology* (Boulder, Colo.: Westview Press, 2000); and Leonardo Boff, *Cry of Earth, Cry of the Poor* (Maryknoll, N.Y.: Orbis, 1997). See the extensive bibliography in these works. Here I limit myself to commenting on David Toolan's wonderful essay, in the spirit of the Ignatian Contemplation, "Praying in a Post-Einsteinian Universe," *Cross-Currents* (Winter 1996/97): 437–70. Numbers in parenthesis in the text refer to pages of Toolan's essay.

11. Cf. Buckley, "The Contemplation," p. 102.

12. Cf. Lera, "Pentecostés ignaciano," p. 173.

13. Ibid., p. 184. The quotation is from *Const* 288.

Chapter 24. Introducing Prayer

1. See Ignacio Ellacuría, "La contemplación en la acción de la justicia," in idem, *Fe y justicia,* Estudio introductorio de Jon Sobrino (Bilbao: Desclée de Brouwer, 1999), pp. 207–16. Along with many contemporary thinkers, Ellacuría understands action (praxis) to be the defining characteristic of human existence. See Ignacio Ellacuría, *Filosofía de la realidad histórica* (San Salvador: UCA Editores, 1991). Contemplation is a moment of praxis understood in this broad sense.

2. Ignatius uses the term "contemplation" in this narrower sense, and especially to refer to the imaginative re-presentation of gospel scenes that characterizes the Second to Fourth weeks of the Spiritual Exercises. See chapter 9 of this book.

3. As was discussed in the previous chapter.

4. Cf. Mark 3:35; Matt. 23:9; and compare the two lists in Mark 10:29–30.

5. This was not exclusively a child's expression, "so the 'Daddy' interpretation for Jesus' usage should be dropped" (Raymond E. Brown, *Death of the Messiah: From Gethsemane to the Grave, a Commentary on the Passion Narratives in the Four Gospels* [New York: Doubleday, 1994] 1:173).

6. Hillesum, *An Interrupted Life* (ch. 5 n. 5 above), p. 105. Etty imagined entitling a quasi-autobiographical novel "The Girl Who Could Not Kneel" (ibid., p. 58).

7. See further Matt. 18:19; Mark 11:22–24; Luke 18:1–8; John 14:13–14; 15:7; 1 John 3:22; 5:14; Eph. 6:18; Phil. 4:6; 1 Tim. 2:1; James 1:5–8.

8. Cf. Peter Schineller, "The Pilgrim Journey of Ignatius" (ch. 22 n. 8 above), p. 25.

9. Xavier Zubiri, *El hombre y Dios* (Madrid: Alianza, 1994), p. 203.

10. See chapter 21, "Resurrection and Holy Spirit."

Chapter 25. School of Prayer

1. Joseph Veale, "Ignatian Prayer or Jesuit Spirituality," *The Way Supplement* 27 (Spring 1976): 8.

2. Gonçalves da Câmara, *Memorial* (ch. 16 n. 32 above), p. 182 (§256).

3. Letter to Francisco Borja, September 20, 1548, in *Obras,* pp. 831–32; cf. *LettIgn,* p. 181.

4. See chapter 15 above.

5. See chapter 2 and José María Castillo, "Tercera manera de humildad" (ch. 12 n. 7 above), pp. 127–28.

6. Anthony de Mello's *Sadhana: A Way to God. Christian Exercises in Eastern Form,* 5th ed. (St. Louis: IJS, 1978) contains helpful suggestions for centering and concentration in prayer.

7. See "Contemplating the Life of Jesus" in chapter 9.

8. In [66–70] one "sees" and "feels" flames, "hears" weeping and cursing, "tastes" tears, "smells" smoke and sulfur. These are biblical symbols of the anti-reign.

9. Hugo Rahner, S.J., "The Application of the Senses," in idem, *Ignatius the Theologian* (ch. 22 n. 16 above), pp. 181–213 at 182. In this section, I am following Rahner and, even more, Pousset, *LFF,* pp. 51–54, 96–109. Both are excellent sources.

10. Letter of September 11, 1536, *Obras,* pp. 734–35; cf. *LettIgn,* pp. 24–25.

For other types of prayer not examined here, see *Spiritual Exercises* [238–60] and the commentaries.

11. See the beautiful reflections of Jean Vanier, founder of the L'Arche movement, for example, his *Tears of Silence* (Toronto: Griffin House, 1970), and idem, *Eruption to Hope* (New York and Ramsey, N.J.: Paulist Press, 1971).

12. Cf. Dermot Mansfield, "The Exercises and Contemplative Prayer," in Philip Sheldrake, S.J., ed., *The Way of Ignatius Loyola* (ch. 17 n. 12 above), pp. 191–202.

13. Joan Scott, "The Experience of Ignatian Prayer," *The Way Supplement* 82 (Spring 1995): 56. "We are no longer interested in whether any one kind of prayer is higher and in some mysterious way closer to God than another. . . . In the end the only possible criterion of choice is where I feel drawn and where I feel most at home" (ibid., pp. 55–56).

Chapter 26. Worldly Prayer

1. Ignatius's trusted interpreter, Jerónimo Nadal, so characterized him: ". . . in all things, actions, and conversations, he would sense and contemplate the presence of God and attraction to spiritual things, as a contemplative person even while in action [*simul in actione contemplatiuus*] (something which he used to express as 'finding God in all things')" (J. Nadal, "In examen annotationes," *Epistolae et Monumenta* (ch. 23 n. 9 above), vol. 5 [1962], p. 162).

2. *Const* 723, 813; Gonçalves da Câmara, *Memorial* (ch. 16 n. 32 above), p. 140 (§175).

3. So did Francis de Sales, Mary Ward, and the Reformers in different ways. Three centuries before Ignatius, Thomas Aquinas argued that in a sense it was more perfect to interrupt contemplation with God in order to share its fruits with one's neighbor. Cf. *S.T.* II-II, q. 188, a. 6. Meister Eckhart argued for the priority of action over contemplation more generally. Ignatius specified that the action in question is following Jesus. See J. Matthew Ashley, "La contemplación en la acción por la justicia: La contribución de Ignacio Ellacuría a la espiritualidad cristiana," *Revista Latinoamericana de Teología* 51 (September-December 2000): 211–32.

4. I am grateful to Miguel Elizondo, who trained generations of Jesuits in Latin America (and also guided Archbishop Oscar Romero through the Spiritual Exercises), for showing me the importance of this shift in language. Elizondo uses the formula "united to God in seeking and finding God's will." See also Joseph Veale, "Saint Ignatius Speaks about 'Ignatian Prayer,'" *SSJ* 28, no. 2 (March 1996). Gervais Dumeige ("El Problema de la acción y de la contemplación: La solución ignaciana," *Cursus Internationalis Exercitiorum Spiritualium* [Rome, 1969], pp. 192/1–7) prefers the formula "in actione *unitus cum Deo*" to Nadal's "contemplativus in actione" (ibid., p. 192/5, emphasis in original).

5. E. Edward Kinerk, "When Jesuits Pray: A Perspective on the Prayer of Apostolic Persons," *SSJ* 17, no. 5 (November 1985), p. 6, citing Gregorius Rosephius, *Fontes Narrativi de S. Ignatio de Loyola,* MHSI, vol. 3, p. 515.

6. To Manuel Godinho (January 31, 1552), *LettIgn,* pp. 254–55; *Obras,* p. 906.

7. Through his personal secretary Polanco, Ignatius wrote that he desired of members of the Society "that if possible they find no less devotion in any work of charity or obedience than in prayer or meditation; for they ought not do anything except for love and service of God" (Letter to Urbano Fernandes, June 1, 1551, in *Obras,* p. 892; cf. *LettIgn,* p. 236). Cf. also *Const* 340.

8. *Commentary on Romans,* chap. 1, lect. 5. I alter the translation in George Ganss, *The Constitutions of the Society of Jesus* (St. Louis: IJS, 1970), §340 n. 4, and Joseph Veale, "Saint Ignatius Speaks," p. 15.

9. Letter 4,012, *Epistolae et Instructiones S. Ignatii de Loyola,* vol. 6, *Monumenta Ignatiana,* vol. 33 (Madrid: MHSI, 1907), p. 91; cited in Veale, "Saint Ignatius Speaks," p. 15. In the words of a longtime associate of Ignatius: "he desired that all in the Society accustom themselves always to find the presence of God in everything and that they learn to raise their hearts not only in private prayer but also in all of their occupations, carrying them out and offering them in such a way that they would feel no less devotion in action than in meditation. And he used to say that this method of prayer is very profitable for all and especially for those who are much engaged in exterior things of the divine service" (Pedro Ribadeneira, *Vita Ignatii Loyolae,* in *Fontes Narrativi,* vol. 4, p. 743; quoted by Kinerk, "When Jesuits Pray," p. 7).

10. Walter J. Burghardt, S.J., "The Richness of a Resource," in *A Spirituality for Contemporary Life: The Jesuit Heritage Today,* ed. David L. Fleming (St. Louis, Mo.: Review for Religious, 1991), p. 14.

11. *Epistolae et Monumenta,* vol. 5 (note 1 above), p. 29; quoted in Kinerk, "When Jesuits Pray," p. 13. Nadal wrote of Jesuits and their prayer: "All should strive in the Lord, as they walk in the way of prayer and the spiritual life, to find God in all their ministries and labors. The delight, the love of prayer which would incite them to seek seclusion and a solitude beyond what is imposed, would not seem appropriate for the Company. What is appropriate is a prayer that incites to the labors and ministries of our vocation and especially to the prefect obedience which our institute requires.... [The prayer proper to the Company] consists in this: that, with the grace of Jesus Christ, the light of the understanding, the good inclinations of the will, steadfast union with God (apart from prayer in the strict sense) accompany and guide all our actions, in such a way that we find God in everything.... That our prayer be such that it increases in us spiritual delight for [apostolic] labors... and that these labors increase virtue and joy in prayer. Thus... Martha and Mary will be united and they will help each other in the Lord" (*Epistolae et Monumenta,* vol. 4, pp. 673–74). "In this way, what was the starting point of prayer is also its end, that is, charity" (ibid., p. 651). See the marvelous reflections of Ignatius's companion, Pierre Favre, on apostolic prayer, in P. Favre, *The Spiritual Writings of Pierre Favre* (St. Louis: IJS, 1996), p. 141.

12. "When you stretch out your hands [in prayer], I will hide my eyes from you; even though you make many prayers, I will not listen; your hands are full of blood" (Isa. 1:15; cf. 1 John 4:8, 20). According to Nadal, it is characteristic of the Ignatian style to "easily" prefer service to our neighbor to the delights that might come from long hours of contemplative prayer. Cf. Nadal, "In examen annotaciones" (note 1 above), p. 163. To be sure, Nadal was defending the discipline of the Jesuits against those who exaggerated the need for long hours of contemplative prayer—a rare temptation today.

13. Ignacio Ellacuría, "Lectura latinoamericana de los Ejercicios Espirituales de San Ignacio," *Revista Latinoamericana de Teología* 23 (May–August 1991): 111–47, especially 142–47; idem, "La contemplación en la acción de la justicia" (ch. 24 n. 1 above), especially p. 214. On Ellacuría and Ignatian spirituality, cf. J. Matthew Ashley, "Ignacio Ellacuría and the *Spiritual Exercises* of Ignatius Loyola," *Theological Studies* 61, no. 1 (March 2000): 16–39; idem, "Contemplación" (note 3 above).

14. Among many fine resources in this spirit, see William Reiser, *To Hear God's Word, Listen to the World: The Liberation of Spirituality* (New York: Paulist Press, 1997).

15. "There is a centeredness found only through quiet and solitude which will elude the busy apostle. But there is another kind of centeredness which does not consist in eliminating all 'noise' from the world, but in sorting it before God, in 'prioritizing' it; and this second type of centering lies at the heart of apostolic prayer" (Kinerk, "When Jesuits Pray," p. 11).

16. Letter to Francisco Borja, September 20, 1548, in *Obras,* p. 830; *LettIgn,* p. 180; and letter to Borja, July 1549, in *Obras,* p. 859; *LettIgn,* p. 211.

17. Letter to Antonio Brandão, June 1, 1551, *Obras,* pp. 885–86; cf. *LettIgn,* p. 240. The same doctrine, with the familiar expressions (e.g., "finding God in all things"), is incorporated into *Const* 288.

18. See chapter 23.

19. *Sancti Ignatii Epistolae et Instructiones,* vol. 3, *Monumenta Ignatiana* (Madrid: MHSI, 1903–11), p. 502; cited by Kinerk, "When Jesuits Pray," p. 3.

20. Gonçalves da Câmara, *Memorial,* p. 149 (§146). Gonçalves was unsure whether Ignatius actually said ninety-nine were deceived.

21. Ibid., p. 148 (§195).

22. Ibid., pp. 148–49 (§195–96); cf. pp. 181–82 (§256).

23. Ibid., pp. 181–82 (§256). For Jesuit students Ignatius stipulated a total of one hour of daily prayer in addition to Mass. The hour included two fifteen-minute periods of examen (*Const* 340–43; on the examen, see below). Because he believed that the amount and kind of prayer were such personal matters, he provided no uniform rule for formed Jesuits on these subjects (*Const* 582)—a radical departure from the practice of all other religious orders. Each Jesuit was to work out a suitable practice in dialogue with his superior. Ignatius's *Constitutions* also grant broad latitude in these matters to those responsible for novices and students (*Const* 279, 343). "Father Ignatius desired very much that in spiritual things regarding God's service we be moved and inclined by devotion and interior impulse, and he used extrinsic principles as little as possible in such matters" (Gonçalves da Câmara, *Memorial,* p. 138 [§171]).

24. See George A. Aschenbrenner, S.J., "Consciousness Examen," in *Review for Religious* 31 (1972): 13–21 at 21.

25. Cf. de Guibert, *The Jesuits* (ch. 22 n. 15 above), pp. 39–40, 66–67.

26. Cf. Tetlow, *Choosing Christ in the World* (ch. 7 n. 7 above), p. 210. On the examen in general, besides Aschenbrenner's classic article, "Consciousness Examen," see Joseph Tetlow, S.J., "That Most Postmodern Prayer," *SSJ* 26, no. 1 (January 1994). Donald St. Louis, "The Ignatian Examen," in Sheldrake, ed., *The Way of Ignatius Loyola* (ch. 17 n. 12 above), chapter 13, provides a rich commentary on the text of the *Spiritual Exercises* treating the examen [43].

27. See, especially, chapters 6 and 15.

Appendix I. The Kingdom Meditation?

1. Peters, *SpEx,* p. 71.

2. William Peters, "The Exercise in Jesuit Tradition" in *The Way* Supplement 18 (Spring 1973), *The Kingdom,* p. 30. *"Del Rey"* = "On the King" (cf. Peters, *SpEx,* p. 73).

3. Santiago Arzubialde, S.J., *Ejercicios Espirituales de S. Ignacio: Historia y análisis* (Bilbao and Santander: Mensajero and Sal Terrae, 1991), p. 221.

4. Cf. Ganss, *Spiritual Exercises* (ch. 2 n. 2), p. 159.

5. See Nadal's talk at Alcalá in 1554 in MHSI, *Fontes Narrativi,* I. 305.

6. William Peters, "The Kingdom: The Text of the Exercise" in *The Way* Supplement 18 (Spring 1973), *The Kingdom,* p. 11.

7. Peters, *SpEx,* pp. 71–72.

8. Peters, "The Exercise," passim; idem, "The Text," p. 12.

9. Ignatius "simply names [this exercise] *the call.* This curious observation puts us on the track of the meaning and finality which the exercise pursues. The whole life of Jesus, even its last details, is 'call.' Therefore people have to discern how to listen to it and how to respond to it" (Arzubialde, *Ejercicios Espirituales,* p. 221; emphasis in original). So, too, Peters: "The object of the consideration is undoubtedly the call" ("The Text," p. 9).

10. See Peter Schineller, "The Pilgrim Journey of Ignatius: From Soldier to Laborer in the Lord's Vineyard and Its Implications for Apostolic Lay Spirituality," *SSJ* 31, no. 4 (September 1999).

11. Cusson, *BibTheol,* p. 201.

12. Although the exercise contains echoes of medieval chivalry, the theme is fundamentally biblical and messianic. See Hervé Coathalem, *Ignatian Insights: A Guide to the Complete Spiritual Exercises* (Taichung, Taiwan: Kuangchi Press, 1961), pp. 134–35.

13. Peters, "The Text," pp. 9–10; idem, *SpEx,* pp. 72–73; Arzubialde, *Ejercicios Espirituales,* p. 221.

Appendix II. The Meaning of the Two Standards

1. I referred to the interpretation of Michael Ivens in chapter 10. David Fleming paraphrases *Spiritual Exercises* [142] as follows: "people find themselves tempted to covet *whatever seems to make them rich.*" (Fleming, *Draw Me into Your Friendship* [ch. 7 n. 7 above], p. 113; my emphasis). After recognizing that "the possession of material goods . . . is what [Ignatius] means by 'riches'" here, Karl Rahner adds that the "desire to possess" that Ignatius has in mind is actually "'wealth' in the broadest sense; it embraces not only material goods, but also spiritual values such as success, honor, cultural accomplishments" (Karl Rahner, *Spiritual Exercises* [New York: Herder & Herder, 1965,], p. 173). In a similar way, while poverty is first of all detachment from material riches, it includes detachment from "spiritual values such as a career, a reputation, and so forth" (ibid., p. 176). Similarly, Cusson, *BibTheol,* pp. 255–56; Dyckman et al., *The Spiritual Exercises Reclaimed* (ch. 1 n. 2 above), p. 198.

2. Luis Teixidor, "Un pasaje difícil de la meditación de Dos Banderas, y una cita implícita en el mismo de Santo Tomás de Aquino," *Manr* 3 (1927): 298–309. From this point, I follow the line of argument in my essay, "Downward Mobility: Social Implications of Saint Ignatius's Two Standards," *SSJ* 20, no. 1 (January 1988), "Appendix I: Thomistic Influence on Ignatius's Two Standards," pp. 41–48.

3. *S.T.,* 1a 2ae, 84, 1 ad 3. Quotations from the *Summa* are taken from St. Thomas Aquinas, *Summa Theologiae,* Latin text and English translation, Introduction, Notes, Appendices, and Glossaries (London and New York: Blackfriars/Eyre & Spottiswoode/ McGraw Hill, 1965–), with an occasional slight alteration.

4. "In the definitive verbal formulation of the meditation on the Two Standards, Ignatius, without doubt, had consulted the results of the theological investigations of his own time" (Hugo Rahner, S.J., *The Spirituality of St. Ignatius Loyola: An Account of Its Historical Development,* trans. Francis John Smith, S.J. [Westminster, Md.: Newman Press, 1953], p. 94). See also pp. 89–90 and idem, *Notes on the Spiritual Exercises,*

trans. Louis Mounteer (Woodstock, Md.: Woodstock College Press, 1956), pp. 286–87, 323.

5. Ignatius provides few particulars about the accusations, but he does tell us that in Salamanca in 1527, when questioned by the Dominican subprior, he answered that he and his companions taught about *virtues and vices* and that this raised the suspicions of his interrogators. See *Autobiog* 65. Did questioning like this spur Ignatius to seek theological support for the triads of virtues and vices in the Two Standards meditation?

6. For example, Augustine in *De Div. Quaest.* 83, 33 and 35; PL 40, 23–24.

7. Cf. *S.T.* 2a 2ae, 118, 2, where Thomas treats covetousness itself. See 2a 2ae, 119, 2 ad 1. Compare [23], the Foundation.

8. Augustine is the fundamental authority in the West. The sin of the angels was one of pride (*City of God,* xii, 6), as was the sin of Adam and Eve (ibid., xiv, 13). Thus, the earthly city is based on pride, "love of self extending to contempt of God" (ibid., xiv, 28). For the East, see Basil, Homilies 20.1 and John Chrysostom, *In Joan.* 9.2. Feminist theology has challenged this thesis.

9. See also *S.T.,* 2a 2ae, 162:3.

10. *S.T.* 1a 2ae, 84, 3 ad 1.

11. See 2a 2ae, 162, 8, and 1a 2ae, 84, 4 ad 4.

12. See *Const* 553–54. Ignatius considered the evangelical counsels as privileged means to concretize the standard of Christ. He believed that many religious orders in his day needed reform because they had grown lax in the practice of poverty ordained by their founders. To avoid this for the Society of Jesus, he stipulated that professed Jesuits were to promise not to change the statutes on poverty in the Society, except to make poverty more strict.

13. Jesuits promise not to seek prelacies and to report Jesuits who do to superiors.

14. The idea of "spiritual poverty" could also refer to our absolute poverty before God, as it frequently does in the *Imitation of Christ.*

15. "Riches" in the Two Standards cannot include "honor" because the two words occur in series in [142] and [146].

16. See José Calveras, "¿De qué humildad se habla en las Dos Banderas?" *Manr* 9 (1933): 12–22 and 97–106.

Select Bibliography of Ignatian Resources in English

The following list includes only translations of primary sources and secondary sources of a more general nature. The secondary sources include only books, not articles or individual chapters.

Collected Works of St. Ignatius

Ganss, George E., S.J., ed. *Ignatius of Loyola: The Spiritual Exercises and Selected Works,* with the collaboration of Parmananda R. Divarkar, S.J., Edward J. Malatesta, S.J., and Martin E. Palmer, S.J. Classics of Western Spirituality (Mahwah, N.J.: Paulist Press, 1991). Contains the *Spiritual Exercises,* the *Autobiography,* selections from the *Spiritual Diary,* selections from the *Constitutions* of the Society of Jesus, selected letters, additional texts and commentary.

Texts of the Spiritual Exercises *(with Commentary)*

The more readily available English versions of the *Spiritual Exercises* include:

Fleming, David L., S.J. *Draw Me into Your Friendship: A Literal Translation and a Contemporary Reading of "The Spiritual Exercises."* (St. Louis: IJS, 1996). Includes the literal translation by Elder Mullan of 1914.

Ganss, George E., S.J. *The Spiritual Exercises of St. Ignatius: Translation and Commentary* (Chicago: Loyola University Press, 1992). An excellent translation and commentary.

Ivens, Michael, S.J. *Understanding the Spiritual Exercises: Text and Commentary. A Handbook for Retreat Directors* (Herefordshire/Surrey: Gracewing/Iñigo, 1998).

Puhl, Louis J. *The Spiritual Exercises of St. Ignatius: A New Translation Based on Studies in the Language of the Autograph* (Chicago: Loyola University Press, 1951). A highly accurate English translation.

Tetlow, Elizabeth M. *The Spiritual Exercises of St. Ignatius Loyola: A New Translation* (Lanham, Md.: College Theology Society, 1987). Uses inclusive language and modifies military language and imagery.

Yeomans, William. *Iñigo Texts: The Spiritual Exercises* (London: Iñigo Enterprises, 1989).

Wolff, Pierre. *The Spiritual Exercises of Saint Ignatius* (Liguouri, Mo.: Triumph, 1997). This is a translation, with commentary by Wolff, of the official Latin version, "V," officially approved in 1548. (The preceding versions in this bibliography are all translations of the Spanish Autograph, ca. 1534.)

Directories of the Spiritual Exercises

Palmer, Martin E., S.J., ed. *On Giving the Spiritual Exercises: The Early Jesuit Manuscript Directories and the Official Directory of 1599* (St. Louis: IJS, 1996).

The "Autobiography" of St. Ignatius

Divarkar, Parmananda R. *A Pilgrim's Testament: The Memoirs of Ignatius of Loyola* (Rome: Gregorian University; Chicago: Loyola Press, 1983). Also in Ganss, ed., *Ignatius of Loyola.*

O'Callaghan, J. F. *The Autobiography of St. Ignatius Loyola with Related Documents.* Introduction and Notes by J. C. Colin (New York: Harper and Row, 1974).

Tylenda, Joseph N. *A Pilgrim's Journey: The Autobiography of Ignatius of Loyola,* with introduction and commentary (Wilmington, Del.: M. Glazier, 1985).

Yeomans, William, trans. *Iñigo: Original Testament: The Autobiography of St. Ignatius Loyola,* introduction by William Hewett, Iñigo Text Series 1 (London: Iñigo Enterprises, 1985).

Young, William J., S.J. *St. Ignatius' Own Story as Told to Luis González de Cámara,* new ed. "With a Sampling of his Letters" (Chicago: Loyola University Press, 1968).

Letters of St. Ignatius

Ganss, George E., ed. *Ignatius of Loyola,* which is the first entry in this bibliography, also contains selected letters.

Munitiz, Joseph A., ed. *Ignatius Loyola: Letters Personal and Spiritual,* Iñigo Texts Series 3 (Hurstpierpoint, England: Iñigo Enterprises, 1995).

Rahner, Hugo, ed. *St. Ignatius Loyola: Letters to Women.* Trans. K. Pond and S. A. H. Westman (New York: Herder & Herder, 1960).

Young, William J., S.J., ed. *Letters of St. Ignatius of Loyola* (Chicago: Loyola University Press, 1959).

The Constitutions of the Society of Jesus

The Constitutions of the Society of Jesus and Their Complementary Norms: A Complete English Translation of the Official Latin Texts (St. Louis: IJS, 1996).

Ganss, George, S.J., trans. and ed. *The Constitutions of the Society of Jesus* (St. Louis: IJS, 1970). This version includes excellent notes.

Ganss, George E., S.J., ed. *Ignatius of Loyola,* which is the first entry in this bibliography, contains selections from the *Constitutions.*

The Spiritual Diary

Ganss, George E., S.J., ed. *Ignatius of Loyola,* which is the first entry in this bibliography, contains selections from the *Spiritual Diary,* as well.

Munitiz, Joseph A., ed. *Iñigo: Discernment Log-Book; The Spiritual Diary of Saint Ignatius Loyola.* Iñigo Texts Series 2 (London: Iñigo Enterprises, 1987).

Ignatian Spirituality (including Commentaries on the Spiritual Exercises*)*

Coathalem, Hervé. *Ignatian Insights: A Guide to the Complete Spiritual Exercises* (Taichung, Taiwan: Kuangchi Press, 1961).

de Guibert, Joseph, S.J. *The Jesuits: Their Spiritual Doctrine and Practice; A Historical Study.* Trans. William J. Young, S.J., 3rd ed. (St. Louis: IJS, 1964).

Dister, John E., ed. *A New Introduction to the Spiritual Exercises of St. Ignatius* (Collegeville, Minn.: Michael Glazier, 1993).

Dyckman, Katherine, Mary Garvin, and Elizabeth Liebert. *The Spiritual Exercises Reclaimed: Uncovering Liberating Possibilities for Women* (New York: Paulist Press, 2001).

Egan, Harvey D. *Ignatius Loyola the Mystic* (Wilmington, Del.: Michael Glazier, 1987).

———. *The Spiritual Exercises and the Ignatian Mystical Horizon* (St. Louis: IJS, 1976).

English, John. *Spiritual Freedom,* 2nd ed. (Chicago: Loyola University Press, 1995).

Fleming, David L., ed. *Notes on the Spiritual Exercises of St. Ignatius of Loyola [The Best of the Review]* (St. Louis: Review for Religious, 1981).

———, ed. *A Spirituality for Contemporary Life: The Jesuit Heritage Today* (St. Louis: Review for Religious, 1991).

Ganss, George E., S.J. See above under "Collected Works" and "Texts of the *Spiritual Exercises.*"

Harbaugh, Jim. *A 12-Step Approach to the Spiritual Exercises of St. Ignatius* (Kansas City, Mo.: Sheed & Ward, 1997).

Ivens, Michael, S.J. See above, under "Texts of the *Spiritual Exercises.*"

Lonsdale, David. *Eyes to See, Ears to Hear* (London: Darton, Longman and Todd, 1990).

Modras, Ronald. *Ignatian Humanism: A Dynamic Spirituality for the Twenty-first Century* (Chicago: Loyola Press, 2004).

Muldoon, Tim. *The Ignatian Workout: Daily Spiritual Exercises for a Healthy Faith* (Chicago: Loyola Press, 2004).

Peters, William A., S.J. *The Spiritual Exercises of St. Ignatius: Exposition and Interpretation* (Jersey City, N.J.: Program to Adapt the Spiritual Exercises, 1968).

Pousset, Édouard, S.J., *Life in Faith and Freedom: An Essay Presenting Gaston Fessard's Analysis of the Spiritual Exercises of St. Ignatius.* Trans. and ed. Eugene L. Donohue, S.J. (St. Louis: IJS, 1980).

Rahner, Hugo, S.J. *Ignatius the Theologian.* Trans. Michael Barry (New York: Herder and Herder, 1968).

Segundo, Juan Luis. *The Christ of the Ignatian Exercises* (London: Sheed & Ward, 1988).

Sheldrake, Philip, S.J., ed. *The Way of Ignatius Loyola: Contemporary Approaches to the Spiritual Exercises* (St. Louis: IJS, 1991).

Silf, Margaret. *Inner Compass: An Invitation to Ignatian Spirituality* (Chicago: Loyola Press, 2000).

Tetlow, Joseph A. *Choosing Christ in the World: Directing the Spiritual Exercises according to Annotations Eighteen and Nineteen. A Handbook* (St. Louis: IJS, 1989).

Toner, Jules J., S.J. *A Commentary on St. Ignatius' Rules for the Discernment of Spirits* (St. Louis: IJS, 1982).

———. *Discerning God's Will: Ignatius of Loyola's Teaching on Christian Decision Making* (St. Louis: IJS, 1991).

For articles, specialized works and particular themes, see the notes in the individual chapters of this book and references in the following bibliographies.

Bibliographies

Begheyn, Paul, S.J. "A Bibliography on St. Ignatius's *Spiritual Exercises,*" *SSJ* 23, no. 3 (May 1991).

———. "Bibliography on the History of the Jesuits: Publications in English, 1900–1993." *SSJ* 28, no. 1 (January 1996).

Ivens, Michael, S.J. *Understanding the Spiritual Exercises* (see above under "Texts of the *Spiritual Exercises*"). Contains an extensive, up-to-date bibliography on the Exercises.

About the Author

Since 1990, Dean Brackley has taught theology and ethics at the Universidad Centroamericana (UCA) in El Salvador, Central America.

Born in upstate New York in 1946, Brackley entered the Jesuit Order in 1964 and was ordained a Catholic priest in 1976. He received his doctorate in theological ethics at the University of Chicago in 1980. In the 1970s and '80s, Brackley worked in social ministry and popular education on Manhattan's Lower East Side and in the South Bronx. He taught at Fordham University in 1989–90 before joining the staff of the UCA. In addition to teaching there, he has administered the university's School for Religious Education and collaborated in schools for pastoral formation sponsored by the UCA. He does pastoral work in an urban community in San Salvador.

Besides texts on popular education and articles on theology and society, his published works include *Etica social cristiana* (UCA Editores, 1995) and *Divine Revolution: Salvation and Liberation in Catholic Thought* (Orbis Books, 1996).